PRAISE FOR

From Outrage to Courage

"This book brings together a review of most of the major issues that have engaged the global women's movement over the last three decades. Seeking to "make injustice visible" Anne Firth Murray locates her analysis in the experience of grassroots women and the issues that affect their lives, including persistent poverty, unequal access to food, education, health care and money and pervasive violence against women. Throughout, she looks at the power of women's activism, going beyond victimhood to agency to bring about social change."

—Noeleen Heyzer, Former Executive Director,
    United Nations Development Fund for Women (UNIFEM)

"In her passionate and thought-provoking book, Anne Firth Murray documents the tremendous discrimination and inequities poor women face in the developing world at every stage of life. These injustices are manifested in high rates of deaths and illnesses and unequal access to food, health care, education, and employment. Interwoven throughout the book are inspiring stories of courageous women who are joining forces to fight for human rights and build the foundation for a brighter future."

—Elizabeth Maguire, President and CEO of Ipas and former Director of
    USAID's Office of Population

"Anne Firth Murray has done the near impossible in taking a critically important topic—the health of women in poor countries—which has been dealt with in a limited, fragmented, piecemeal fashion and given us a passionate, coherent, shocking, truthful, engaging, and utterly persuasive story that should turn your view of women in poor countries in the right direction. The book will make you sad, it will make you angry, but it will also give you hope because of the courage and actions of women in poor countries throughout the world. This book should be read and widely shared by anyone concerned about justice and our world."

—Philip Lee, MD, Professor of Social Medicine (Emeritus) and Senior Advisor,
    Institute for Health Policy Studies, School of Medicine, UCSF

From Outrage
to Courage

Women Taking Action for Health and Justice

ANNE FIRTH MURRAY

COMMON COURAGE PRESS

MONROE, MAINE

Cover design by Erica Bjerning
Cover photo by Esther B. Hewlett, used by permission

Interior design by Chris Hall/Ampersand

ISBN (paper): 978-1-56751-390-5
ISBN (hardcover): 978-1-56751-391-2

Library of Congress Cataloging-in-Publication Data
is available from the publisher by request.

Common Courage Press
P.O. Box 702
121 Red Barn Road
Monroe, ME 04951

207-525-0900
fax: 207-525-3068

www.commoncouragepress.com
info@commoncouragepress.com

SECOND PRINTING
Printed in Canada

To the women who teach courage and resilience.

In the midst of death, life persists;

in the midst of untruth, truth persists;

in the midst of darkness, light persists.

—Gandhi

Contents

Foreword

ANNE FIRTH MURRAY'S NEW BOOK is three things at once: a catalogue of abuses, an analysis of their causes and consequences, and a chronicle of courage under fire. It is the seamless blending of these strands that make *From Outrage to Courage* a tremendous contribution to all those who wish to understand how poverty and gender inequality conspire to make life miserable and short for so many, and, at the same time, a roadmap for those who wish to do something about it.

Anne Firth Murray is one of America's best practicing intellectuals. For a physician, the term "practice" has specific connotations: I first met Anne when she was creating the Global Fund for Women, which like her latest book moves from outrage—a necessary but unstable sentiment—to action by supporting small groups of women taking action in the most pragmatic and important ways. This book tells the story of these efforts and many others, taking us across the globe and inspiring all those who wish, who need, to take heart in the face of unjust suffering.

Murray draws on decades-long experience linking the disparate worlds that are in fact one world: the world of the affluent (which has generated its own, often blinkered feminism of glass ceilings) and that of the poor (where women face very different challenges, from lack of water and food to death in childbirth or, through sex-selective abortion, death before birth). Through her scholarship and activism, she has bridged this growing gap in ways that few others have.

It is also a work of sound scholarship, but free of the jargon that mars so many studies of this topic. *From Outrage to Courage* focuses on the social and health conditions of the world's poorest women, a topic neglected in the feminist literature of the affluent world. Anne Firth Murray is not content to look at only part of our wounded planet: from Latin America to Africa to the United States, from war zone to refugee camp, from village to slum, she relates the strength and resilience of unknown but exemplary women struggling to transform their lives and their societies. Anne is one of those rare writers able to link individual experience—the stories of real women facing very real problems—with the less visible structural constraints, many of them rooted in an unjust and globalized economy—against which they must struggle. Her writing is never the dry language of the academic sociologist, but the vibrant writing of a scholar in touch with the everyday dilemmas of women living in, and struggling against, poverty.

In sum, this book is both a call to action and a prescription for "turning the world rightside up," to use her felicitous phrase. Without paying attention to the information, the revelations, and the lessons of Murray's tour de force, we are condemned to live in an upside-down world in which poor women—connected to all of us in the ways so carefully detailed in *From Outrage to Courage*—continue to suffer unnecessarily and die untimely deaths. We are deeply in her debt.

PAUL FARMER, MD
Harvard Medical School and Partners in Health

Spare no effort, struggle unceasingly,
That at last peace may come to our people.
And jeweled dresses and deformed feet
Will be abandoned.
And one day, all under heaven
Will see beautiful women,
Blooming like fields of flowers,
And bearing brilliant and noble human beings.

  —Ch'iu Chin, China, 19th Century[1]

Prologue: Darkness and Light

BEING BORN FEMALE is dangerous to your health. This reality may not be true for many readers, but for most women living in poorer countries[2] around the globe, it is devastating.

The dangers start before birth. Sex-selective abortion is widespread, as parents decide for various reasons that they cannot bring another girl into the world.[3] Hundreds of thousands of girls have "disappeared," unbalancing sex ratios in countries like China, India, and Korea.[4] Every person in poverty is at a disadvantage, but the gender differences are staggering. Ninety million girls worldwide, compared with twenty-five million boys, do not go to school.[5] Some two million girls, most of them in Africa, are at risk of being genitally mutilated each year.[6] HIV/AIDS is spreading fastest in one population: adolescent girls and young women.[7] More than half a million women die each year from almost completely preventable childbirth-related injuries and illnesses.[8] One fourth to one half of women worldwide suffer violence at the hands of an intimate partner.[9] Three out of four fatalities of war are women and children.[10] Most older women in poorer countries are illiterate and living with illness, challenges also faced by many men. But unlike their male counterparts, these women are more isolated (rarely remarrying after the death of a spouse) and often are saddled with arduous care-giving roles.

Women's health is so much more than a medical issue; it is cultural, political, economic, and—above all—an issue of social justice. Improving women's health and advancing the status of women is often seen as a powerful means to solve economic problems rather than as a route toward true justice. It is both, to be sure. However, I write this book to make the case that social justice has for too long been eclipsed by concerns for "development." My experience indicates that the basic reality of women as "the other," or persons of lesser power (in many senses, not just economic power), emerges as central. Health issues are one prism through which to view the human rights of all.

In this book I describe this outrage, the darkness of persistent poverty and the low status of women, and the scandalous injustices that ravage the health of poor women in many poorer countries. Yet there is another side to this story. Change is possible, brought on by the courage of women to shine a light in the darkness and take action. These efforts are represented here by the poetry of women and the work of women's groups. They are also expressed through the images of the *koru* used throughout the book. *Koru*, in the Maori language of New Zealand, symbolizes not only the unfolding of the fern frond striving toward the light, but also a new beginning, renewal, and hope for the future. To fully grasp the depth of women's courage requires understanding the outrage in all its heinous aspects, a fact that has led me to concentrate on describing the details of their plight.

On a trip to Kenya in 2002, I met Janet,[11] one of many women who have left lasting impressions on me and inspired me with hope. In the face of the systematic attack on the health and rights of women, some remain undaunted. Janet, a forty-year-old woman who lives in Butula, Western Kenya, is a community health worker, walking barefoot from village to village to tell others of the value of being tested for HIV/AIDS, and helping those who test positive to live fully and those who test negative to stay that way. She has four children under the age of twelve, has lost her husband to AIDS, and is HIV positive herself, having contracted the virus from her husband. She earns twenty dollars a month for her outreach work; not enough to feed, clothe, and educate her children. "I hope that they will be looked after when I die," she says, "I worry about my children, but otherwise my life is good." I asked Janet if it had been difficult to be open about her status in a country where people who are HIV positive or who have AIDS are stigmatized. She told me that being open about being HIV positive had made her feel free—to seek help, to live more joyfully, and to help others.

Janet is illiterate; she is an "ordinary" woman and may even be said to be "typical" of many women in poorer countries in the world today. Some 38%

of women in the developing world are illiterate (a figure that rises to 48% in Africa), compared with 24% of men.[12] The vast majority of these women are poor, live in rural areas, and suffer ill health. Great numbers of these "ordinary" women, however, are strong and resilient. Janet, like many women I have met around the world, brings light to the world's darkness, and has found meaning and fulfillment in her capacity to go beyond herself to help others.

I am a fortunate person to have had the chance to meet people like Janet, to be inspired by them and to have learned from them. So, too, the students in my classes at Stanford: their enthusiasm and commitment to positive change have spurred me to move beyond the classes to describe in this book some of the outrageous situations of women contrasted with the compelling stories of women who are making change around the world. Hundreds of students eagerly learn about the situation of women worldwide and just as eagerly wonder "What can be done?" "What can I do?" I hope that by learning about the situation of women and of the efforts that women's groups are making to ensure that life, truth, and light persist in the face of death, untruth, and darkness, we will join together to try to complete the work of positive social change.

Critical Issues Faced by Resource-Poor Women

To understand the situation of women's health in poorer regions, particularly life-or-death health issues whose outcome depends on whether women can exercise their basic human rights—in other words, be empowered—one only need listen to women at the grassroots levels. At forums, in their writing, in proposals to donor agencies, and increasingly in interviews with journalists, they identify the critical issues affecting their lives and their health, which can be summarized thus:

- the demeaning and disempowerment of girls and women
- the persistence of poverty
- unequal access to education, food, health care, and money
- pervasive violence.

This book begins with a chapter on women, poverty, and human rights, for this reason: If we are interested in transforming our societies by promoting women's health, it is important to make the concept of human rights and justice central, as the basic context for all of our programs to assist girls and women.

The promotion of women's health is not just a good economic or development decision; it is the right thing to do. All aspects of a woman's life are involved with her health, especially if we define "health" broadly, as does the World Health Organization (WHO), as "a state of complete physical, mental and social well-being and not merely the absence of disease or infirmity."[13]

Subsequent chapters are concerned with the enormity of the world's grief as it is expressed through women's lives—the issues of son preference, unequal access to education and food, the vulnerability of adolescent girls, the scandals of maternal injury and illness, the prevalence of violence in the home, and the reality of unequal access throughout life, into older age. A current force affecting women's health is the economic power of globalization, which is explored in Chapter 8, in the context of women's labor and need for access to the cash economy. The universal and under-studied problem of mental health is raised throughout the book. "We women worry too much!" as Avotri and Walters quote in their study of Ghanaian women's perceptions of their health.[14] Yes, we do, and that can be both an unhealthy behavior and one that spurs us to action.

Examples of some of the thousands of community-based women's organizations addressing these health and human rights issues are inserted throughout the chapters to highlight the strength of women like Janet and to provide hope for change.[15] To provide context for the descriptions of women's groups that serve as illustrations throughout the book, a final chapter describes women's activism and the international women's movement and offers some thoughts for the future.

Through stories and descriptions, poetry and statistics, I seek to augment the overview provided by this book. Many issues of women's health have long been invisible, and considered too "private" to discuss. Here we try, as Gandhi counsels, to "make injustice visible."

Who is Worth Studying?

Few books focus on the situation of women and their health globally, though some describe specific health topics and health status in general. All too often there is no mention or description of how many issues (violence, HIV/AIDS, and aging, for example) affect women and men differently. Some of this neglect is a carryover from earlier times in which women were not studied, and the situation of men, mostly white men, was seen to be the norm or standard against which to measure others. Some of the neglect is simply a reflection of priorities: who and what is worth studying?[16]

In the book *Engendering Health Equity*, Gita Sen and her colleagues explain that although public health researchers have been concerned with health inequity (mostly based on determinants such as class or race) since the early nineteenth century to the present, there is still not significant study of gender-based inequities in health.[17] Early in their book they suggest that it is important to pay attention to health differences between men and women for the simple reason that differences do exist. They write: "Despite these empirical differences and growing attention to health inequity generally, it has taken much longer for gender to be recognized as a contributing social factor than, say, socioeconomic class, race, or caste. In part this is because of the still common fallacy of conflating gender with biological difference."[18] They explain that when one refers to gender one looks beyond biological differences to understand the deeper social foundations of power and inequality. The authors write (and I have taken to heart in this book): "Understanding the way in which biological and social factors interact in different aspects of health becomes central to our understanding of how gender operates in health."[19]

Many of the topics raised here have not been studied extensively and therefore appear to be "new," even though they may represent "tradition" in some countries. To discuss such issues, I have drawn from a diversity of sources, including the publications of multinational agencies and grassroots women's groups, journalists' accounts, and academic studies, where they exist. Some studies on the situation of women were done in preparation for the Fourth United Nations Conference on Women held in Beijing, China, in 1995, but since that time relatively little money has been made available to enable formal research and analysis on the situation of women and their health worldwide and in individual countries. Journalists' accounts, some UN statistical material, and applied studies by women's groups offer some information and current perspectives.

Turning a Blind Eye to Key Issues

How is it that women's health—the situation of about half of the world's population—has failed to be a focus of study? Here are some thoughts about why there is limited financial support and very little research on certain topics.

- Female infants' and children's access to food and/or medical care has been neglected because researchers either view the household as a single entity with uniform internal distribution or treat newborns as a sex-neutral category.

- Beyond a focus on fertility/childbearing behavior, the health lives of adolescents have not been studied extensively, perhaps because of a preoccupation with population pressure and sexuality.

- The extent of sex trafficking has been little known, perhaps because this phenomenon is tied in intricate and hidden ways to international corporate and business interests.

- Until very recently, the special vulnerability of women in war and refugee situations has been seen to be a "natural" byproduct of war—"collateral damage."

- Almost no attention has been given to older women in poorer countries, perhaps because, in the scheme of things, older women have been considered unimportant and unproductive.

- The mental health of women and girls (and men and boys) in poorer countries has been virtually unstudied, probably because of the difficulties of definition and the overwhelming nature of the problems.

In short, until very recently, little was studied—and therefore learned about—women in poorer countries, beyond their roles as producers of children and as mothers. Even the issue of violence against women within the home and community—so central to women's health—was taboo until the past ten to fifteen years.[20]

Much of the violence that has been done to women and girls has been invisible or taboo. Certainly it has not been accessible to outsiders in many societies, particularly those where women's place has not been public but always private, closed, behind doors. A man's home is his castle, in which live women and children—the "subjects" of the lord and master—whose lives are not to be seen. Private, secret things go on behind the walls. This separation of the "public" and "private" spheres has resulted in injuries inflicted on women and children in private not being viewed as human rights abuses and essentially remaining invisible. These have included such violations as unsafe childbirth practices, female genital mutilation, the buying and selling of young girls, honor killings, dowry deaths, and domestic violence.

When we look at women's lives and their health from infancy through old age we are stunned by the degree of injustice and outright harm that occurs. Governments struggle to provide for their people in the face of many conflicts and very difficult economic circumstances. Tough choices are made at the government, community, and family levels, choices that directly affect the health of individual men, women, and children. The situation is dire, and it is easy to be dragged down by the difficulties that face many societies and individual people these days. Reading the daily newspaper can be a "downer," as we learn of corruption and lying by governments and corporations, the slaughter and rape of innocent villagers in war-torn countries, the competition and greed that drives officials and so-called leaders, and the violence that characterizes our time.

Despite many indications, however, there is a lot of good news, much of it going unreported in a media structure bent on emphasizing despair. Women in Afghanistan gather together to cast their votes, risking public ridicule. A village woman, Mukhtaran Bibi, in Meerwala, Pakistan, chooses to take a gang of rapists to court rather than to commit suicide out of shame, and she receives the support of women's groups in her country and beyond. Local groups of women in Chennai, India, turn up at the home of a victim of domestic violence to silently but publicly shame her attacker. Grandmothers in Mali and Senegal add orphans to their already heavy load of responsibility; they meet to strengthen one another.

Seldom reported are the amazing accomplishments of individuals and groups at the grassroots level of societies. Women's groups, in particular, have proliferated in every country in the world. People are coming together with strength in villages and cities to address practices rooted in tradition (such as female genital mutilation and early marriage) and problems exacerbated by current forces (such as trafficking of women and girls and unhealthy labor practices). Examples of such initiatives appear throughout this book.

Around the world the rights of individuals are increasingly being recognized. With the promulgation of the Universal Declaration of Human Rights in 1948 and subsequent conventions and actions of the United Nations, individual people and governments are beginning to accept the possibility of change.[21] Furthermore, as civil society grows in strength, in the form of thousands of "third" sector (non-governmental, not-for-profit) organizations, and in particular women's groups, movements for social justice are becoming stronger and marginalized people are demanding their rights.

The descriptions throughout this book provide hope that poor women working to create change—even against overwhelming odds—constitute a strong and inevitable force. To ensure their success, we need to learn from them, join them, and be there for them at home and globally. I take guidance from this quote from the Talmud: "Do not be daunted by the enormity of the world's grief. Do justly, now. Love mercy, now. Walk humbly, now. You are not obligated to complete the work, but neither are you free to abandon it." The way we do our work is key. By never failing to put justice at the center of our efforts, we can realize the hope that Ch'iu Chin offered a hundred years ago—that "one day, all will see beautiful free women."

Birth, old age,
Sickness, and death:
From the beginning,
This is the way
Things have always been.
Any thought
Of release from this life
Will wrap you only more tightly
In its snares.
The sleeping person
Looks for a Buddha,
The troubled person
Turns toward meditation.
But the one who knows
That there's nothing to seek
Knows too that there's nothing to say.
She keeps her mouth closed.

—Ly Ngoc Kieu, Vietnam, 1041-1113[1]

Where, after all, do universal human rights begin? In small
places, close to home—so close and so small that they cannot be
seen on any maps of the world. . . . Such are the places where
every man, woman, and child seeks equal justice, equal oppor-
tunity, and equal dignity, without discrimination.

—Eleanor Roosevelt, U.S.A., 1958[2]

Women's Health, Poverty, and Rights

EVERY TWO SECONDS, somewhere in the world, eight babies are born, about half of them girls.[3] Some 81% will live in poor countries. As we shall see in this and the next chapter, their births are all too often something more to be endured than to be celebrated.

Let us put a human face on the numbers. Think of Hope, the mother of Mary, a baby girl born in western Kenya. Hope was in her mid-thirties and already had five children when I visited the area in 2004 and heard about her from a traditional birth attendant at the local health clinic. Hope was disappointed to produce yet another girl, another mouth to feed, and she was feeling weak and very tired. Her other five children—three girls and two boys—were all under age twelve. To try to pay for the daily costs of her family, her husband searched for work in a nearby town even though he had been feeling very sick, while Hope sold vegetables in a local market. She struggled up after giving birth, thanked the village midwife who had helped her at the birth, and gave the new baby a breast to be shared with a sibling.

Several thousand miles north and east, in a rural village near Lucknow, India, baby Kamla was born in a small house made of clay and palm fronds. Kamla's young mother, Laxmi, age seventeen and already the mother of another little girl, was unhappy. Because she had not borne a son, she had failed as a wife.

Her one-year-old and the new baby were weak because the family she had married into was poor and she had not had sufficient good food to nurture a growing fetus and provide enough milk for her baby. Laxmi had gone to school for a year, not quite enough time for her to learn to read. Her parents arranged her marriage when she was twelve, and she went to the home of her husband when she was fourteen. Her in-laws were mistreating her and resented her for giving birth only to girls. When Laxmi's husband judged that she had not been working hard or keeping the house in order, he sometimes struck her. And here she was with Kamla, another girl, another burden.

My companion on this trip was a woman from BETI (Better Education through Innovation), a women's group working in the Lucknow area. She explained that not all stories of girls' births in India and other poorer countries are sad; many girls are welcomed into the world. But the hard truths are that most women in the world who are giving birth today are poor and illiterate, with little access to health care; that most girls in our world will face discrimination, poverty, unequal access to education and health care, and unequal pay for equal work. And about a third of women giving birth today will face violence at the hands of a partner, a violation of human rights that all too often happens in "small places, close to home, so small and so close that they cannot be seen on the maps of the world."

Women's health cannot be understood or improved without understanding the contextual relationship—the subordination of women, poverty, and violence, resulting in unequal access to education, food, health care, and paid employment.

Women and Poverty

What does poverty mean? The World Bank, in its 2000-2001 report on poverty, offered this description:

> Poor people live without fundamental freedoms of action and choice that
> the better-off take for granted. They often lack adequate food and shelter,
> education and health, deprivations that keep them from leading the kind of
> life that everyone values. They also face extreme vulnerability to ill health,
> economic dislocation, and natural disasters. And they are often exposed to
> ill treatment by institutions of the state and society and are powerless to
> influence key decisions affecting their lives.

In an attempt to document the extent of poverty, the report continues:
The world has deep poverty amid plenty. Of the world's 6 billion people,
2.8 billion—almost half—live on less than $1 a day, with 44% living in
South Asia. In rich countries, fewer than one child in one hundred does
not reach its fifth birthday, while in the poorest countries, as many as one
in five children do not. And while in rich countries fewer than 5% of all
children under five are malnourished, in poor countries as many as 50%
are. . . . The average income in the richest twenty countries is 37 times the
average in the poorest twenty—a gap that has doubled in the past forty
years. . . . In East Asia the number of people living on less that $1 a day
fell from around 420 million to around 280 million between 1987 and
1998. . . . Yet in Latin America, South Asia, and Sub-Saharan Africa, the
numbers of poor people have been rising. And in the countries of Europe
and Central Asia in transition to market economies, the number of people
living on less than $1 a day rose more than twenty fold during that period.[4]

The World Bank report notes further that experiences of poverty are very
different at sub-national levels in countries and for minorities and women.
Based on measures of school enrollment and infant mortality rates, women
face more severe disadvantages than do men.[5] Worldwide, women's wages,
when women have access to the formal economy, are about two-thirds of
men's. The majority of women are in low-wage situations or work informally
for part-time wages with little or no benefits. In this age of globalization,
which touts the spread of democracy and equality through market forces,
the wage gap between men and women persists and is so prevalent that it is
now commonly referred to as "the feminization of poverty." Rural women,
in particular, have suffered; over the past two decades, the number of rural
women worldwide living in absolute poverty rose by nearly 50%.[6]

The Human Poverty Index (HPI), introduced in the 1997 Human Development Report from the United Nations Development Programme (UNDP),
attempts to quantify poverty in the world today by accounting for and trying to measure aspects of poverty beyond income, including lack of access
to opportunities and resources.[7] The report suggests that the HPI provides
a better, though still incomplete, measure of women's experience of poverty.
Though the practice of measuring by entire households makes it difficult to

WOMEN'S COURAGE: BEIJING, CHINA. The Beijing Cultural Development Center for Rural Women, also known as Rural Women Knowing All (RWKA) was formed to address the reality that rural women in China have little access to health services, independent income, and even education. RWKA works across China to improve women's literacy and expand educational opportunities for poor women. It does this through various media projects, including RWKA's magazine—the only magazine for rural women in China—which reaches millions of women using an appropriate level of written language for people with minimal reading skills.

RWKA's television and film projects include a documentary film series which deals with rural women's economic and social rights, environmental protection in China, education, and the construction of the legal system in China. The organization's reach has grown tremendously in recent years and now includes micro-credit programs, migrant women's clubs, literacy education, and reproductive health examinations. RWKA's vision is to inspire Chinese women by introducing them to positive role models and programs for financial and social empowerment.

discern bias and different levels of poverty within the home, "it is clear that poverty strikes women particularly harshly."[8]

Poverty's greater burden on women has been known for years. It was described in the Platform for Action of the UN Fourth World Conference on Women, 1995: "In the past decade the number of women living in poverty has increased disproportionately to the number of men, particularly in the developing countries. In addition to economic factors, the rigidity of socially ascribed gender roles and women's limited access to power, education, training and productive resources . . . are also responsible."[9] It is clear that poverty affects households in general, but because men and women do different work and have different responsibilities for the household, women bear a greater burden as they manage consumption, some production, and scarce resources.

Many conditions of women's lives set them up to have fewer financial resources than their male counterparts, and poverty in turn can influence these conditions. For example, level of school enrollment, one measure of

WOMEN'S COURAGE: PHNOM PENH, CAMBODIA. Urban Poor Women Development (UPWD) initiates projects to help poor women in urban regions of Cambodia improve their economic situations. Many unskilled rural women migrate to Phnom Penh in search of jobs, where they endure poor living conditions in the slums of the city.

Formed in 1997, UPWD offers training to female workers in the city to increase their employability and their rights awareness. Working at the community level, the group gives funds to start small women's businesses, provides workshops on leadership skills, and offers training sessions for non-governmental organizations. UPWD hopes to lift Cambodian women out of poverty and increase their economic and social status.

poverty, reveals that more women than men are denied the education and skills to support themselves. Worldwide, 69% of females over the age of fifteen are literate, compared with 83% of males. In less developed countries the percentages are 66% and 81% respectively.[10] More examples of challenging conditions for women are addressed in more detail in later chapters.

Unsurprisingly, the percentages of women in the paid labor force in virtually all countries are consistently lower than the percentages of men. For example, 37% of women are in the labor force in North Africa compared with 82% of men; 45% in Latin America and the Caribbean, compared with 86% of men.[11]

If a mother is undernourished, often because she is poor, her baby is likely to be underweight and may even be born with a smaller brain. Maternal mortality, another measure of women's poverty, persists: complications of pregnancy and childbirth, when met with inadequate medical care at the time of delivery, can be deadly. Quality care saves lives, and it doesn't have to be done in a very wealthy country, as Malaysia and Chile have demonstrated. Skilled personnel attended 96% and 100% of births in those countries, respectively, resulting in the deaths of thirty-nine and thirty-three women per 100,000 live births. In Niger, by comparison, where only 18% of births are attended by skilled personnel, 920 women died per 100,000 live births in 2004. In Indonesia, 56% of births were attended by skilled personnel, and 580 women died per 100,000 live births.

Discrepancies in infant death rates illustrate women's disadvantaged status in poorer countries, as is discussed in the next chapter. Their disadvantaged status is also expressed in the situation of young women with regard to HIV/AIDS, discussed in a subsequent chapter, where it is noted that the HIV/AIDS epidemic has had a profound impact on the lives of women, especially those whose economic dependence on men and low social status leave them powerless to avoid risky sexual behaviors.

Access to money matters. Poverty is directly correlated with poor health. In a study of socioeconomic status and health, Nancy Adler et al. state: "Throughout history, socioeconomic status (SES) has been linked to health. Individuals higher in the social hierarchy typically enjoy better health than do those below. . . . The effects of severe poverty on health may seem obvious through the impact of poor nutrition, crowded and unsanitary living conditions, and inadequate medical care. . . . There is evidence that the association of SES and health occurs at every level of the SES hierarchy. . . . Not only do those in poverty have poorer health than those in more favored circumstances, but those at the highest level enjoy better health than do those just below."[12]

Health Defined

Now it becomes clear why a narrow definition of health that would refer only to physical fitness and/or an absence of illness would not help much with understanding the situation of women and their health and taking action to improve it. In contrast, the concept and ideal of health defined by the World Health Organization (WHO) as "a state of complete physical, mental and social well being and not merely the absence of disease or infirmity" makes a lot of sense. Indeed, it is the definition used in this book as not only illnesses (e.g., HIV/AIDS) but also other conditions affecting health (e.g., education and work) are discussed.

Using the WHO definition of health raises the challenge of *measuring health status* across societies and groups that are very different one from another in terms of culture, economy, history, demography, and medical history.[13] Nevertheless, the United Nations and other multinational agencies have attempted to measure health status; in combination they provide the best statistics and information currently available on the subject. Drawing from many sources, including as careful work as possible by various multinational, governmental, and nongovernmental agencies, researchers and officials have no doubt that in no society today, including our own, do women enjoy the same opportunities as men. As a 1997 UN Development Programme report notes: "This unequal status leaves considerable disparities between how much women contribute to human development and how little they share its benefits."[14] Three years later, another UN report, *The World's Women 2000: Trends and Statistics*, showed some gains but still found persistent disparities between women and men worldwide in six areas: health, human rights and political decision-making, work, education and communication, population, and families.[15]

The extent of poverty and ill health discussed above contrasts with a genuine revolution in human health and well being in the world as a whole. People are living longer—average life expectancy at birth in many developed countries nearly has doubled, from about 45 in 1900 to about 78 in 2003, and poorer countries have also experienced dramatic improvements in terms of declines in mortality—although this positive trend has reversed in some African countries as a result of the HIV/AIDS pandemic.[16] There have been great improvements in health in general and success at controlling such diseases as smallpox and cholera. At the same time, however, the health of people around the world has been threatened by illness-causing substances, including some, like smoking and high-fat diets, that encourage unhealthy behavior. HIV/AIDS and TB have become scourges in more and more countries, threatening whole populations and weakening societal structures.

We live in a paradoxical world: while there have been tremendous health gains in some parts of the world and among some populations, these are counterbalanced by stagnation and decline in others. Health improvements have been unevenly distributed.[17] Gro Brundtland, former head of the World Health Organization, in a 1998 press release, was quoted as follows: "Never have so many had such broad and advanced access to healthcare. But never have so many been denied access to healthcare. The developing world carries 90% of the disease burden, yet poorer countries have access to only 10% of the resources that go to health."[18] Had Brundtland been highlighting women's health, she might have added that women carry the majority of the ill health burden but have access to a minority of resources to lighten it.

Women and Human Rights: A Slow Dawning

The reports mentioned above hint at but do not explicitly indicate the dire consequences that the persistent discrimination against women has for their health status. Jonathan Mann, who spent his life as a champion of human rights and health, made the link clear: "Discrimination against ethnic, religious, and racial minorities, as well as on account of gender, political opinion, or immigration status, compromises or threatens the health and well-being and, all too often, the very lives of millions. . . . Discriminatory practices threaten physical and mental health and result in the denial of access to care, inappropriate therapies, or inferior care."[19] Being born female is a health hazard, at times a fatal one.

Mann is, to be sure, talking more broadly about human rights, a concept that first became a worldwide preoccupation after the Second World War, when representatives of the newly formed United Nations tried to identify and agree upon what governments should not do to people and what they should assure to all. Out of these discussions came the Universal Declaration of Human Rights, promulgated on December 10, 1948.[20] But as significant as this achievement was, the Universal Declaration was a product of its time. The concept of "universal" human rights was, after all, developed by a particular set of people, people who were in positions of power at that time. For the most part, they were male, with the notable and inspiring exception of Eleanor Roosevelt. In subsequent decades, as individual people and groups—previously marginalized and certainly not party to the earlier discussions—began demanding their "rights," the UN had to rethink its definitions, broadening them to include the needs of people whose special vulnerabilities were not taken into consideration in the past—women, children, indigenous people, the disabled, and so on.

Despite progress, the process was slow. These days, the idea that "women's rights are human rights" seems obvious, but it was not until 1993, when the UN held a conference on human rights in Vienna, that the member states began to talk about abuses such as rape and domestic violence as "human rights" violations. It took even longer and prodding by women's and human rights organizations for the UN Security Council to recognize the particular violations of women's human rights in situations of war and armed conflict, including systematic rape as a policy of war and sexual slavery for the "comfort" of soldiers. As Human Rights Watch noted, "Combatants and their sympathizers in conflicts, such as those in Sierra Leone, Kosovo, the Democratic Republic of Congo, Afghanistan, and Rwanda, have raped women as a weapon of war with near complete impunity."[21]

The problem, though, was much deeper and broader than had been recognized. As Human Rights Watch put it:

Millions of women throughout the world live in conditions of abject deprivation of, and attacks against, their fundamental human rights for no other reason than that they are women. . . . Men in Pakistan, South Africa, Peru, Russia, and Uzbekistan beat women in the home at astounding rates, while these governments alternatively refuse to intervene to protect women and punish their batterers or do so haphazardly and in ways that make women feel culpable for the violence. As a direct result of inequalities found in their countries of origin, women from Ukraine, Moldova, Nigeria, the Dominican Republic, Burma, and Thailand are bought and sold, trafficked to work in forced prostitution, with insufficient government attention to protect their rights and punish the traffickers. In Guatemala, South Africa, and Mexico, women's ability to enter and remain in the work force is obstructed by private employers who use women's reproductive status to exclude them from work and by discriminatory employment laws or discriminatory enforcement of the law. In the U.S., students discriminate against and attack girls in school who are lesbian, bisexual, or trans-gendered, or do not conform to male standards of female behavior. Women in Morocco, Jordan, Kuwait, and Saudi Arabia face government-sponsored discrimination that renders them unequal before the law—including discriminatory family codes that take away women's legal authority and place it in the hands of male family members—and restricts women's participation in public life. . . . Abuses against women are relentless, systematic, and widely tolerated, if not explicitly condoned. Violence and discrimination against women are global social epidemics, notwithstanding the very real progress of the international women's human rights movement in identifying, raising awareness about, and challenging impunity for women's human rights [and health] violations.[22]

In response to ever-louder criticisms and complaints, the UN promulgated two conventions of particular importance to women and girls: the Convention on the Elimination of All Forms of Discrimination Against Women (known as CEDAW or the women's convention, adopted in 1979 by the UN General Assembly)[23] and the Convention on the Rights of the Child (adopted in November 1989 and entered into force in September 1990).[24] Both of these conventions laid out guidelines to protect the rights of women and children, but like many such documents, they lack enforcement mechanisms that are indispensable to creating meaningful change.

The Universal Declaration and other UN documents spelling out human rights are not as far removed from the everyday health concerns of women as they may seem. After all, as Mann wrote, "Human rights and public health are two complementary approaches, and languages, to address and advance human well-being."[25] Invoking international agreements like these lends strength to women's groups and others who try to encourage governments to improve conditions that affect women's health. In 1992, for example, at a Global Fund for Women meeting of a women's circle working to eliminate trafficking in women, some American participants asked activists from South and Southeast Asia what they (the Americans) could do to help the most. Expecting the activists to say that they needed more money for their work, the eager donors were awakened by the answer: "The most important thing that you and other Americans can do to help is to get the U.S. Government to ratify the women's convention [CEDAW] and the Convention on the Rights of the Child, both of which address the issue of trafficking in women and girls." The activists explained that without U.S. ratification of such conventions, it was difficult, if not impossible, for them to lobby their governments for legal change in such countries as Nepal, the Philippines, and Thailand.

The UN may seem distant to many of us, and its ways are often bureaucratic, but women's groups around the world have used the UN system to lobby for change in their own countries. These activists were saying that around the world, caring women and men must join together to demand full human rights for all women. (As of 2007, the U.S. Government has not ratified CEDAW or the Convention on the Rights of the Child. For information, see section on "Some Useful Resources," pp. 277–283.)

For decades, women's health issues have been approached as purely "development" issues (i.e., improving economic and social development). This focus is an instrumental one (i.e., improving women's health in order to increase productivity or providing family planning in order to reduce population levels). Why now complicate things by shifting to a human rights framework? The answer highlights a critical difference: The human rights approach moves the intention away from a broad instrumental approach to an individual, human approach—to improving women's health and/or providing family planning simply for the sake of justice.

The stories of Kamla and Mary, the little girls born in India and Kenya, would not have been relevant if we were to take a strictly developmentalist approach to their situations without addressing their rights as human beings. Recall that both were born into poor families, that one of the mothers had suffered violence, and that just because they were born female, both were destined to have problems gaining access to education and other services. Arguing a development rather than a human rights approach would result in the idea that the poor will always be with us, that governments should try to educate girls in order to increase national productivity, and that domestic violence is a private rather than a public matter and need be considered primarily to calculate a society's health costs.

A human rights perspective demands that we recognize that providing education for girls, for example, is not only a good development decision but also a question of justice, of individual rights. It leads us to see that tolerating sexual abuse is not just a bad economic choice, in terms of health costs, but also a violation of a woman's right to bodily integrity. A human rights view reveals that maternal mortality is not only a tragedy because it deprives children of a caregiver but an abrogation of the right of a woman to basic health care.

The rights to "life, liberty, and security of person" and to freedom from "slavery or servitude" and "cruel, inhuman, or degrading treatment or punishment" in articles 3, 4, and 5 of the Universal Declaration were to be guaranteed to every person. Who could take issue with that? The problem is the context: these words referred to civil and political prisoners, not to people who were subjected to "slavery," "torture," or "cruel, inhuman, or degrading treatment" in their homes or places of work. It was the human rights advocates who highlighted the importance of equality and freedom from bodily harm for individual people whose circumstances were not recognized in early international conventions on human rights. It was women's advocacy groups who proclaimed at the 1993 UN Conference on Human Rights in Vienna: "Women's rights are human rights." This is an idea that Eleanor Roosevelt would surely have fully understood, but it is an idea that did not make its way into public consciousness until the 1990s.

Why Focus on Women?

The discrepancies in opportunity and access for women already highlighted here may be reason enough to focus a discussion on women. But there are other reasons to learn more about the experiences of women and their health. Women, whether healthy or not, are at the heart of family and society. A woman's health affects every area of her life and therefore of her family and community. Today, for a variety of reasons, women often end up as the sole supporters of their children. While percentages vary around the world, in many countries more than 30% of households are headed by single females.[26] Women are not just productive members of a family; often they are its safety net. If the truth of women's lives, in all their complexity, is hidden from us, change is unlikely.

The subordination of women as well as the persistence of poverty, the proliferation of violence, and continuing gaps in access to food, health care, education, and living wages are in their breadth and depth like a war on women. These inequalities—these violations of the human rights of women— stem from a basic dislocation in society that distorts the lives of both men and women. This dislocation has to do with the way we conceive of ourselves in relation to others. Focusing on and learning more about the situation of women may help us transform our "either/or" way of thinking and change the way that we view and treat each other in this world.

At the moment, we are caught in a paradigm of behavior that is unhealthy. It is an either/or paradigm that leads us to categorize people and then assign values to the various categories—black versus white, male versus female, strong versus weak, educated versus uneducated, rich versus poor. Instead of appreciating and welcoming such differences, we use these dichotomies to separate ourselves and even pit ourselves against one another. Although there is nothing inherently unequal or even negative about assigning categories—perhaps a natural human tendency—it is the destructive value judgments that follow that need to be eliminated. This paradigm of see- ing people who are different from ourselves as the "other" and possibly of lesser value has resulted in the marginalization and subordination of certain groups over the years (groups such as people of color, indigenous people, differently abled people, and women). The result has been the development of hierarchical social structures, structures that have subordinated more than half of the world's population—women and groups of marginalized men as well. We need to understand and work to change the paradigm of "either/or" to "both/and."

The "either/or" paradigm is perfectly illustrated by the significant statements: "It's a girl!" or "It's a boy!" Society's different and value-laden reactions to these two statements will determine the course and health of a person's life.

The subordination of women is deeply ingrained in the lives of both men and women. Sometimes it is explained in terms of biological differences.[27] Over time, culture, religion, and most social systems, including educational, legal, and medical systems, which in both traditional and modern forms tend to be hierarchical in structure, have assigned less status and power to women and other marginalized groups.[28] The subordination of women and girls takes many forms. At the moment of birth, celebrations may differ according to the sex of the baby. In childhood, girls' and boys' access to food, health care, and education often differs. Later in life, women's subordination is illustrated in the objectification of women's bodies, the gendered division of labor, and persistent abuse of women and girls.

As the realities of women's lives demonstrate, the state of women's health is critically connected to the subordination of women. Throughout this book, many examples of this subordination will be cited and described. However, it is important to remember, as Gerda Lerner argues in *The Creation of Patriarchy*, that:

> While women have been victimized by . . . many other aspects of their
> long subordination to men, it is a fundamental error to try to conceptual-
> ize women primarily as victims. To do so at once obscures what must be
> assumed as a given of women's historical situation: Women are essential
> and central to creating society; they are and always have been actors and
> agents in history. Women have "made history," yet they have been kept
> from knowing their history and from interpreting history, either their own
> or that of men. . . . The tension between women's actual historical experi-
> ence and their exclusion from interpreting that experience I have called
> "the dialectic of women's history". . . . [which] has been a dynamic force,
> causing women to struggle against their condition. . . . This coming-into-
> consciousness of women becomes the dialectical force moving them into
> action to change their condition and to enter a new relationship to male-
> dominated society.[29]

WOMEN'S COURAGE: ACCRA, GHANA. The African Women's Development Fund (AWDF) raises money and gives grants to projects initiated by African women for African women. Founded in 2000, the Fund is one of about twenty women's funds around the world that have formed in the last ten years to provide support to women's human rights organizations in their countries or regions. AWDF gives grants ranging in size from about $10,000 to $25,000 to strengthen and link smaller women's groups throughout Africa. The Fund also provides technical assistance in organizational management and assistance in communications and networking.

The Fund helps women's groups defend and improve women's rights in areas such as reproductive health, political participation, access to healthcare, and employment. Between 2000 and 2007, AWDF provided grants to groups in more than thirty-two African nations.

The examples of women's groups inserted throughout the text in this book represent this "coming-into-consciousness" of women, that force that is moving them into action to change their condition.

A final and important reason to understand the complex health situation of poorer women is to better appreciate our global interconnectedness. William Budd, a physician, writing about typhoid in 1931, noted: "This disease not seldom attacks the rich, but it thrives among the poor. But by reason of our common humanity we are all, whether rich or poor, more nearly related here than we are apt to think. The members of the great human family are, in fact, bound together by a thousand secret ties, of whose existence the world in general little dreams. And he that was never connected with his poorer neighbor, by deeds of charity or love, may one day find, when it is too late, that he is connected with him by a bond which may bring them both, at once, to a common grave."[30] Adding SARS, avian flu, or HIV/AIDS along with one or two politically correct changes in pronouns makes this quote timely today.

Women in poorer countries are much more vulnerable to the kinds of infectious diseases alluded to in the previous paragraph than are people in richer countries. Still, women around the world deeply feel their shared struggles around such health issues as domestic violence, reproductive rights, and equal access to paid employment.

But the clarion call in Dr. Bud's statement, to me, is the phrase *"by reason of our common humanity* [my emphasis] we are all, whether rich or poor, more nearly related here than we are apt to think." Though women and men may share vulnerabilities and struggles relating to issues of health and human rights, our true bond of interconnectedness is in our common humanity. We can choose to live by universal standards of justice, and we can choose to create change to make that justice possible for all.

To improve women's health we must treat specific health problems, but the conditions of women's lives must also change so that we women can gain more power over our lives and our health. At the base of such social change is extending women's capacity to be in charge of our own lives, to exercise our human rights.

We focus on women, therefore, because women's experiences are different and under-studied, because societies need women to be healthy and fully engaged, because it is only fair that women have full equality in their societies. And we focus on women because understanding their unique challenges is a prerequisite to justice.

She was a girl who arrived when
everyone was expecting a boy.
So since she was such a disappointment
to her parents,
to her immediate family,
to her tribe,
nobody thought of recording her birth.
She was so insignificant.

—Buchi Emecheta, Nigeria, 1983[1]

From the Beginning: A Deadly Preference

THE JOURNALIST ELISABETH BUMILLER paints a vivid picture of a village in Tamil Nadu, India, where the literacy rate of women is higher than the national average and "women do not veil their faces." And yet, in this valley and another beyond it, "families sometimes poisoned their newborn daughters. . . . I met four couples, all poor farm laborers, who told me that the hardships in their lives and the astronomical expense of marrying off daughters had forced them to murder their infant girls. 'I don't feel sorry that I have done this,' Mariaye, one of the four mothers, told me quietly. 'Actually, I think I have done the right thing. Why should a child suffer like me?'"[2]

"Global women's health" may bring to mind thoughts of access to prenatal care, vulnerabilities to sexually transmitted diseases, and the need for better nutrition and education. True enough, these issues, among others, are very important. But such a picture omits a powerful force that must be reckoned with if women's health is to be improved: the widespread preference for male children. Both poverty and the demeaning of women account for practices such as infanticide, neglect, and sex-selective abortion, all of which are discussed in this chapter. These practices are powerful, to the point that they have skewed male/female ratios worldwide and produced millions of "missing girls." Where poverty is present, it cannot account on its own for the

WOMEN'S COURAGE: SONEPUR, ORISSA, INDIA. Duradarshini Mahila Mahasangha (DMM) was established in 2003 by twenty-nine women's groups that were formed by Solidarity for Social Equality, a non-governmental group in Orissa. DMM is exemplary of many women's groups in South Asia in that it aims to address gender-based inequalities that stem from dowry traditions, including women's economic dependence on men, the lack of reproductive rights and health services available to women, sex-selective abortion, gender-based violence, and trafficking. It has provided health services for rural women, hosted international women's day events, and organized village women to build roads for their community.

choices that parents make to reduce the number of girl children. Devaluing girls is the root cause.

Of the 68 million girls born around the world annually,[3] the majority are greeted with varying degrees of disappointment by relatives hoping for a boy. Birth rituals may be substantially different for males and females. Among Bedouins of the Middle East, for example, a boy's birth demands a feast to which many people are invited. In contrast, upon the birth of a girl, the husband and wife may be consoled by their relatives who express hope that the next baby will be a son. In northern India, at the birth of a male child, women may gather to sing songs of welcome, whereas for a female baby, there may be silence or even abuse of the mother.[4]

Son preference is not just a third-world problem. In America, for example, a team of economists wondering about persistent wage gaps between men and women were quoted thus: "Could the problem stretch far beyond the workplace . . . and all the way back to childhood and the ways that parents treat boys and girls? Was it possible that even in the United States, even in 2003, parents favor boys in a way that has lifelong implications?" The economists found their results "shocking." Ever since the 1940s, couples with girls divorced more often than those with boys. U.S. Census Bureau data showed that the effect was unmistakable: it happened in every region, among all groups, and among people with differing levels of education: parents with an only child that was a girl were 6% more likely to split up than parents with a single boy, and the gap rose for parents with more girls than boys.

The researchers stated: "This research strongly suggests that the age-old favoring of boys is not confined to the past or to developing countries like China and India. It is subtle and less widespread than it once was in the United States, but it still gives boys an important leg up."[5]

Tracking changes in discrimination against women in the United States is not central to this book, and it is clear that huge gains have been made in terms of education and access to leadership positions. The ground is shifting here and elsewhere, particularly with regard to access to education. More girls than boys are entering and graduating from universities in the U.S. today; the first woman president in Harvard's 375-year history was just appointed, and a leading candidate for president is a woman. At the same time, wage differentials persist, favoring men.[6] One out of every three women in the U.S. will experience violence at the hands of an intimate partner—about the same level as for women around the world. Women around the world and even in the U.S. have a long way to go to reach full equality, but there has been progress.

Around the world, preference for sons is alive and well. It results in discrimination and health risks for girls and women. In some regions, particularly in South and East Asia, being conceived a girl presents a major risk up front—the possibility of not being born at all or not surviving infancy—of being one of the millions of girls who have "disappeared" from the demographer's charts as a result of infanticide, neglect, and, among the relatively wealthy, sex-selective abortion. Amartya Sen, the 1998 Nobel laureate in economics, estimates that the number of "missing" girls worldwide ranges from sixty to one hundred million, or about the same number of females born each year.[7]

According to demographic projections, a population where all are treated equally in terms of access to food and health care ought to have at least as many females as males, and among infants, the sex ratio should be approximately 106 males to 100 females.[8] However, in large parts of Asia, particularly China and India, the sex ratio among infants is unnaturally elevated to 115 or even 120 males for every 100 females, which indicates that many fewer young girls reach childhood than biology would predict.[9]

Economic and social pressures, both stemming from cultural inequalities in gender roles, induce parents to prevent the survival of female babies.

Bumiller learned that, above all, poverty drove Indian farming families' decisions about whether to bring a child into the world—and in Tamil Nadu, as in many other places, girls are not worth as much as boys in the labor market. She reported that "government-employed midwives who lived in the area told me they feared for a newborn's life if it was so unfortunate as to be the third or fourth girl born into a poor family of farm laborers. Such a family could not possibly afford the price of another girl's dowry. . . . The birth of a daughter had become a devastating blow, one that a family believed could threaten its survival. At best, a family saw a daughter as an investment with little return. She would never earn as much in the fields as a son, and her small contribution from day labor would end when she left her family after marriage. To some villagers . . . 'putting a child to sleep,' as they called it, seemed their only choice."[10]

Resource-poor people also make difficult choices about their living infants. When a mother gives food to her children, she may have to choose who gets more and who less. When children become ill, parents make critical decisions about who will be taken to the health clinic. Gender bias in the culture weighs in the balance. Bias also leads some wealthier parents to use sex selection to prevent the birth of a female child. Their reasons have to do with the social devaluation and subordination of women. Such parents may feel either unwilling to bring a girl into a world hostile to females or unable to face the perceived shame of producing another girl.

How Do Girls Go Missing?

Writing very personally, Charles Feng, a writer and medical student, recorded some of his family's history thus:

> Deep in the heartland of Henan Province, northwest of the Songshan Mountain Range's foothills and just south of the Yellow River, lies the Wang village where my great-grandparents, and their parents, and countless parents before that, came into this world and passed away. . . . It is in this remote locale, some ninety years ago, that my great-grandmother, Shu Wang, gave birth to her first child, a daughter. Understandably depressed—it was the males who perpetuated the Wang lineage—my great-grandfather, Chung Wang, took the little girl on her fifth day of life down to the river and quietly placed her body, headfirst, into the rushing water. Two years later, when their second child came out of the womb,

WOMEN'S COURAGE: MADURAI, TAMIL NADU, INDIA. Women's Cell is a small women's group working to prevent individual cases of female human rights violations and societal systems of discrimination against women. The group works specifically to prevent female infanticide, rape, malnutrition among female children, AIDS, imposed prostitution, the exploitation of women's agricultural labor, and forms of discriminatory marriage customs, including dowry—whether practiced by Hindus, Muslims, or Christians. With the purpose of raising consciousness among women and rendering "invisible" women visible, Cell was begun in 1985 by an English teacher at Fatima College.

The group is particularly interested in raising awareness and confidence among underprivileged women who, according to Women's Cell, suffer the most severe gender oppression in the local area and are "always exploited by police, lawyers" and others because of a lack of information, confidence, and support available to them. The group's programs include organizing rallies, marches, and other nonviolent demonstrations to protest female infanticide, rape, bride burning, dowry, etc.; producing lessons communicated through street theater, poetry, and stories; and collaborating with other groups on literacy programs.

WOMEN'S COURAGE: USILAMPETTI, TAMIL NADU, INDIA. The Indian Council for Child Welfare, Tamil Nadu, has worked since 1953 to protect the rights of deprived, neglected, and exploited children. With the goal of ending female infanticide, the Council has implemented strategies in 307 villages in the Usilampetti region of Tamil Nadu. These strategies involve income-generating activities, women's self-help groups, girl-child support services, awareness campaigns, and adolescent education. Focusing on students between the ages of twelve and sixteen, the Council provides books and uniforms to encourage girls to stay in school and learn about self-confidence and health. The girls use street theater to raise community awareness about women's health.

The group also provides direct monitoring and counseling to all pregnant and at-risk women (defined as those who have one or more daughters) and their family members. If a couple still does not want a girl child, the Council provides a receiving center for female babies, hoping to prevent infanticide. Between 1998 and 1999 the cases of female infanticide in the region dropped from 200 to 22 and have continued to remain low. The Council explains this success in terms of awareness, economic independence, and empowerment of women.

it, too, was a daughter, and so met the same fate—an unmarked grave into which a body, faceless and nameless, was laid to rest. With unswerving ambition and eagerness, Shu and Chung Wang tried again. And, yet again, the same result: a daughter. Unable to cope with the misery of going down to the river a third time, Chung decided they would keep this baby, my grandmother.[11]

Girls go missing because of infanticide, a problem that the world has not outgrown, though statistics on the practice are virtually unavailable. Bumiller has written about it, drawing from interviews and observations in villages in India. A 2004 *Newsweek* article described the work of a woman in Bihar, India, who helps women give birth for a fee equal to about 80 U.S. cents; for an additional, equal amount, if the baby is a girl and the parents so choose, the birth attendant will snap the spinal chord of the newborn and declare her stillborn. "Many couples insist that we get rid of the baby girl at birth," she is quoted as saying. "What can we do?"[12]

Girls also go missing because of neglect. Differential treatment among infants takes three main paths: neglect in allocation of food, of developmentally supportive nurturance, and of medical treatment or health care.[13] Haldar and her colleagues, studying families in India in the late 1960s, observed differential weaning and breastfeeding patterns and found that intervals between births were consistently shorter after the birth of a girl than after the birth of a boy, suggesting that boys were breast fed longer.[14] Longer duration of breastfeeding not only reduces malnutrition but also improves brain development. Furthermore, some research has shown that infantile diarrheal diseases, related to malnutrition in infancy, are more widespread among girls.[15]

The Human Development Report of the United Nations Development Programme (UNDP), 1995, notes that "The perception is widespread that infant boys are fed more adequately than infant girls in poor areas, suggesting a gender bias in favour of male children," but that "nutrition data disaggregated by sex are limited," and that comparisons vary from one country or area to another.[16] For example, whereas in sub-Saharan Africa, measures of moderate or severe underweight were 17% among girls and 32% for boys, the opposite was true "in Latin America and the Caribbean, where 31% of girls were underweight in comparison to 17% of boys. In Bangladesh, girls

WOMEN'S COURAGE: TARAPOTO, PERU. La Federación Provincial de Clubes de Madres de San Martín (The Federation of Mothers' Clubs of San Martin) works with local clubs to teach mothers healthy practices and to help them gain financial independence. One of the Federation's major nutrition programs is "vaso de leche" (glass of milk), a nutrition campaign promoted by word of mouth among members of the clubs and through the Federation's weekly radio program.

Over the years, the program has come to cover such issues as women's legal rights, child nutrition, and mental health. Through the network of mother's clubs and the radio program, many women in Peru have received information about how to start community gardens, raise animals, and generate income. The founders of the Federation were raising families and cultivating farm plots when they met and joined with others in 1994 to advocate for their own rights and the rights of their children.

WOMEN'S COURAGE: VIENTIANE, LAOS. The Gender Development Group (GDG) serves expectant mothers and infants through its outreach programs to promote nutrition for newborns, family planning, and obstetrical care. Formed in 1991 to raise awareness about gender equality in the country, the GDG draws its members from different non-governmental organizations in most regions of Laos. In this country, maternal and infant mortality rates are among the highest in the world. (For example, Laos ranks twenty-fourth out of twenty-eight countries in the region for deaths of children under five.) To address these issues, GDG focuses on women and children's health. However, other programs serve the longer term goals of reducing gender-based discrimination and violence. The group firmly believes that health education and greater equity in the community will empower women to gain control over their own bodies and health choices.

experienced malnutrition somewhat more than did boys: 59% of girls and 56% of boys suffered chronic malnutrition, and 10% of girls and 7% of boys suffered acute malnutrition. In India's rural Punjab, poverty takes a bigger toll on the nutrition of girls than on that of boys: 21% of the girls in low-income families suffer severe malnutrition, compared with 3% of boys in the same families; and low-income boys fare better than upper-income girls."[17]

Differential health care also seems to be a major factor with regard to survival rates of female infants. Indeed, Sen argues that the morbidity and mortality observed in infant girls in India may result more from unequal access to health care than from bias in food distribution.[18] A 1997 UNICEF annual report noted that 250,000 girls die each year, primarily in South Central Asia and China, because they experience some sort of disadvantage relative to boys.[19] And although it is commonly believed that when choices have to be made, boys are taken to doctors more readily than are girls, there is little solid research on infant girls' unequal access to formal medical care.

Unfortunately, it is difficult to precisely determine the relative effects of discrimination on infant girls' access to food and to health care, because most research either views the household as a single entity with uniform internal distribution or treats newborns as a sex-neutral category. Whatever the cause of female infant mortality, however, the pressure of discrimination is so strong that unbalanced ratios of boys to girls continue beyond infancy into childhood.[20]

Finally, sex-selective abortion accounts for many of the missing girls. While poverty partially explains the practices of infanticide and neglect of female infants among poor families, it cannot account for the widespread abortion of female fetuses among wealthier families. That practice is more easily explained by the underlying critical issue relating to all women's health and human rights, namely the devaluing of women and girls. A study of a private hospital in Bombay, carried out by a local women's organization from 1978 to 1982, found that of eight thousand women who came from all over India for a sex-selection test, all but one wanted a son.[21] More generally in India, "after such a test, if the fetus turned out to be female, most women decided to abort," notes Bumiller.[22]

In India and possibly in China and Korea, the preferred method for ensuring the ideal of having sons has become sex-selective abortion. Combining prenatal screening with the abortion of a female fetus may be less shocking to most people than killing a newborn but because it is possible and widely practiced, its effect on skewing the gender balance is greater. In the 1970s, the new technologies of amniocentesis and ultrasound became widely available, allowing those who could afford the tests the opportunity to practice sex-selective abortion.

In India, abortion was legalized in 1971 (through the Medical Termination of Pregnancy Act), but its use for sex selection was outlawed in 1994 by the 1994 Prenatal Diagnostic Techniques Bill. Nevertheless, more and more people use screening and abortion to ensure having a son. In the four years from 1978 to 1982, nearly 78,000 female fetuses were aborted in India. A decade later, that figure had escalated dramatically: in just two years, 1993 and 1994, 360,000 female fetuses were aborted.[23] A 23-year-old woman in Maharashtra, when interviewed about why she had chosen an abortion, said "The hope for a son was so much that I didn't have any other feeling. I felt sad, but what to do? One has to burn one's mind. There are two daughters; what to do with a third daughter? Nothing else, a son is wanted. Only that is in my mind."[24]

Although using amniocentesis, ultrasound, or other methods of prenatal screening (such as sperm sorting for Y chromosomes, an expensive high-tech method) for sex selection is illegal in India, China, Korea, and most other countries, it is increasingly prevalent. Describing the drive for sons and reporting on the practice of sex-selective abortion in one region of China, Chu Junhong, a faculty member of the Institute of Population Research at Beijing University, writes that under the one-child-per-family program, many families control for the sex of their children, particularly the later born, by using prenatal screening and abortion.[25] Although some statistics in China may be unreliable—some village lists leave out girls entirely—Chinese census results demonstrate significant and widening imbalances between male and female births as methods of prenatal screening have become more widely available. Furthermore, most Chinese infants available for adoption are female. Writing on science subjects for *Newsweek*, journalist Mary Carmichael reports that "In Korea, ultrasound is used to identify sex; although it is illegal to use the method for sex selection, it is estimated that some 30,000 Korean female fetuses and virtually no male fetuses are aborted each year. In Korea, the ratio of boys to girls is 110 to 100; among fourth-born children, it is 168 to 100."[26]

In addressing such statistics, a complex issue arises. If abortion is banned for the purpose of sex selection, as it is in most countries, and if the ban is enforced, won't women's access to legal and safe abortion be compromised? While abortion is legal in many countries, access to the procedure remains inadequate in many areas; restricting the procedure may only result in more unwanted pregnancies and another blow to women's health. Balancing a

WOMEN'S COURAGE: NEW DELHI, INDIA. The Sama Resource Group for Women and Health (sama means equality in Hindi and ambience in Urdu) was formed in 1997 to stop sex-selective abortion, advocate for women's reproductive rights, and carry out research on such women's health issues as the relationship between gender and rates of malaria. Sama's concept of health involves linking violence, human rights, livelihood, and health. The group produces informational materials and training programs for partner organizations and individual communities of women.

Started by a group of activists with experience in women's empowerment and health, Sama is a resource center that collaborates with tribal, dalit (sometimes referred to as untouchables, the lowest caste level), and minority forums and women's groups across India on issues relating to gender, health, and violence. Its objectives are to empower women by changing perspectives on health from needs to rights through training and capacity building; to inform women about the availability of health services, including indigenous concepts of reproductive health; to initiate debate and discussion on women's health within a human rights framework; and to establish a network of women's organizations working on reproductive health issues and rights at both the grassroots and policy levels.

Although based in New Delhi, Sama works primarily in the northeast states of Assam, Meghalaya, Nagaland, Orissa, Andhra Pradesh, Bihar, Tamil Nadu, and Uttar Pradesh. Its collaborative campaigns to stop sex-selective abortion have been directed to both women and men.

woman's right to choose to terminate a pregnancy against that choice being based on sex preference is a dilemma for feminists and others working to preserve a woman's right to choose.

Demographic Imbalance and its Societal Effects

Widespread sex selection has resulted in imbalances between the sexes. For example, the China News Service, reporting on census data, said that the proportion of newborn boys to girls had risen from about 109% in 1982 to 117% in 2000,[27] more than ten percentage points higher than the normal ratio of about 106 boys to 100 girls.

The report from the Chinese news agency notes that there are regional differences in these ratios within China, with Tibet and Xinjiang, for example, having relatively normal ratios, and Hainan and Guangdong at the other extreme with ratios of 135.6 (boys to 100 girls) and 130.3 respectively. The greatest disparities in proportions of male and female infants were found in rural areas and between first, second, and third or later births. In 2000, the ratios for first, second, and third or later babies were 107%, 152%, and 159%, respectively. The report goes on to predict that these imbalances "will necessarily lead to the disproportion of [the] male and female population in [the] matrimonial age group, and further the eruption of sharp competition for marriage among [the] masculine population, thereby entailing a series of such problems as swindling and selling women and unstable family relations. And this will further endanger the healthy and stable development of society and economy, for which we must take great account and find out ways and means to solve the problem as soon as possible."[28]

And indeed, 2004 news reports from China and official statements from the China Statistics Administration suggest that one of the results of widespread son preference and the one-child-per-family policy is the emergence of a large class of young, single men, and resultant rising crime and instability in the provinces. The situation is also said to have resulted in increased kidnapping and trafficking of girls from one region to another. Girls may not be valued in individual families, but society needs and demands their presence, so the black market appears to be stepping in to meet a demand. In Beijing in 2004, for example, a court convicted 52 members of a baby-trafficking gang, highlighting "the scale of China's thriving black market in babies," according to the *New York Times*. "The evidence in the case included . . . an incident . . . when twenty-eight baby girls, none older than three months, were found in nylon tote bags aboard a long-distance bus."[29]

Nevertheless, overall, in South and some East Asian countries, cultural practices of female infanticide, limiting food and medical care for baby girls, and sex-selective abortion have, together, seriously clashed with biological principles, distorting the sex composition of some societies.

Signs of Changing Times

To deal with the problem of a shortage of females, some governments have begun to offer monetary incentives to parents. In Huaiyuan County in China, for example, a pilot program gives parents of girls tax breaks; after two years, the program is beginning to be successful—at least in the eyes of local officials: "For every 100 girls born there . . . there are now just 120 boys," reported to be a "better" ratio than before the incentive program, when the ratio was close to 150 boys to 100 girls.[30]

Moreover, there is some evidence that in parts of China, particularly urban areas, as women realize that old traditions of sons looking after elderly parents are beginning to weaken, mothers are beginning to welcome a girl as their one child, thinking that they will be more likely to be looked after by a daughter than a son.

In Japan, the tide of preference has shifted. Increasing numbers of couples (some 75%) want daughters, and many turn to modern methods of sex selection to effect that outcome. "Only a generation ago Japanese society also favored sons. Now, parents want daughters because daughters, they say, are more likely than sons to take care of them in their old age. The Japanese enjoy the highest life expectancy in the world, but the government has only just begun setting up a comprehensive system of care for the elderly. 'One day I hope to live with my daughter and her husband after she marries,' says Chika Okamoto, a twenty-nine-year old with one daughter. 'A son's wife would be like a stranger and harder to ask for help.'"[31] Although using amniocentesis and other such technologies for sex selection is illegal in most countries, it does happen, increasingly, as couples seek to "balance" their families according to their personal and cultural wishes, raising ethical questions in countries both rich and poor.

And so, for various reasons and in some parts of the world, things are beginning to change. Sons are still preferred—because they are still perceived as being more valuable—but girls are beginning to be more welcome.

Education is a lifetime inheritance. It is a lifetime insurance. Education is the key to success, a bus to a brighter future for our people.

—Zukiswa, age 16, Kwa Magxaki Township, Port Elizabeth, South Africa[1]

They shot my father right in front of me. . . . It was nine-o'clock at night. They came to our house and told him they had orders to kill him because he allowed me to go to school. The Mujahideen had already stopped me from going to school, but that was not enough. Then they came and killed my father. I cannot describe what they did to me after killing my father. . . .

—A 15-year-old girl, Afghanistan, 1994[2]

Exhibit C is the young girl
dragged into the bush by the midwives
and made to sing while they scrape the flesh
from between her legs, then tie her thighs
till she scabs over and is called healed. . . .

—Margaret Atwood, "A Women's Issue," Canada, 1981[3]

3

Childhood: The Hope of Education and the Persistence of Discrimination

PHILOMENA, WHO LIVES IN KENYA, was excited because she was going to school with her brother. There were hundreds of children at the school, all hoping to learn and to get a free lunch of porridge every day. The first months went well, and Philomena made friends with some of the other girls who were at the school. She and three other seven-year-old girls crowded together at a little wooden desk, looking at pictures and beginning to read the words in the one book that they shared. In the springtime, Philomena's mother told her that the next day they were going together to do something very special. Some of the other girls were going too. Philomena was nervous and excited at the same time; she had heard that special things happened to girls of her age, but she was not sure what the surprise was going to be.

It turned out to be terrifying and indescribably painful. Her auntie and grandmother held her arms and legs while another older woman cut her between the legs. Finally Philomena fainted. When she awoke, she was lying on a cot, her legs bound closely together to stem the bleeding. She remained resting for several days and finally was allowed to get up, to hobble around until the wound healed. Her mother and other female relatives gave her special food; they treated her in a respectful and admiring way. She felt honored to become a special part of the community. Because of her wounds, she stayed away from school for several weeks, and then it seemed embarrassing to return. Besides, her mother needed her to do chores at home. Philomena never went back to school. Philomena is fifteen now, in 2007; she helps her mother in the fields and looks after her younger brothers and sisters. Soon she will be married.

Philomena's story is not unusual. Female genital mutilation, poverty, and the reality of household and farm work are some of the reasons that cause little girls to drop out of school or perhaps never enroll in the first place.

There are 2.2 billion children in the world today, in 2007; 1.9 billion of them live in poor countries; about half of them—1 billion—live in poverty.[4] Girls in poor countries, made vulnerable by virtue of both their sex and poverty, are in danger of being denied their human rights to health care and basic education.[5] They are also vulnerable to sexual and physical abuse as well as cultural practices such as female genital mutilation. Boys, of course, suffer poverty too, and they are also subjected to child labor and sexual exploitation. But poverty, violence, and unequal access to education and other basic rights have greater effects on girls and demand particular attention. This chapter focuses on these issues as they affect girls in childhood, the years from about four to twelve: restricted access to health care and education, the violent experiences of female genital mutilation, and forced labor and prostitution.

Unequal Access to Nutrition and Health Care

Patterns of care begun in infancy persist into childhood. While a lack of resources forces parents to make difficult choices with regard to food and health care, the perception that girls are worth less than boys often determines the outcome of those dilemmas. If a child is ill, or if food is scarce, how will parents allocate their limited resources? Who will get to go to the doctor? Who will eat first? Which child or adult will receive the last morsel of food on the table?

Studies by Leela Visaria of the Gujarat Institute for Development Research in India have shown that son preference affects these choices. Traditions and social customs in some countries of South Asia, for example, have favored

WOMEN'S COURAGE: IGANGA, UGANDA.   The National Women's Association for Social and Educational Advancement works with girls, parents, and school administrators to decrease negative stereotypes of girls' academic performance. Since its founding in 1992, the Association has focused particularly on raising girls' confidence by teaching them public speaking skills and by encouraging participation in drama and debate groups. The Association has addressed the needs of rural communities, where both admissions and retention rates are low for girls in elementary schools. The group's overarching goals are to give women and girls a voice in society by promoting skills development, training functional literacy, and advocating for justice through human rights and legal education.

feeding men and boys before women and girls.[6] "An Indian girl is five times less likely than a boy to be properly fed or immunized," reports Visaria in her 2002 study on education and health in South Asia, which examined government statistics for more than four thousand children in sixteen states in India. Although levels of vaccination varied "enormously" by caste and religion, with more Hindus vaccinating their children than minority Muslims or dalits (sometimes referred to as "untouchables," the lowest caste level), girls were more neglected than boys in all these groups. Other studies also highlight "the relative neglect of girls compared to boys" with regard to health services generally.[7] Such discrimination is not confined to India, though studies have been much more extensive in that country than elsewhere.

The Great Hope of Education

Although poverty coupled with persistent son-preference often results in parents in some countries choosing not to educate girls, things are changing. Changing social attitudes toward girls are showing up in higher school enrollment for girls and for boys, especially in Asia and Latin America. Girls want to go to school, and parents are beginning to want them to attend.

Education can be offered on a railway platform in Rajasthan, India, and in a private school in the United States; it can be grasped by an eager child in a war-torn building in Kabul or in the mobile schools of Sudan. Somewhere amid the squalor of slum streets and shantytowns are scores of children who want, more than anything, the excitement and potential of an education—an inheritance essential to the dignity and worth of the human person.[8]

I remember a ragged little girl in a village in Nepal in 2001 who had picked up broken English and wanted to practice it with me. She was eight. "What do you want to be when you grow up?" I asked. Without hesitation, she said "A doctor!" What happened to her? Was the women's group I visited sufficiently strong to help her realize her dreams? I hope so.

Trends in Nepal are encouraging. Visaria reports that "the government has subscribed to the goal of achieving universal primary education and has made the five-year primary education program starting at six years of age officially compulsory and free of charge in government schools. . . . Despite these efforts, and a dramatic increase in enrollment at [all] levels of general education . . . available data indicate that girls lag behind boys in school enrollment and in literacy and educational attainment." She attributes this "low level of literacy among females in Nepal . . . to social prejudices against female education, restrictions on their mobility, and their overall low social status." However, while in 1991 37% of girls were in secondary school in Nepal,[9] by the late 1990s female enrollment in secondary school had almost doubled, and the trend has continued.[10]

Progress in Nepal has been mirrored in other parts of the world. In primary school, girls' enrollment either increased or remained stable for almost all countries during the 1990s. In secondary school, the ratios of girls to boys also rose, and in two regions (East Asia and the Pacific and industrialized countries), girls and boys are enrolling in equal numbers.

As the graph on page 35 shows, the countries of Central and Eastern Europe and the Commonwealth of Independent States are close to "gender parity" in education, and in the Middle East and North Africa, the female GER is at 93% of the male GER in primary school and at 90% in secondary school. With female enrollment rates at 95% to 97% of male enrollment rates, Latin America and the Caribbean are close to gender parity in primary school; in secondary school, the female GER exceeds the male GER, which means that more girls than boys continue their education past primary school. In the three remaining regions, there is a larger drop in the index from primary to secondary school. In Eastern and Southern Africa, almost as many girls as boys are enrolled in primary school, but at the secondary

**Primary and secondary school gross enrollment ratios:
female Gender Enrollment Ratio (GER) as a % of male GER, 2000–2005**

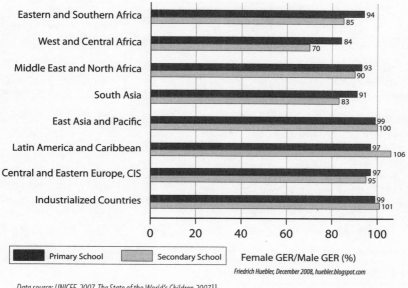

Friedrich Huebler, December 2008, huebler.blogspot.com

Data source: UNICEF. 2007. The State of the World's Children 2007.[11]

level of education, the female GER is only 85% of the male GER. In South Asia, the index is 91% in primary school and 83% in secondary school.

In West and Central Africa, girls are furthest behind boys in terms of school enrollment. The index is 84% in primary school and 70% in secondary school. In addition, total enrollment rates are lower than in any other region of the world. Compared to boys and compared to girls in other region, girls from West and Central Africa are least likely to reap the benefits of a formal school education.

The information cited above does not include absolute levels of school enrollment, information that for some reason is hard to find.[12] Gender parity may exist within the context of very low enrollment levels: i.e., there may be gender parity where only 50% of all children are enrolled. The following chart shows girls' enrollment in primary education over the decade between 1990 and 2000, but it does not show total numbers of children in each region.[13]

Enrollment (millions) in primary education by region (1990 and 2000)

| | Enrollment | | | | | |
| | 1990 | | | 2000 | | |
	Total	Female	%F	Total	Female	%F
World	595.5	273.2	45.9	647.5	302.7	46.7
Developing countries	505.0	229.1	45.4	562.2	261.2	46.5
Developed countries	61.3	29.8	48.6	62.3	30.3	48.7
Countries in transition	29.3	14.3	48.9	23.0	11.1	48.6
Sub-Saharan Africa	62.0	28.0	45.2	85.8	39.9	46.5
Arab States	30.5	13.2	43.4	35.7	16.4	46.0
Asia and the Pacific						
Central Asia	5.1	2.5	49.1	6.7	3.3	48.7
East Asia and the Pacific	206.7	97.4	47.1	211.2	100.9	47.8
South and West Asia	134.9	56.0	41.5	160.5	70.7	44.1
Latin America and the Caribbean	75.0	36.6	48.8	70.3	34.1	48.5
North America and Western Europe	50.1	24.3	48.6	52.7	25.7	48.7
Central and Eastern Europe	31.2	15.1	48.5	24.5	11.8	48.0

Note: Comparisons between the two years should be made with caution as the classification of primary education has changed for many countries. In particular, some countries reported a duration of more than six years in 1990, often equating primary to basic education. The duration for these countries has now been reduced to six grades or less.

At first glance, these enrollment statistics are extremely encouraging, and they bode well for the future of children's education. However, enrollment does not necessarily mean attendance, as we saw in Philomena's case. Philomena, like many girls, enrolled in school but was forced to drop out for health and social reasons. Many widely quoted figures on education are based on enrollment rather than on actual attendance, and in many countries even such data as these are just not available. In other words, the enrollment statistics may paint a picture that is far more positive than what is really taking place.

According to the *World Development Report of 2000-2001*, "The most commonly available indicator, the gross primary enrollment rate, suffers from serious conceptual shortcomings. The greatest is that school enrollment is only a proxy for actual school attendance. Moreover, the gross primary enrollment rate can rise if grade repetitions increase. The much-preferred net primary enrollment rate (showing the ratio of enrolled primary-school-age children to all primary-school-age children) is available only for around fifty developing countries for 1990–1997 and is not always separated by gender—

WOMEN'S COURAGE: KIBAYA, TANZANIA. Initially an informal home-based study group for girls, Jifunze (which in Swahili means "teaching oneself") has become a formal study center staffed with five certified teachers and six full-time volunteers. For the first time, girls in Kibaya have access to a multimedia learning complex, including an educational resource center, a library with gender-sensitive books in Swahili, and a solar-powered lighting system that enables them to study at night. The Jifunze project was founded in 1988 by two women—a Maasai kindergarten teacher and an American resident—to address limitations on girls' higher education in Tanzania, where very few young women graduate from university. Each year in that country, a number of high school girls gain admission to university training; however, they cannot attend because they cannot afford the tuition or because they already have family responsibilities. In addition to strengthening girls' primary and secondary schooling, Jifunze has established a scholarship fund for girls to enter and complete university.

not enough to make reliable aggregations by region. A number of ongoing survey initiatives, however, are improving the quantity and quality of data on health and education."[14] Given major efforts over the past five years by international agencies and individual governments with regard to access to education, more up-to-date and more reliable information should be available by about 2009. Despite these limitations, there are enough data to know that school enrollment and attendance by both girls and boys is growing around the globe. They also show that girls' participation in formal education continues to lag behind boys' in the poorest regions of the world.

Unequal access to education in the past has resulted in discrepancies in literacy among women in most regions around the world. Worldwide, about 875 million adults, two-thirds of whom are women, cannot read or write. Figures from the Population Reference Bureau for 2002 reveal that in Africa, 52% of women were literate compared with 70% of men. In much of South Asia, the comparable figures for literacy were 45% female compared with 67% male. Moreover, that the populations of these two regions are among the world's fastest growing suggests that the absolute number of illiterate and poorly educated women in these regions will continue to grow.[15] Slightly more recent figures from UNESCO, shown in the graph on page 38, indicate

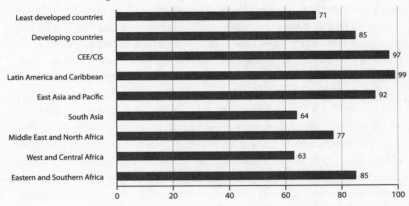

Regional Literacy Rates for Women, 2000-2004

Least developed countries — 71
Developing countries — 85
CEE/CIS — 97
Latin America and Caribbean — 99
East Asia and Pacific — 92
South Asia — 64
Middle East and North Africa — 77
West and Central Africa — 63
Eastern and Southern Africa — 85

Adult literacy rate: females as a percentage of males, 2000–2004*

Note: Adult literacy rate refers to the percentage of persons aged 15 and over who can read and write.
*Data refer to the most recent year available during the period specified.
Source: UNESCO Institute of Statistics.

that in sub-Saharan Africa and South Asia—where almost one-third of the world's women live—the gender gap continues to be wide with regard to literacy. Regional literacy rates for women compared with men, for example, are shown in the graph above.

EDUCATION AS A DEVELOPMENT STRATEGY

Increasingly, UN agencies and the World Bank are coming to regard educating girls as a central strategy for poverty alleviation, health improvement, and development. In his role as the World Bank's chief economist, Lawrence Summers stated that "investment in girls' education may well be the highest return investment available in the developing world."[16] His report focuses mainly on the benefits of girls' education to society in general:

> First, educating women reduces child mortality. . . . The evidence that mothers channel much more of their income to expenditures on children than their husbands do is overwhelming. Education also increases the willingness to seek medical care and improves sanitation practices. . . . Studies done at the micro level within individual countries also show that more educated women have healthier children. . . . In Africa, for example, the child of a woman who has not been to school has a one in five chance of

dying before the age of five; a child whose mother attended five years of school has a mortality risk that is over 40% less. . . . Second, educating women reduces fertility. . . . Educated women want to have fewer children and are better able to attain their desired level of fertility. . . . Third, educating women reduces maternal mortality. . . . one can calculate that an additional year of school for 1,000 women will prevent two maternal deaths. Fourth, educating women helps prevent the spread of AIDS. . . . Educated women are more likely to enter into stable marriages and look out for their reproductive health, and much less likely to become prostitutes. Each of these factors is crucial in stopping the spread of AIDS.[17]

This last point on AIDS is somewhat suspect, given recent data from East Africa indicating that, for women, a major risk factor for their contracting HIV is being married (a topic discussed in the next chapter).

In his presentation, Summers focuses on the benefits that go beyond those that individual women and girls receive, and, indeed, the education of women and girls is inextricably linked with solving broader societal problems. He continues, "Fifth, educating women has important environmental benefits. . . . Educating women contributes to reduced fertility. By raising the opportunity cost of women's time, it discourages them from clearing forests, and it increases their ability to manage natural resources efficiently."[18] Estimating how much it would cost to produce similar health and fertility benefits using medical and family planning interventions, he concludes that educating girls is a particularly cost-effective approach to many health and social problems. "Considering the very low cost of equalizing educational opportunities for men and women, the question is not whether countries can afford this investment, but whether countries can afford not to educate more girls."[19]

The economic and social benefits of female education are coming to light, but the neglected sister in the literature from international development agencies is the clear recognition of girls' fundamental right to education as a matter of social justice. Perhaps the utilitarian economic emphasis thus far has been based on the notion that advocating social justice and human rights does not necessarily result in the allocation of bigger budgets. I found as I raised money to create The Global Fund for Women (the overarching

WOMEN'S COURAGE: DAR ES SALAAM, TANZANIA. The Child Concern Consortium (C3) was founded in 1999 in Dar es Salaam with the goal of providing help to vulnerable women and children (especially girls) living in abusive circumstances. The group's mission is to increase access to quality social services (education, health care, nutrition, clean water and sanitation) for women, girls, and the youth of Tanzania.

The group's ongoing work involves working directly with women and youth on economic and legal rights; sensitizing parents, teachers, and law enforcement officials of the rights of girls; establishing and improving social service facilities, such as clinics and schools; and promoting the elimination of child labor and abuse. C3 has raised awareness of women's and adolescents' sexual and reproductive health through a variety of initiatives, including public rallies to sensitize people to women's health and rights issues. The group has had some success in influencing government to be more aware of the needs of girls, and it has also implemented an HIV/AIDS prevention program in secondary schools which reaches some fifteen schools and some twelve thousand youth.

interest of which is the human rights of women) that a simple economic development argument was easier for donors to understand and respond to than a human rights/social justice argument.

Of course these approaches to funding girls' education programs are not mutually exclusive. The support of girls and women can be advocated both in terms of justice—"It isn't fair that girls' education has been so neglected!"—and in instrumental terms—educating girls enables a country's economic goals. Both approaches are reasonable.

But if we are interested in transforming our societies by changing the ways we relate to each other, it is imperative that we make the concept of justice central, as the basic context for all of our programs to assist girls and women. Advances in civil rights during the 1960s and 1970s in the U.S. were not made on the basis of the argument that giving African Americans access to education and employment on an equal footing with whites would solve the U.S.'s economic problems. Rather, the advancements were made by an appeal to justice. As long as we work exclusively within the framework of "economic development," we will prevent the formation of more profound solutions based on social justice.

WOMEN'S COURAGE: ISLAMABAD, PAKISTAN. The Working Women Association started out in 1975 as the first hostel for working women in Pakistan, responding to the housing and other needs of young professional women. Over time, the Association has grown to the point of having offices in all provinces of Pakistan and members throughout the country. In recent years, the group began to support women and girl domestic workers, mainly providing them with informal education through free education centers.

Millions of girls in Pakistan do not attend school, many of them because they must work to provide for their families. Once they begin to work, it is difficult for them to enroll in regular government-run schools because of scheduling and access issues. The gender gap in girls' education in Pakistan is one of the highest in Asia. The Association's non-formal girls education centers are unique because they provide education for girls while they are on the job. The objective of these centers is to eliminate child labor and prepare girls for semi-skilled occupations, such as teaching and nursing.

Through its programs the girls also receive medical checkups and basic medical services. Focusing on self esteem and self confidence as well as formal education, the schools have succeeded in providing basic education to some 2,000 children, mostly girls, and some 20% of the girls have mainstreamed into government schools in order to receive additional education.

WOMEN'S COURAGE: KABUL, AFGHANISTAN. The New Afghanistan Women Association (NAWA, meaning "voice" in Dari) was formed to address the problem of very high rates of illiteracy among Afghan women and girls. Its major programs are home schools for girls and training centers for women to become journalists and to learn about the media. NAWA was formed in 2002, bringing together the Afghan Women Journalists Association and the Afghan Feminine Association (AFA), groups that had developed during the 1990s. NAWA's overarching goal is to further democracy and women's rights by encouraging women to become active partners in reconstructing a new democratic Afghanistan.

EDUCATION AS A HUMAN RIGHT

Certain international meetings, most notably the Fourth United Nations Conference on Women, held in China in 1995, have represented the education of girls and women as both a human right and a strategy for development.

WOMEN'S COURAGE: GARISSA, NORTHEASTERN PROVINCE, KENYA. Womankind Kenya, also known as WOKIKE, promotes education in rural farming communities in the northeastern province of Kenya, where illiteracy and poverty are widespread. Traditional practices persist in this region. For this reason, WOKIKE emphasizes women's and girls' rights, specifically with regard to ending such traditional practices as female genital cutting and early marriage. Focusing on education since its founding in 1989, WOKIKE has built primary schools and learning centers for orphaned girls, so they can grow and prosper in safe environments. WOKIKE also provides business training for women and programs to train health and legal workers, with the overall purpose of raising awareness of women's rights in the community.

The Conference in China highlighted literacy as the key to women's full participation in societal decision-making and to improving the well being of families. Education earns community respect, and being respected builds confidence and encourages participation.

Recognizing individual people's right to education as well as the economic benefits of an educated population, governments have tried different approaches to boost girls' education. Several countries in recent years have reversed the earlier strategy of imposing school fees, with remarkable results. In Kenya, after fees were abolished, children's enrollment in school increased by 1.3 million. In Uganda, enrollment went from 2.5 million in 1997 to 6.5 million in 2000.[20] A 2003 *New York Times* article on girls' education in Africa reported the irony that "School fees, which were a fixture of World Bank-led economic reform packages for the last decade [were singled out] as the largest obstacle to girls' education. In societies where girls are considered unworthy of the investment, many poor parents pay for their sons, not their daughters, to go to school."[21] Ensuring that every child gets free primary or basic education is of utmost importance; even if secondary education is not feasible, primary education at least affords literacy and, with it, a sense of empowerment. Eliminating school fees has made a huge difference.

Adding a free meal to free primary school programs should further increase the likelihood that children are allowed to enroll and remain in school. In India, where primary education is free, schools offer a mid-day

WOMEN'S COURAGE: PESHAWAR, NORTHWEST FRONTIER PROVINCE, PAKISTAN. The Afghan Institute of Learning (AIL) has created a network of schools, medical clinics, and training programs in Peshawar, with the purpose of improving Afghan women's access to education and health. Through its programs, AIL reaches more than 350,000 women and girls each year. AIL has also established the first Afghan Women's University in Peshawar, Pakistan, giving Afghan women access to post-secondary education and providing them with training to become teachers and health workers. The women of AIL believe that the key to Afghanistan's future lies in an educated populace. Through human rights and leadership workshops, the Institute teaches within the context of Islam, drawing support from the Quran for women's rights and education. The group also encourages Afghan women's participation and leadership as the keys to rebuilding the nation.

meal for girls up to grade seven.[22] Similarly, in Kenya, free primary education and one meal a day has boosted enrollment, though the costs of books and uniforms and secondary school fees still force some children of poor parents to stay home or leave school.

Worldwide, free education is possible. According to OXFAM, "to provide basic [primary] education for every child [in the world] would cost . . . U.S.$5.6 billion a year—the equivalent of less than three days of global military spending."[23] This would be a useful investment for both girls and boys. Educated children in the Kibera slums of Nairobi, Kenya, the favelas of Brazil, and rural areas of West Africa and India bring learning and the possibility of change home to others in their families.[24]

One of the major goals of the United Nations Educational, Scientific, and Cultural Organization (UNESCO) is to provide free primary education for all children by the year 2015. Doing this will be a challenge. According to UNESCO, in 2000, about 104 million children were out of school, nearly all of them living in resource-poor countries; of these, 57% were girls, a better percentage than in 1990, when 63% of all out-of-school children were girls. Over the same decade, however, the actual number of children out of school in Africa increased by 17% to an estimated total of 6,378,000 more children without the chance to obtain primary education.[25]

CHALLENGES TO GIRLS' EDUCATION

Although in many parts of the world, especially in Asia and Latin America, girls are beginning to be enrolled in school in much greater numbers, girls are often unable to stay in school, given cultural traditions like female genital mutilation and the demands on girls to help at home and in the fields. According to a 1995 report by the Forum for Women African Educationalists, 50% of the girls enrolled drop out of school by the fourth grade, only 34% of girls complete primary school, and 64% drop out before they are fully literate.[26] The demands on girls to do housework and fieldwork make doing schoolwork difficult or impossible, which results in poorer grades and higher dropout rates for girls than boys and finally leads to the conclusion that girls' education is not as good an investment as boys'. Parents find value in the domestic labor of girls, whereas they incur costs in time and money when children travel to school and pay school fees.[27]

In addition, traveling to school can be a particular problem for girls, whose families often fear for their safety. To solve this problem, an innovative project in rural Benin, Africa, set up a ferry service that helped rural girls cross rivers and get to school rather than travel other, more dangerous and circuitous routes. Ed Allan of World Learning for International Development, the NGO that worked with local groups to launch the ferry service, summed up an important lesson: "Not all education problems need education solutions."

It is becoming more widely understood that the HIV/AIDS epidemic, especially in Africa, is creating legions of orphans. UNICEF reported that in 2003, fifteen million children on the continent had lost one or both of their parents to AIDS.[28] What is less well known is that this crisis affects girl orphans differently from boys, and poses additional burdens. Many orphans live in houses run by other children or are left to beg on the streets. According to UNAIDS, because of social stigma concerning the disease, these orphans are at greater risk of malnutrition, illness, sexual exploitation, and HIV infection than children orphaned by other causes.[29] HIV positive children who have lost their parents to the disease or been abandoned may be shunned by their societies and forced out of school. Many of the girls who are AIDS orphans become heads of households. This thrusts them deeper into poverty, blotting out their dreams of education and a paying job as they are sidelined into care-giving roles precisely at the time they should be in school.

WOMEN'S COURAGE: YOGYAKARTA, INDONESIA. The Institute for Women and Children's Studies teaches gender equality to children in their homes and schools by working with local radio stations, religious centers, parent groups, and pre-school teachers. Part of a network of non-governmental organizations in Yogyakarta that focuses on women and children's rights, the Institute directs its messages to both boys and girls, with the vision of children developing strong and positive images of girls and women. Over the years, the Institute has expanded its programs, particularly by collaborating with Mbangum Deso ("develop our village"), a popular television program directed toward rural children aged between five and eighteen. The program uses humor and facts to inform people about such issues as women's status, HIV/AIDS, family planning, education, and environmental degradation.

Beyond the problem of how to enroll and retain more girls in school lies that of what schools teach girls (and boys) about their possibilities for achievement. Education that is not gender-neutral often teaches girls subjects and skills that may be considered unimportant or less marketable. Different tasks may be assigned to girls and boys, based on traditional notions of gender. For example, gender stereotypes sometimes prompt teachers to instruct girls to clean the classrooms and bathrooms.[30] Being assigned less challenging academic tasks and being made to conform to gender roles can affect a child's self-confidence. A much debated issue in discussions on global education is the nature and quality of the education girls may receive. In the course of learning to read, are girls and boys using texts that reinforce girls' lesser status? By not calling on girls as often as boys, do teachers perpetuate the subordinate roles of women? What perspectives on gender are presented in social studies? Whose history is taught? These questions are applicable worldwide as educators strive to communicate messages that accord with their values. As girls attempt to move out of subordinate positions in society—through the primary means of education—the answers to such questions are critical, though certainly not obvious.

Quality of education is of utmost importance, and yet it is one of the hardest variables to standardize and achieve. Therefore the question persists: when faced with uphill battles about allocation of resources, is it better to send girls to school so that they at least have the tool of literacy—even if their subordinate roles may be reinforced—or to hold out for more appropriate education? There seems little doubt that basic literacy is at least one key to girls' and women's empowerment and freedom. Even if the quality of education is poor or the environment is not gender sensitive, learning to read is part of the path to liberation. Pushing for higher female school enrollment and retention rates is a positive step in the direction of eradicating the gender gap in education and in society. Beyond that step, however, it is also important to confront and eliminate the barriers that prevent girls from being educated even when they attend school. Ultimately, addressing the quality and nature of education is crucial so that girls and boys can derive the maximum benefit from their time in school.

Other important challenges to girls' education are the fear of going against sexual taboos and the reality of sexual predation and violence. For example, in parts of the Middle East and North Africa, as well as South and East Asia, even casual, social contact with male teachers and students may violate social norms of chastity. In Benin, as we have seen, the obstacle was concern over girls' safety on the journey to school; the solution, a local ferry service. In Guinea and Nigeria, among other countries, providing separate bathroom facilities for girls significantly increased female school enrollment, according to the UN. Similarly, according to ActionAid, a South Africa-based NGO, separate schools for girls helped assure parents in Pakistan that their daughters could attend school and be safe.[31]

An especially serious threat to girls is the fact that some find no other way to pay for their education than to sell their bodies. The "sugar daddy" syndrome, which the next chapter considers further, is common in parts of East Africa, where girls are so eager to attend school that they will pay school fees through "transactional sex" with male teachers and other older males. Addressing the problems of transactional sex and gender violence requires recognizing the special needs of girls, particularly with regard to their vulnerability to predation. Strategies to reduce or eliminate the gender gap in education must, therefore, take into account these needs if universal female education and literacy are to become realities.

A Violent Practice: Female Genital Mutilation

In some societies, traditional coming-of-age ceremonies or rites of passage to womanhood have limited girls' human rights in the sense of both violating their bodily integrity and limiting access to education and other choices. Female genital mutilation (FGM) is one such practice that stems from the social norms of a girl's tribe or ethnic group and serves to define her in the context of her community.[32] Some two million girls every year are at risk of undergoing the procedure, which involves the excision of female genitalia for aesthetic and/or cultural purposes.[33] It is estimated that about 130 million women, mostly in Africa, have undergone the FGM ritual during the last fifty or sixty years.[34]

To clarify the terminology: "female genital mutilation" is the phrase currently used by UN agencies, including the WHO, to identify the ritual cutting of female genitalia. A term used in the past was female circumcision, which implied that the surgery bore some resemblance to male circumcision. This is a misleading comparison because male circumcision involves removing only part of the foreskin of the penis without impairing sexual function.[35] The practice experienced by girls is a clitoridectomy—the partial or complete removal of the clitoris, a female sexual organ, with lifelong side effects and significant sexual impairment. To better reflect the true debilitating nature of the practice, the term female genital mutilation is now widely used both by the World Health Organization and by many African groups advocating the elimination of the practice. Some organizations working for the eradication of the practice refer to it as "female genital mutilation/female cutting" out of respect for those women who have undergone the ritual and do not wish to consider themselves mutilated.

Female genital mutilation (FGM) is prevalent in about twenty-eight African countries and among a few minority groups in Asia. The prevalence rate ranges from 5% in countries like Uganda and Zaire to 98% or almost 100% in Somalia, Sudan, Djibouti, Ethiopia, and Eritrea. It also occurs in some Middle Eastern countries, such as Egypt, some parts of Oman and Yemen, and among some groups in Saudi Arabia. A very limited form of the practice also occurs among some groups in Indonesia and Malaysia. Moreover, "Some immigrants practice various forms of FGM in other parts of the world, including some countries in Europe, the United States, Canada, New Zealand, and Australia. Most countries have enacted laws banning the practice."[36] FGM is illegal in fifteen of the twenty-eight African countries in which it is practiced, and it has also been made illegal in eleven industrialized countries. Percentages of women and girls affected vary from country to country, and so does the nature of the procedure.[37]

WOMEN'S COURAGE: BUEA, SOUTHWEST PROVINCE, CAMEROON. The Association of Ejagham Women of Vision in Buea, founded in 1998, works to end the practice of female genital cutting in the Manyu division of Cameroon by offering scholarships to young girls from poor backgrounds in order to promote their education. It also carries out programs in HIV/AIDS prevention by providing condoms for the large number of sex workers in this poor area of Cameroon.

The group encourages legal and legislative change by urging the Parliament to eradicate the practice of female genital cutting, which is traditional in the Manyu division of the southwest province. The southwest province borders Nigeria; that geographic fact, combined with poverty, means that sex trafficking and prostitution are especially widespread in the region as women and girls turn to prostitution for income to support their families. By making education more feasible and by providing information about HIV/AIDS, the organization strives to encourage positive change for women in Cameroon.

Female genital mutilation has no health value. Still, the value of a girl in some societies is closely tied to this tradition. Once the procedure has been carried out, parents and the larger community and often the girls themselves begin to see school as an unnecessary part of life that belongs more to the realm of childhood than to womanhood, which by virtue of the traditional practice, a girl may be said to have entered.[38]

Apart from its negative effects on girls' health and school attendance, FGM abrogates a person's basic right to bodily integrity. The practice has been condemned in several United Nations conventions and declarations and by the WHO, which views FGM as a major health risk.[39] Activists and public health officials, including locally based women's groups working to eliminate the practice, predict that it will disappear within the next two or three generations.

Like some other traditional practices, most notably foot binding, a practice that no longer exists but was prevalent in China even to the mid-twentieth century, female genital mutilation not only disfigures a woman but also inhibits her full participation in society. Similarly, when Chinese girls' feet were tightly bound from a very early age, they became deformed and dysfunctional. This painful process was carried out to cater to men's sexual desires; apparently small feet, or "lotuses," were considered sexually attractive. An important effect, of course, was that women with bound feet could not wander freely; they were confined to the home and dependent on others who could venture forth. The practice died out in the mid-twentieth century largely because of the advent of communism in China and the need for women's labor. Foot-binding had never been a practice of the lower socio-economic classes; working class people and rural peasants needed the labor of able-bodied and able-footed women to produce and feed the population. Yet, in Hong Kong in the 1960s, one could still see very old women tottering around on tiny feet, leaning on canes or being carried by young family members. Like foot-binding, female genital mutilation involves disfiguring and disabling a girl to make her more marriageable and attractive to men.

FEMALE GENITAL MUTILATION DESCRIBED

The World Health Organization has divided female genital mutilation into three categories. The first type, which involves excision of the prepuce, with or without partial or complete removal of the clitoris, is sometimes called sunna circumcision. When the entire clitoris, the prepuce, and some or all of the labia minora are removed, the term used is clitoridectomy. About 80% of all cases are of this type. The third and most extreme form of female genital mutilation involves a clitoridectomy followed by stitching up of the vulva; this type is referred to as infibulation. It is estimated that 15% of all cut women have undergone this most severe form of female genital mutilation, infibulation, which involves the stitching and narrowing of the vaginal opening. About 80% to 90% of all circumcisions in Djibouti, Somalia, and Sudan are of this type. In this procedure, a small opening is left to allow urine and menstrual blood to pass. This type is intended to ensure that a girl is a virgin at the time of marriage, when the area is either torn or cut open to allow sexual intercourse. Similarly, at the time of childbirth, the wound is opened either surgically or by tearing for passage of the baby, and is sewn closed again after the birth.

In their comprehensive writing on female genital mutilation, Anika Rahman and Nahid Toubia explain that the reasons for female genital mutilation are "complex, related to each other and woven into the beliefs and values communities uphold. Hence it is extremely difficult to isolate explanations for the practice. [FGM] represents not a singular value, but a single way to demonstrate physically otherwise socially constructed concepts like gender and sexuality." They enumerate the "four most common justifications for the practice," as follows:

- Custom and tradition: In many communities, circumcision is performed as a rite of passage from childhood to adulthood. . . . [FGM] represents an act of socialization into cultural values and a connection to family, community members, and previous generations. . . .

- Women's sexuality: A fundamental reason advanced for [FGM] is the need to control women's sexuality. . . . For many communities that practice [it], a family or clan's honor depends on a girl's virginity or sexual restraint. This is the case in Egypt, Sudan, and Somalia, where [FGM] is perceived as a way to curtail premarital sex. . . . In other contexts, such as in Kenya and Uganda, where sexual 'purity' is not a concern, [it] is performed to reduce the woman's sexual demands on her husband, thus allowing him to have several wives. . . . [it] is intended to reduce women's sexual desire, thus promoting women's virginity and protecting marital fidelity, in the interest of male sexuality. . . .

- Religion: It is important to note that [FGM] is a cultural, not a religious, practice. The practice predates the arrival of Christianity and Islam in Africa and is not a requirement of either religion. In fact, [it] is practiced by Jews, Christians, Muslims, and indigenous religious groups in Africa. However . . . it is strongly identified with Islam in several African nations, and many members of the Muslim community advocate for the practice. . . . during the 1998 International Conference on Population and Reproductive Health in the Muslim World at Egypt's Al Azhar University, a traditional center of Islamic scholarship, it was agreed that certain harmful practices, including [FGM], were the result of misunderstandings of Islamic provisions. . . .

- Social pressure: a common explanation for [FGM] is social pressure. In a community where most women are circumcised, family, friends, and neighbors create an environment in which the practice of circumcision becomes a component of social conformity. . . . Fear of community

WOMEN'S COURAGE: GAOUA, BURKINA FASO. L'Association pour la Promotion Feminine de Gaoua (The Association for the Promotion of Women in Gaoua) works to eradicate female genital mutilation and since its founding has transformed FGM practices throughout the Gaoua region of Burkina Faso. Begun in 1990 by thirty-one women, the group initially organized a series of meetings with traditional "circumcisers." The circumcisers explained that the ritual was a matter of moral obligation to the ancestors: they really wanted to do something to help, but they also wanted to adhere to cultural traditions. After much negotiation, the Association successfully persuaded the circumcisers to maintain all of the sacred and initiatory elements of the rite, performing all of the same gestures and preserving the ritual, but not carrying out the actual excision. These changes resulted in the circumcisers being able to feel and demonstrate that they had acted appropriately while also respecting the health of the girls. At the request of a chief from a neighboring village in Ghana, who had heard of the group's work on a radio program, members of the Association have now expanded their innovative work across the border into Ghana.

judgment, such as men's refusal to marry uncircumcised women, contributes to this pressure. . . .[40]

The World Health Organization identifies two additional perceptions:
- Hygiene and aesthetic reasons: the external female genitalia are considered dirty and unsightly and are to be removed to promote hygiene and provide aesthetic appeal.

- Myths: enhancement of fertility and promotion of child survival.[41]

Girls of various ages undergo the procedure, which differs from one region to another. In some countries, such as Somalia and Sudan, infant girls may be cut at eighteen months or two years. In most African countries where the practice is prevalent, the majority of girls undergo FGM at about age six or seven. Elsewhere, FGM is done to adolescents as an initiation into womanhood, sometimes in the days before marriage. Practices differ from country to country, as well as within countries. Generally, the ritual is quite secret, and is perpetuated and practiced almost entirely by women, often older women, who may be well paid to carry out the practice.[42]

HEALTH CONSEQUENCES

"The immediate and long-term consequences of female genital mutilation (FGM) vary according to the type and severity of the procedure performed," according to the WHO. "Immediate complications include severe pain, shock, hemorrhage, urine retention, ulceration of the genital region and injury to adjacent tissue. Hemorrhage and infection can cause death."[43] Moreover, pelvic infections emerging as a consequence of this practice can lead to irreversible damage to the reproductive organs, resulting in infertility.

The WHO reported in 2000 that:

> Although few reliable data exist, it is likely that the risk of maternal death and stillbirth is greatly increased, particularly in the absence of skilled health personnel and appropriate facilities. Female genital mutilation may have adverse effects on a healthy reproductive life and also be associated with long-term maternal morbidity. . . . Genital mutilation may leave a lasting mark on the life and mind of the woman who has undergone it. . . . The loss of trust and confidence in care-givers has been reported as a possible serious effect. In the longer term, women may suffer feelings of incompleteness, anxiety, depression, chronic irritability, and frigidity. They may experience marital conflicts because of sexual dysfunction. . . . Many girls and women, traumatized by their experience but with no acceptable means of expressing their fears, suffer in silence.[44]

Those speculations by the WHO were validated a few years later, when the first large medical study of FGM, conducted by members of the WHO Study Group on FGM and Obstetrical Outcome, found that the procedure raises by 50% the risks of mothers and infants dying. The study was conducted with the help of more than 28,000 women in six African nations from 2001 to 2003; the women were examined to document the degree of genital damage, and were followed until after they had given birth.[45]

Public health officials have worried further that, because sterilization procedures are not commonly available and a single razor blade or sharp stone may be used on several girls, FGM may spread HIV. Studies so far have not been conclusive on this point.

Poverty, educational level, and female genital mutilation are closely linked. Where pre-adolescent and adolescent girls undergo the practice as an initiation into womanhood, a girl is believed to be mature enough for marriage.

WOMEN'S COURAGE: NOUAKCHOTT, MAURITANIA. The Reseau Mauritanien pour la Promotion des Droits de la Femme (The Mauritanian Network for the Promotion of Women's Rights) works at both the policy and community levels to eradicate female genital mutilation (FGM) and HIV/AIDS. Members of the Network have developed proposed national policies on FGM and have presented these to the President of the Republic. At local levels, the group provides education for girls and training and education programs on health, FGM, and HIV/AIDS. Since its founding in 1998, the Network has had a vision of improving women's lives politically, socially, and economically.

She may gain newfound respect and status in her community, which can be empowering for young women in Africa. This attitude often translates into the belief, on both her part and that of the community, that she needs "no more education." Missing school because of pain during healing and subsequently dropping out results in lower educational levels and fewer economic prospects for "cut" women. They may marry when educationally and economically disadvantaged and at an age that is biologically too young to be safe. (Consequences of early marriage and childbearing are discussed in the next chapter.) Women's reduced sexual pleasure or perceived "passivity" sometimes triggers dissatisfaction in spouses and can promote polygamy, infidelity, or divorce, further impoverishing women.

PREVENTION

Although action against female genital mutilation began slowly, it has progressed significantly in recent years. In the early 1900s, colonial administrations and missionaries in Burkina Faso, Kenya, and Sudan passed laws and church rules to stop the practice, but such actions backfired and provoked anti-foreign sentiment. Then, in the mid-1940s, the governments of Egypt and Sudan attempted to restrict the practice, also without success. In the 1960s and 1970s, African activism, in many countries led by women's groups, began to develop. At this time, some doctors began to document the procedure and its effects. Subsequently, some activity by the UN, particularly by the WHO, and increasing activism by women's groups and public health workers, stimulated legal and human rights action and educational programs.

Today many women's groups, particularly in Africa, are addressing FGM at various levels, including introducing alternative rituals as the health dangers of the practice become more widely understood. The Inter-African Committee on Traditional Practices Affecting the Health of Women and Children and its affiliates have been actively opposing FGM for two decades,[46] and numerous other women's groups protesting the practice have grown in strength over the last ten years. Furthermore, young, educated people are taking matters into their own hands, young women by publicly proclaiming that they refuse to undergo FGM, and young men by stating that they do not want to marry women who have experienced the cutting. In recent years, pressure from locally-based groups on African officials to ban the practice has increased, and, as noted above, fifteen African governments have passed laws outlawing the practice in varying degrees.[47]

"Having laws on paper is one thing, while implementation is another. Yes, half of the countries practicing FGM in Africa have laws; but they fail to implement them. Yet if they took advantage of the laws, the problem would reduce drastically," said Taina Bien-Aime, Executive Director of Equality Now, a non-governmental group that works to eliminate FGM, among other goals.[48] Kenya has been cited as a country where laws have been used to good effect: the ban on the practice was contained in the Children's Act passed in 2001. The Centre for Human Rights and Democracy, a non-governmental organization based in Nairobi, has been "using Section 14 of the Act, which criminalizes FGM, and Section 115, which gives the civil right to anyone who comes across a girl under threat of being genitally cut to move to court. These two provisions," says its executive director, Ken Wafula, "have enabled us to obtain court orders barring anyone to touch the girls."[49]

In other places without such laws, informal fines have sometimes been imposed by local communities or chiefs. Isnino Shuriye, a former circumciser from Somalia who has been in the trade for 25 years, told journalists that she was threatened with a fine of forty camels for every girl she cut. "Anti-FGM campaigners in Somalia told me over and over again about the harm I was doing to young girls and women. At first I did not listen; but when they told me about the camels—and indeed I recalled the girls I had cut, and some who had hemorrhaged to death—I heeded their advice," she said. Shuriye has since joined the campaign to eradicate the practice. Another former circumciser, Mariam Bagayako of Mali, remembered with sadness how she had removed the genitalia of various girls and women for ten years.

"I have now laid my knife down, and I am trying to come to terms with the ills that I committed on fellow women and young girls," she told Inter-Press Service News. Mali has not yet passed legislation banning FGM, but local groups are advocating change.[50]

The exemplary work of some community-based women's groups is highlighted in the accompanying descriptions in this chapter. Their strategies have met with more success in stopping female genital mutilation than have efforts that make use of negative financial incentives such as fines. Programs to empower women through education, paid employment, and greater decision-making opportunities in families and communities offer promising strategies for change.[51]

Interestingly, approaches that focus primarily on the negative health effects of female genital mutilation do not always succeed in changing people's attitudes toward the practice. Some people argue that rather than attempting to abolish FGM, thereby alienating those who consider it an essential element of their culture, communities and physicians should make the procedure safe, bringing it into the medical system, to be done under sterile conditions.[52] Doing so, they argue, will ensure that the procedure is performed under hygienic conditions in hospitals, clinics, or other health facilities, and ideally with anesthesia and sterilized surgical instruments. Unfortunately, however, even if some people do approve of "medicalizing" the procedure, such facilities are beyond the reach of many poor and rural people among whom the practice continues.

Human rights groups, including those highlighted in this chapter, and others, such as the Center for Reproductive Rights, Equality Now, and Human Rights Watch, along with groups like the Inter-African Committee on Traditional Practices Affecting the Health of Women and Children, reject the practice entirely, performed under sterile conditions or not, as a violation of human rights. They cite "the rights to non-discrimination, health, and bodily integrity," and "to life, liberty, and security of person" in their condemnation of the practice. The Convention on the Rights of the Child and the Convention on the Elimination of All Forms of Discrimination against Women both recognize FGM as a human rights violation.

Other Current Challenges: Child Labor and Trafficking

Girls are also deprived of the right to control their physical person through exploitation for labor, particularly for prostitution. Child labor and prostitution are linked to poverty, lack of education, and violence. In some areas around the world—for example, Nepal, the Philippines, Thailand, Central and Eastern Africa, and some regions of Latin America—poverty and the devaluing of girls drives parents and relatives to sell girls into slavery, sexual or otherwise.

Child trafficking is a lucrative business worldwide, linked with criminal activities and corruption. It is always hidden and hard to address. Some estimate that as many as 1.2 million children are trafficked every year. The children and their families are often unaware of the dangers, believing that leaving home for a job will improve their situations. The UN Children's Fund (UNICEF) reported in 2005 that "large numbers of children are being trafficked in West and Central Africa, mainly for domestic work but also for sexual exploitation and to work in shops or on farms." Such trafficking of girls is also prevalent in Nepal, the Philippines, Thailand, and parts of Latin America. "Nearly 90% of these trafficked domestic workers are girls. Children from Togo, Mali, Burkina Faso, and Ghana are trafficked to Nigeria, Ivory Coast, Cameroon, and Gabon. Children are trafficked both in and out of Benin and Nigeria. Some children are sent as far away as the Middle East and Europe." UNICEF also estimates that 1,000 to 1,500 Guatemalan babies and children are trafficked each year for adoption by couples in North America and Europe.[53] Moreover, as the Dutch writer Sietske Altink points out, enforced sexual slavery of children to satisfy the demands of pedophiles is also an unfortunate feature of the sex trade worldwide, as is child pornography and the market to which it caters.[54]

Amnesty International describes trafficking as "modern-day slave trading [that] involves transporting people away from the communities they live in by the threat or use of violence, deception, or coercion so they can be exploited as forced or enslaved workers. When children are trafficked, no violence, deception or coercion needs to be involved: simply transporting them into exploitative conditions constitutes trafficking."[55] (This practice is discussed further in Chapter 8.) Such trafficking is a global problem affecting large numbers of children.

As with FGM, trafficking is a fundamental abuse of human rights. It denies the rights to life, liberty, and security of the person; physical and mental integrity; dignity; freedom from slavery, slave-like practices, torture

WOMEN'S COURAGE: LIMA, PERU. The Grupo de Trabajo Redes works with girls and teen domestic workers to preserve their cultural identity and resolve problems relating to domestic labor in Peru. A study on household workers in Peru revealed that 41% of household workers had been abused in their workplace and had experienced this before the age of fifteen. Although many rights are guaranteed to domestic workers, such as holidays and rest days, most workers do not know about or fail to take advantage of these rights. Formed in 1989 by twelve former and/or current household workers, the group works with girls and teens to provide training, education, health information, and legal and psychological counseling. The group has recently strengthened its work by creating a physical base for its work (Casa de Panchita) and by expanding its educational outreach to young workers.

and other inhuman or degrading treatment; family life; freedom of movement; privacy; the highest attainable standard of health; and safe and secure housing. Trafficking always violates the child's right to grow up in a family environment. In addition, children who have been trafficked face a range of dangers, including violence and sexual abuse.

Documenting child labor and prostitution is difficult, given the problems of gathering reliable statistics in all countries. Nevertheless, the International Labor Organization (ILO), using available data and reporting on labor markets around the world, comes up with shocking numbers relating to children. Without separating the data by gender, the ILO estimates that 246 million children (about one out of six children in the world today) are child laborers, about 73 million of whom are under ten years old. In sub-Saharan Africa, where three quarters of the population—about five hundred million people—live on less than U.S.$2 a day, a third of the children under age fourteen, or about 48 million, work to support themselves or their families. This is the largest group of child laborers in the world.[56]

UNICEF reports that, of the 246 million children engaged in child labor worldwide, "almost three-quarters (171 million) work in hazardous situations or conditions, such as working in mines, working with chemicals and pesticides in agriculture, or working with dangerous machinery. They are everywhere, but invisible, toiling as domestic servants in homes, labouring behind the walls of workshops, hidden from view in plantations. . . ."[57] And with regard to female children in particular, "Millions of girls work as domestic servants and unpaid household help, and are especially vulnerable to exploitation and abuse. Millions of others work under horrific circumstances. They may be trafficked (1.2 million), forced into debt bondage or other forms of slavery (5.7 million), into prostitution and pornography (1.8 million), into participating in armed conflict (0.3 million) or other illicit activities (0.6 million). However, the vast majority of child labourers—70% or more—work in agriculture."[58]

Where statistics allow, the following picture of various regions emerges, according to UNICEF: The Asian and Pacific regions harbor the largest number of child workers in the five-to-fourteen age group, 127.3 million in total; 19% of all children work in this region. Sub-Saharan Africa has an estimated 48 million child workers: about one child in three below the age of fourteen (29%) works. Latin America and the Caribbean have approximately 17.4 million child workers; 16% of all children work in the region. Approximately 15% of children work in the Middle East and North Africa. About 2.5 million children are working in industrialized and transition economies.

Poverty, ill health, unequal access to education, and violations of human rights continually interact to generate extreme misery for children and their families. And although female genital mutilation is a violent practice that seems to be in decline, trafficking in children is increasing, as traffickers benefit from modern communications, the persistence of poverty, and flawed governmental systems. This topic is raised again in a subsequent chapter on globalization and women's work.

"Childhood is entitled to special care and assistance" declares the United Nations' Convention on the Rights of the Child.[59] The rights of every child include health, education, and an adequate standard of living. Childhood is a vulnerable time: "the child, by reason of . . . physical and mental immaturity, needs special safeguards and care, including appropriate legal protection, before and after birth."[60]

Unfortunately, the ideals expressed in the Convention are far from being realized in most regions of the world, particularly for female children.

From the moment of birth, as we have noted, gender socialization starts, and son preference endangers the welfare of girls. Subsequent chapters describe how girls continue to be less valued as they move out of infancy and child-hood and into adolescence and adulthood.

A Tartar chief forced me to become his wife,
And took me far away to Heaven's edge.
Ten thousand clouds and mountains
Bar my road home.
And whirlwinds of dust and sand
Blow for a thousand miles.
Men here are as savage as giant vipers,
And strut about in armour, snapping their bows.
As I sing the second stanza I almost break the lutestrings,
Will broken, heart broken, I sing to myself.

—Ts'ai Yen, China, ca. A.D. 200[1]

A woman approached a Buddhist monk and said: "When I was twelve, my parents, who were very poor, sold me to a brothel, and I have had to do this work ever since. I must beg your forgiveness for my sin." The monk replied: "It is I and the world who should beg forgiveness, for we have not done enough to protect you. Please forgive me and the world for having failed to protect you in the first place."

—Bhikkhu, a Thai Buddhist monk[2]

4

Adolescence: Change and Vulnerability

KHUNYING KANITHA, an activist from Thailand, arrived at a women's meeting held in 1992 in Singapore[3] with this story: "Twelve years ago I began working with twelve-year-old girls sold by their parents to people who trafficked them across the border from Burma and from northern areas of Thailand to Bangkok. They were promised jobs in restaurants, as workers or even dancers. But they were enslaved as prostitutes. When they contracted HIV, they were dumped into the streets. Our organization, the Association for the Protection of the Status of Women, works with them, to try to rehabilitate them, teach them skills, and help them return to their families. We built a center, with a dormitory. We teach and we counsel. Now, twelve years later, there are many more twelve-year-olds than there were before. The number is always growing. We help individual girls, but our efforts to address the problem and the causes of the problem have resulted in frustration and exhaustion. We have come here to rest and to learn. We hope to leave this meeting with renewed strength and perhaps with some ideas for change."

The issues underlying the plight of the young women on whose behalf Kanitha works are many, complex, and intertwined. Trafficking in girls and women is just one of the brutal problems that arise at the intersection of poverty, unequal access to education and health care, violence, and growing up female.

Adolescence: A Time of Change

This chapter focuses on people in the stage between childhood and adulthood, who, according to UN agencies, specifically the World Health Organization (WHO), are variously described as "youth" (those between fifteen and twenty-four years of age), "young people" (between ten and twenty-four), and "adolescents" (between ten and nineteen). In this chapter we draw from sources that have used these various definitions, using the terms interchangeably in this discussion and using the agencies' own terms when citing their data.[4]

Adolescence is a time of great change. In most parts of the world, youth are now considered a separate group to be studied and dealt with according to their unique needs, but until recently they have been neglected as a distinct group and subsumed under the promotion of "family, women's and child welfare and health."[5] Some view adolescence as a Western construct, believing that it is an artificial phase characteristic of industrial society—a kind of enforced delay of maturity. Considering this phase of life as separate from childhood is a relatively recent idea.

In the past, in many countries, children moved from childhood to adulthood—from girls and boys to women and men—in a matter of hours or days, as they went through rituals that conferred on them a new status: womanhood or manhood. In some twenty-seven countries in Africa, including Kenya, Sudan, Somalia, and Tanzania, female genital mutilation is seen as conferring adult status. In parts of Niger, girls let go of girlhood and prepare for childbearing by participating in the Iria rite, during which the young women's bodies are painted with beautiful designs and subjected to public scrutiny by the elder women; the girls are then methodically fattened and taught the responsibilities of womanhood; finally the girls run through the village and fields pursued by young men.

Many such rituals have disappeared as more people have accepted the idea of delaying adult status. "As the concept of secondary education for people in general spread, so did prolongation of childhood," write Joseph Stone and Joseph Church in *Childhood and Adolescence*. "As society grew more complex, the number of adult roles multiplied, and the young person, instead of moving in the parental footsteps, had to make a choice . . . had to define an identity."[6] It seems that when children faced adulthood with a clear vision of their future lives, they were reasonably well prepared and did not have the anxiety and confusion of making life-defining choices. In such cases, perhaps it was possible to be a child and then suddenly become an adult. These days, however, in most societies, life is unpredictable; it seems necessary for children to go through a significant transition to reach adulthood, if only by receiving education or training in order to participate fully in a complex world.

Since the defining trait of adolescence worldwide is change—physical, intellectual, and emotional—it is not surprising that adolescents experience major alterations in both physical and mental health as they move toward their adult identity. Until recently, very little has been written about girls in this phase of their lives. Terri Apter points out that "if, as Anna Freud said, adolescence was the 'stepchild' of psychoanalysis, the forgotten subject, the subject most easily neglected and glossed over . . . then female adolescence was at a double disadvantage: not even a stepchild but the abandoned child. . . . When one psychoanalytic scholar was asked to write a chapter on female adolescence for a textbook, she concluded there was not enough good, recent material to supply a separate chapter."[7] This was in 1980, in the United States. In the last twenty or thirty years, however, many studies have appeared, particularly about adolescent fertility, and more is being learned about other aspects of young people's lives.

Youth make up about one-sixth of the world's population, for a total of 1.1 billion, the largest number in history. Youth are indigent: 85% of them live in resource-poor countries. They are under-educated: in the developing world, almost a third are illiterate, and fewer girls than boys have access to education. Worldwide, youth are under-employed or unemployed: "the number of unemployed fifteen- to twenty-four-year-olds worldwide has risen sharply over the last decade, leaving about one-third of the world's young people without jobs or in abject poverty," according to the International Labour Organization.[8] Youth are sexually active and suffer the highest infection rates from HIV/AIDS and other sexually transmitted diseases.

This sexual activity also results in about seventeen million young women aged fifteen to nineteen giving birth every year, and they have more children than women who delay childbearing. Moreover, some 4.4 million adolescents undergo abortions every year—about 40% of which are performed under unsafe conditions. The risk of birth complications is 25 times higher for girls under age fifteen and twice as high for those between ages fifteen and nineteen than for older women.[9]

According to the International Center for Research on Women, since "hundreds of millions of youth—especially young women—lack education, skills and job training, employment opportunities, and health services, effectively limiting their futures at a very early age . . . . youth may react by unleashing risky or harmful behavior against themselves or society." On the other hand, the report continues, "Although youth may often be perceived as contributing to society's problems, they are, in fact, important assets for the economic, political, and social life of their communities."[10]

Maria, born thirteen years ago to Consuela in Lima, Peru, did not have the chance to fully participate in her community, being disadvantaged from the start. Her birth weight was low because her mother, Consuela, was only fourteen when she had the child. It took major efforts on the part of Maria's grandmother, Conchita, to bring the tiny baby through the dangers of infancy. When the child was about two, Consuela and Conchita realized that she was not developing normally. They took her to doctors and finally learned that Maria, like many children born to very young women, was developmentally disabled.[11] Nevertheless, Conchita was determined to give her child and granddaughter as much opportunity as possible for a satisfactory life. While her daughter, Consuela, attended school, Conchita cared for Maria. When Consuela finished high school and became a secretary, she was able to help support her mother and daughter. Although she did not marry, she had a regular boyfriend. She hoped to be able to get more job training and to rise in the ranks of her company.

In the meantime, however, Maria had major challenges: at twelve, she was just beginning to show signs of womanhood, and she was mentally delayed. The local school did not have facilities to address her problems. She tagged along with her grandmother, who worked as a maid. One day, playing alone, she was raped by the teenage son of her grandmother's employer, becoming one of the 20% to 48% of girls whose first sexual experience is forced.[12]

Maria became pregnant, and this time Conchita was determined to avoid another birth of a child to a child. Despite her concern about an illegal procedure, she took Maria to an abortionist. Three days after the procedure, Maria started bleeding; she was taken to the hospital, but it was too late. Maria died, becoming one of the women and girls in Peru for whom unsafe abortion is the leading cause of maternal death, and one of the five thousand women in Latin America and the Caribbean who die each year as a result of complications from unsafe abortions.[13]

Early Childbearing and Early Marriage

Complications related to pregnancy and childbirth constitute the leading cause of death among adolescent girls in the developing world, where about one in six births is to a girl aged fifteen to nineteen.[14] Most of these babies are born in Asia (about six million) and in sub-Saharan Africa (about five million).[15]

"Both biologically and socially, the consequences of sexual activity in adolescence are considerably more onerous for young women than for their male peers," notes a report by the Alan Guttmacher Institute, a leading source of research on reproductive and sexual health.[16] Nevertheless, married or unmarried, by choice, coercion, or force, throughout "most of the world, the majority of young women become sexually active during their teenage years. The proportion is roughly one-half to two-thirds in Latin American and Caribbean countries, reaches three-quarters or more in much of the developed world, and exceeds nine in ten in many sub-Saharan African countries. In some societies, women begin having sex during adolescence because they are expected to marry and begin childbearing at an early age. In others, marriage typically occurs later, but premarital sex is common. Undoubtedly, some societies are in transition from one social norm to the other. Regardless of the norm that influences young women, beginning sexual activity during the teenage years carries certain risks."[17] Women who marry young often have little control over fertility-related decisions, and they may miss opportunities to attend school or develop job skills. Unmarried women who become pregnant are faced with decisions about whether to have an abortion or try to support their child out of wedlock. Sexually active women, whether married or unmarried, are vulnerable to sexually transmitted diseases, and those who bear children very early or frequently risk impairing their health.

WOMEN'S COURAGE: CALABAR, NIGERIA. Dreamboat Development Theatre Foundation promotes social change for women through theatrical productions, mass media, and education. The group conducts theatrical performances in settings ranging from prisons to religious communities. Formed in 1987, the group has reached Nigerian children, adolescents, and women in different areas through its creative methods to raise awareness about sexual and reproductive health. The group's soap opera series—"Because I am a Woman"—reaches a wide audience in Nigeria because it is broadcast in different Nigerian dialects as well as in English. In addition to its media work, the Foundation operates two gynecological clinics to provide healthcare services to women and their babies. Because of early marriage and childbearing, as well as limited healthcare, Nigeria has one of the highest rates of maternal deaths in the world. The Foundation is addressing these challenges by reaching out to adolescent girls and women to help improve their health and raise awareness.

Physically, a girl's body is not fully prepared to undergo childbirth until about age eighteen. Babies born to mothers younger than eighteen or even twenty are more likely to be born underweight and also more likely to die within their first year; childhood mortality is also higher when the mother is young.[18] Maternal mortality is estimated to be twice as high for women aged fifteen to nineteen than for those aged twenty to twenty-four, and 25 times as high if the girl is under the age of fifteen, as Maria was.

The proportion of women who have their first child by age eighteen ranges from 1% in Japan to 53% in Niger. Predictably, the lowest percentages of early childbearing (under 10%) occur in more industrialized or transitional countries such as Japan, Germany, Poland, Great Britain, the Philippines, and Thailand. Countries with the highest concentration of births to adolescents, where more than 35% of women have their first child before the age of eighteen, include Bangladesh, Cameroon, Mali, Liberia, Cote d'Ivoire, Uganda, the Central African Republic, Malawi, and Nigeria.[19]

Socially, early pregnancy contributes to a cycle that keeps young women in poverty. With early childbearing and higher maternal and infant death rates come higher illiteracy rates and a higher incidence of domestic violence.[20] Women who begin childbearing as adolescents are more likely to be kept

WOMEN'S COURAGE: NAIROBI, KENYA. The Centre for the Study of Adolescence has a three-pronged approach to improving adolescent girls' health in the Suba district of Kenya, an area with high rates of early marriage and teenage pregnancy: It conducts research on young women's attitudes toward sexuality and addresses socio-medical problems that may arise during adolescence. It trains peer educators to reach out to young women seeking health care. And it encourages government agencies to develop public health policies that address the health needs of adolescent girls. Since its establishment in 1988, the Centre, among other achievements, has carried out the first women's health assessment on a national level and developed policies and programs to promote sexual health and contraceptive methods. In recent years, CSA has also emphasized access to education as a key factor in discouraging early marriage and pregnancy.

isolated in the household and held in low esteem, and much less likely to have access to appropriate healthcare information and secondary schooling.[21]

Early pregnancy does not necessarily have to do with rising rates of premarital sex; rather, it correlates with poverty and higher rates of early marriage.[22] In many families, girls are viewed as economic burdens. Parents may marry their daughters off in order to gain needed money for themselves as well as for their children. Lack of education and limited job opportunities also limit adolescents' choices. By contrast, where girls' education has increased, giving them better economic and social options, then tend to marry later.[23] Moreover, those who marry later are likely to have fewer and healthier children.[24]

The majority of the seventeen million adolescent girls giving birth this year live in poorer countries and are married. Child marriage—marriage before the age of eighteen—though less prevalent than a generation ago, is still relatively common in the developing world. In 2001, the percentage of girls in Niger who were married before the age of eighteen exceeded 82%. In Bangladesh, Chad, and Yemen, more than 60% of girls were married before eighteen.[25] In Kebbi State, Nigeria, for example, the average age of marriage in 2003 was eleven. Early marriage means early pregnancy, since many societies pressure brides to prove themselves capable of childbearing.

WOMEN'S COURAGE: PHNOM PENH, CAMBODIA. The Girl Guides Association of Cambodia has worked to improve the status of women since 1994 by educating adolescent girls to be "the agents of change." Through the use of age-appropriate activities, the Association teaches young Cambodian girls about important issues such as domestic violence, gender equity, and women's health. The group offers a variety of services to empower girls and young women. In addition to access to non-formal education, girls can attend the Guides' weekly meetings and get the chance to participate in community projects and camping trips. These activities help girls develop self-esteem, an appreciation for leadership, and concrete roles as responsible members of society.

As well as bearing children dangerously early, young wives are susceptible to domestic violence. A 2003 study, for example, revealed that in Egypt, 29% of married adolescent girls were subjected to domestic abuse, 41% beaten while pregnant.[26] Similarly, a 2001 study shows that in Jordan, 26% of domestic violence cases concerned female victims under eighteen.[27] UNICEF reports that in areas of Bangladesh, Egypt, Jordan, and Turkey, "honor killings"—the killing of young women who go against the wishes of their parents by either running away from violent marriages or marrying a husband not chosen by their parents—continue to occur.[28]

Premarital sex is on the rise globally, bringing with it the problem of unwanted pregnancy for many women, particularly young women. Its prevalence varies greatly by region; for example, the percentage of women having premarital sex by age twenty ranges from 20% in Latin America and 43% in sub-Saharan Africa to 72% in France.[29] Almost all pregnancies among unmarried young women are unwanted; and, as Maria's story demonstrates, can involve the risk of stigma in some countries, and possibly resorting to illegal and unsafe abortion.

In the face of the dangers and burdens surrounding early marriage and childbirth, what can be done? Most of the steps to be taken involve addressing entrenched problems that seem overwhelming. And yet, as some of the examples of women's groups illustrate, there are ways to address these issues of the health and human rights of adolescents. Providing education and training can result in girls having more choices about their lives. It can also increase

WOMEN'S COURAGE: KISUMU, KENYA. Integrated Community Health Services (INCHES) provides women in Kisumu with information about sexual health and life skills and raises public awareness about women's social status. Formed in 2003, the group has taken on the challenge of elevating women's social status and improving women's health in a region where many adolescent girls are at risk for unwanted sex, early pregnancies, and unsafe abortions. Collaborating with other organizations to raise awareness about the challenges that Kenyan women encounter, INCHES has distributed a film called "The African Widow," which depicts the particular difficulties experienced by widows. In an effort to reach adolescent viewers, INCHES has produced a soap opera called BrooKenya which focuses on teen health issues.

self esteem, thereby providing greater strength to resist violence and coercion. As contraception and especially condoms become more widely available, young women can protect themselves against unsafe sex, and especially now, against sexually transmitted diseases, including HIV and AIDS.

The Female Face of HIV/AIDS

Depending on the actions of richer nations and individuals around the world, AIDS may soon surpass the Black Death as the greatest plague ever to devastate humanity. Its prevalence reveals the deeply ingrained inequalities of our societies, as it strikes hardest at those already systematically deprived.

The face of HIV/AIDS is increasingly a female face, and the spread of this disease is nothing short of a disaster. More than forty million people worldwide are living with HIV/AIDS, and 5.8 million people contract the disease each year. Women, particularly young women, are at greater risk for HIV/AIDS than men, both biologically and socially. The expanse of soft tissue in women's bodies provides greater opportunity for infection by the virus, and women's subordinate status strips them of power to negotiate in sexual encounters.

That adolescent women are the fastest growing group contracting HIV/AIDS around the world is an outrage, and is beginning to be seen as such at the highest levels. Stephen Lewis, the former UN Special Envoy on HIV/AIDS in Africa, makes the situation clear:

. . . the problem is that the phenomenon of women's acute vulnerability did not happen overnight. It grew relentlessly over the twenty years of the pandemic. What should shock us all, what should stop us in our tracks, is how long it took to focus the world on what was happening. . . . Why have we allowed a continuing pattern of sexual carnage among young women so grave as to lose an entire generation of women and girls?. . . The reason we have observed . . . this wanton attack on women is because it's women. . . . It amounts to the ultimate vindication of the feminist analysis. When the rights of women are involved, the world goes into reverse.[30]

In sub-Saharan Africa, according to the Population Reference Bureau, more than twice as many young women as young men (5,700,000 young women compared with 2,800,000 young men) ages 15-24 are living with HIV/AIDS. In South and Southeast Asia, the respective numbers are 930,000 young women to 590,000 young men. In North Africa and the Near East, the figures are 110,000 young women to 41,000 young men.[31] Even though the pandemic affects all ages, HIV/AIDS is especially urgent for adolescents, and especially girls.

Consider Bhanu, age fifteen, who lives in rural India. Her parents, who have brought five children into the world, three of them girls, could no longer support all their children. They arranged for Bhanu to marry a local village man, Nagaraj, age twenty, who was lucky enough to have a job as a truck driver. The couple began their life together and consummated the marriage, though Nagaraj mostly satisfied his sexual desires on the road, with prostitutes who frequented nearby truck stops. Bhanu wanted to have a baby, and so they tried. Nagaraj, who had begun to feel ill and to lose weight, visited a local clinic, newly created as a "voluntary counseling and testing" center, and he learned he was HIV positive. The clinicians urged him to bring in his wife for a test. Bhanu understood little and was afraid to be tested. Still, her husband insisted, and they spoke with a counselor. Bhanu explained that she had had sex only with her husband and only a few times. The counselor replied that, in any case, learning one's status is important in order to be able to live in a healthy way as an HIV positive or negative person. She prepared Bhanu for the possibility of bad news by saying that women, especially girls, are more susceptible to contracting HIV from a sexual encounter than are men and boys. The test was taken, and Bhanu learned that she did not have HIV.

The counselor explained to the couple that they must, without question, use condoms to protect Bhanu from the disease. But Bhanu insisted that she wanted to have a baby with Nagaraj; she wanted to be fully a woman. He lovingly vowed not to have unprotected sex with Bhanu, in order to protect her from the disease. But Bhanu continued to plead to become pregnant, no matter the risk. Finally Nagaraj relented, and she conceived, was tested again, and was found to be HIV positive. At the birth, neviropine was administered to both the mother and the baby, and the baby was born HIV negative.

Both Nagaraj and Bhanu are now learning to cope with being HIV positive. If they are lucky, they will be able to receive antiretroviral drugs. The counselors have explained that important as drugs can be, equally important is how well they eat and whether they are able to surround themselves with other people who provide support and hope. She tells Nagaraj about a "positive" young man's club and puts Bhanu in touch with a young women's support group. They want to stay healthy, for their baby.[32]

Babies can be infected by HIV positive mothers either at birth or through breast feeding. Some 20% of babies born to HIV positive mothers will be infected as they are born unless neviropene, which reduces the risk by about 50%, is administered to both mother and child at the time of birth.[33] Another 15% will be infected through breast milk. However, the health risks of not breastfeeding and using formula may be even higher, given the protection provided through breast milk against other health risks as well as the costs of buying formula and the risks of using water that may be contaminated.

According to the United Nations, girls make up about 62% of youth who are HIV positive in the developing world, and the rates are rising.[34] Teenage women are becoming infected with HIV at twice the rate of teenage men worldwide.[35] In 2002, about twelve million youth aged fifteen to twenty-four worldwide were living with HIV/AIDS.[36] In sub-Saharan Africa, females make up two thirds of infected youth, a proportion that is growing. A recent study of three countries in that region showed that girls between the ages of fifteen and twenty-four years are at least three times more likely to be infected with HIV than boys the same age.[37]

The numbers are staggering. Worldwide, about forty million people are living with HIV/AIDS; nearly half of the infected adults are women. In 2004, more than three million people worldwide died of AIDS. Five million were newly infected.[38] The AIDS pandemic is ravaging the globe, spreading farther and faster than predicted, expected, or feared. AIDS is the leading cause of death in sub-Saharan Africa, where it is devastating every level of society and leaving hundreds of thousands of orphans in its wake.[39] Because of stigma, they are at greater risk of malnutrition, illness, sexual exploitation, and HIV infection than are children orphaned by other causes.

But the virus is wreaking havoc in many other regions of the world too, including the Caribbean, with prevalence rates higher than anywhere outside of Africa, Southeast Asia, and Central and Eastern Europe, where HIV is spreading faster than anywhere else in the world.[40] India and China, home to more than one third of the world's population, present worrying signs of the seeds of an epidemic. So far four million people in India and about one million in China are reported to be infected, and these numbers are likely to be underestimated.[41] These countries present enormous possibilities for a disaster of at least the same magnitude as the current situation in sub-Saharan Africa because of the sheer numbers of vulnerable people and the subordination of women.

Since it is hard to grasp the effects of this unprecedented calamity by just reading numbers, it may help to consider a few of the people devastated by the disease—people who span the generations:

- Forty-year-old Justine Ilboudo of Burkina Faso, infected by her husband, had lost two children to AIDS when her husband threw her out of their house and locked the door; she survived because her brother and his wife accepted her into their family.

- Zanele Mavana of South Africa lacked family support and access to health care when she became infected, even though she was an AIDS home care worker herself. Because her family was ashamed of her condition, Mavana had no one to look after her as she suffered through the late stages of AIDS. In 2003, at age twenty-six, she was dying of tuberculosis and her relatives could not even leave her at the hospital because it was not accessible without a car. She did not know what would happen to her children, all HIV positive, after her death.

- Thousands of miles away in the former Soviet Union, Natasha and Maria confronted the reality of the virus they contracted through their husbands, who were intravenous drug users. Meanwhile, their country's government and media largely ignored the prospect of an AIDS epidemic, as did officials in neighboring China.

▪ Like many infected people in China, Zhao Liyang, a resident of Henan province, may have contracted HIV from a local blood collection center while selling or receiving blood. And, like Zanele Mavana, Zhao Liyang worries about the next generation. "It doesn't matter if we die, but what will become of our children?"[42]

It is not likely that these people are all still alive. While these particular people have received some international attention, millions of nameless young women, largely in sub-Saharan Africa but increasingly elsewhere around the world, continue to die from this disease, which primarily affects the most vulnerable, poorest, least educated, and most disempowered in society.

AIDS flourishes in regions with the greatest gender inequality, where women cannot negotiate safe sex because of their traditionally subordinate status. The virus affects young women already disadvantaged many times over by their gender, age, and poverty. Women are more likely to contract HIV through heterosexual intercourse than through any other means of transmission.[43] Through sexual intercourse, women are not only biologically more susceptible to contracting HIV than men, but in regions where women lack empowerment, they are also imprisoned by cultural expectations, and thus unable to defend themselves against the virus by refusing sex or insisting that their partners use a condom.

In Eastern and Southern Africa, the main risk factor for women contracting HIV is being married,[44] since cultural norms permit and even encourage men to have several sexual partners outside marriage but deprive women, married or not, of control over their sexual relations. Wives are directly affected by the past and present promiscuity of their husbands. A recent *New York Times* article about young African brides reported that teenage brides in a number of African nations are becoming infected with AIDS at higher rates than sexually active unmarried girls. These young brides acquire HIV and AIDS from their husbands, who tend to be older and have had many more sexual partners.[45]

In Asia, there is a similar trend. Infection rates among Asian women "are soaring; and being married is one of the biggest risk factors," according

WOMEN'S COURAGE: MANKON, MEZAM DIVISION, CAMEROON. Cornerstone Vision Center was established in 2002 in northwest Cameroon as a private fitness club for women looking for a way to meet their health needs. It is now a major resource for women and girls who, unable to obtain medications for HIV/AIDS, are learning other ways of remaining negative or living with a positive diagnosis. The Center is located in the province that has the highest HIV prevalence rate in Cameroon, where three women are infected for every two men. Patriarchal attitudes deny women the authority to negotiate for condom use during sex, meaning that women cannot protect themselves and prevalence rates continue to climb. As the poorest of the poor, women with AIDS cannot afford treatment for infections.

The Center recognizes that good nutrition is essential for people living with AIDS to stay healthy and to ward off infections, and its educational and counseling activities play an important role in a context where access to formal health care is limited. Within six months of the Center's founding, more than fifty women—most with a variety of health concerns, including HIV/AIDS—had joined its training sessions. Cornerstone has since grown into a public center that offers fitness training to about seventy clients each day and provides nutrition counseling to more than two hundred people a month, the vast majority being women and girls.

Serving rural and urban women, women and girls living with HIV/AIDS, and pregnant and lactating mothers, the Center's fitness club provides women a safe space to exercise and focus on their health. Its community-based nutrition and counseling program provides advice on matters relating to HIV/AIDS, nutritional deficiencies, weight management, diabetes, hypertension, osteoporosis, breastfeeding, and pregnancy. Cornerstone is committed to providing such counseling to HIV positive women, regardless of their ability to pay. The Center, which regularly partners with other organizations and is now beginning to publish manuals on health issues, has become a new resource on health for the region.

to UNAIDS deputy executive director Kathleen Cravero. In 2004, she said: "women's infection rates in the region have jumped 10% in the past two years ... with many husbands having several extra-marital partners and their wives powerless to object. In Thailand, 40% of new infections occur between spouses, with 90% of them from husband to wife, and we have seen a similar trend in other countries such as India." Cravero identified as a major factor "the culture of silence," in which women cannot ask about sex or the sexual behavior of their partners. She went on to warn "that the epidemic in Asia could develop into a situation similar to sub-Saharan Africa, where of the 29.4 million people with HIV/AIDS, some 58% are female."[46] Clearly, engaging in a sexual relationship that they think is monogamous is not enough to protect young girls and women from HIV.

Healthcare is also unbalanced for HIV positive males and females. For example in couples infected with HIV, even if both partners are aware of their HIV status, the male is more likely to receive care. In one study in Tanzania, for example, twice as much money was spent on male victims than on females in the same household.[47] Thus the cycle continues: although contracting HIV is outside a woman's control, bound as she is by economic and social constraints, once infected, she will likely have little or no access to reliable health care, discrimination against her may increase, and the poverty in which she lives will deepen as her health worsens. The effect on adolescent girls is magnified: not only are their infection rates increasing, but as more women are lost to the disease, girls lose the mothers and teachers who would have served as their role models during adolescence, a difficult time under most circumstances.

Biologically speaking, women have a higher risk of becoming HIV positive than men. The virus can enter the female body through tiny cuts that can open up on the sensitive skin in the genital areas during intercourse. Because of their expanse of soft tissue, women of any age are at least twice as likely as men to contract HIV than men in an unprotected sexual encounter.[48] In addition, the virus has an easier time surviving in the protected environment of the vagina than on the surface of the penis, and the viral load of HIV in a man's semen is much larger than the viral load in vaginal fluids.[49] The more cuts and scrapes that occur during intercourse, the more likely that a woman will become infected with HIV. Teenage girls are especially vulnerable because of the immaturity of the cervix especially during violent or coerced intercourse, during which the skin is more likely to tear.[50]

HIV/AIDS epitomizes, more than any other disease, the intersection of health and human rights. It is a disease. It is also a symbol and symptom of an unjust world, where young and poor women in developing countries are deprived of control over their lives and their bodies, and, once infected, left to die.

WOMEN'S COURAGE: KATHMANDU, NEPAL. In 1987, a group of women in Kathmandu, Nepal, joined forces and created ABC (Agroforestry, Basic Health, and Cooperatives) "to create awareness about the problem of the trafficking of girls and AIDS, and create employment opportunities and income-generating activities, so that women can be self-reliant." The group's main emphasis is on public awareness of the problem of trafficking and AIDS through orientations, training programs, booklets, storybooks, audiocassettes, and non-formal education classes.

The group also organizes street plays to create understanding and public discussion about the issue. Since its founding, ABC has empowered individual communities to address income generation, health, and, most notably, girl trafficking, in public discussions. In the late 1990s, ABC started to mobilize youth as peer educators. Through school workshops on AIDS and sexual health, ABC implemented its strategy of "putting power into girls' hands."

Although biological differences between women and men account for some of the heightened risk women face, research has shown that social, gender-related factors are the main reason why women, especially young women, are at greater risk.[51] Poverty makes young women and girls particularly vulnerable because it reduces the range of choices they have in their lives, particularly as they seek education in order to move into paid employment. In Mozambique, for example, about 16% of young women aged fifteen to twenty-four are HIV positive, compared with 6% of men in the same age group.

The biological explanation—that a woman is more likely to be infected from sex with an HIV positive man than vice versa—is not sufficient to explain this large difference. David Melody and Gorik Ooms of Doctors Without Borders have described other major factors: "In Mozambique there is a pattern of intergenerational sexual relationships—young women having sex with older men—in which the women have little or no say. Economic, cultural and even physical pressure means that they are frequently forced to have sex with older men. Education ought to be a way out for these young women, offering the hope of an independent future and more control over their lives, especially in terms of sex. But in Mozambique education has its own pitfalls. School fees and uniforms might be paid for by an uncle or friend of the family—who then expects sexual favors in return. Even within schools the sexual menace is present. According to a survey by the Ministry of Education, 91% of secondary school girls personally knew other pupils who had had a sexual relation with a teacher."[52]

Once infected, most women have few options for dealing with the disease. First, women may have no knowledge of the symptoms or the modes of transmission of HIV. It is estimated that nine out of ten HIV positive women in developing nations do not know that they are infected.[53] They may transmit the disease unknowingly to their infants during childbirth. Mother-to-child transmission can be cut in half with known and relatively inexpensive medications, but access to and distribution of such medicines continue to be major hurdles.[54] If a woman knows and admits that she has the virus, she may be shunned or even abused by her family. As with all sexually transmitted infections, women are often considered at fault for contracting and spreading AIDS.[55] Stigma is a huge problem when dealing with HIV/AIDS because it perpetuates ignorance.[56] Even when ignorance is not a factor, the fear of discrimination drives people to avoid voluntary testing, which in turn creates an environment where the virus flourishes.

Moreover, social factors such as unequal access to education significantly contribute to higher HIV transmission in young girls, since their access to information may be limited. As discussed in the previous chapter, girls are more likely to drop out of school because of early pregnancy, early marriage, the effects of female genital mutilation, or care responsibilities at home. While school enrollment for girls has increased worldwide in recent years, in countries with a high prevalence of HIV, school enrollment for girls has decreased because young girls are likely to be required to leave school to care for sick relatives. AIDS doesn't just kill the infected people; it also kills educational opportunities for girls, even when they are not infected. The burden on a girl whose sick relatives rely on her for care can impinge on or eliminate the girl's ability to continue her schooling. Without basic education, women have no hope of pulling themselves out of poverty. They therefore must continue to rely on men, in relation to whom they lack power because of their lower social status.

In addition, in various places, such as Afghanistan, China, and many Muslim countries, it is culturally inappropriate for girls to be knowledgeable about sex or sex-related subjects. According to a study conducted by UNICEF in seventeen countries, more than half of the adolescents surveyed could not

WOMEN'S COURAGE: XINING CITY, QINGHAI, CHINA. The Am Kham Women's Group raises awareness of reproductive health and women's rights issues among Tibetan women in the region, offering free STI and HIV tests, condom distribution, and health education. In addition, the group provides vocational and literacy training to Tibetan women in an attempt to help them develop sources of income that will provide alternatives to prostitution. Tibetan women in this region are poorly educated and lack access to paid work, especially since they are in competition with migrants from other regions. As a consequence, they sometimes turn to prostitution to support themselves and their families.

In addition to its direct service work, Am Kham is politically active: the group recently conducted a research project on reproductive health, sexual practices, and domestic violence in order to better inform policy makers of the pressing need for public programs to address women's health and rights.

WOMEN'S COURAGE: HARARE, ZIMBABWE. The Girl-Child Network is a series of clubs throughout Zimbabwe designed to bring girls together with mentors and peers to address issues of self-esteem, health, and education. The clubs expand girls' access to arts, sports, and science programs, and they encourage girls to challenge discrimination and further their education. After its founding in 1999 by Hazviperi Betty Makoni, a high school teacher, and six of her students, the Network grew rapidly, and now has a membership of more than twenty thousand girls in more than one hundred clubs across Zimbabwe.

Within each club, girls of all ages, classes, colors, and religions discuss their successes and challenges and devise strategies to deal with such issues as rape, sexual harassment, HIV/AIDS, body image, and prostitution. They play and study together, and in many regions the girls are the first female members of their families to attend secondary schools. In October 2004, the Network launched the Women as Role Models Program, creating a space for prominent women and young girls to share experiences and learn from each other. The program encourages female mentors to support the education of needy girls, so that they may "walk in their full potential as future women."

name a single method of protection against HIV, and in all instances girls knew less than boys.[57] Studies have shown that people who have grown up with accurate information about sex tend to be more likely to make responsible choices, such as using condoms or postponing sex until later in life when protection may be more feasible.[58] Lack of basic education and sexual knowledge also maintains the power imbalance between women and men. A study of poor married women from Bombay, India, reported that before marriage, many had no knowledge whatsoever of sex.[59]

VIOLENCE AND PREDATION

In most poorer countries, women develop HIV/AIDS nearly ten years earlier than men.[60] That shocking differential has both a biological component and a large social component related to women's limited power in those countries. Women are at greater risk because they have limited power to negotiate safe sex with partners who themselves may have many partners, greater risk from ignorance and social stigma, and greater risk brought on by economic dependence on men, which results in transactional sex

Women, and especially young girls, lack control over their sexual relationships and even their own sexuality. As noted earlier, between 20% and 48% of women aged ten to twenty-four worldwide say their first sexual encounter was forced.[61] Furthermore, of women sexually assaulted in 2001, between one third and two thirds were under the age of fifteen.[62] Even if they have access to knowledge of their own bodies and the diseases that may attack them, they have no power to insist on safe sex. Young women are particularly vulnerable, both physiologically and socially. Older men may coerce girls into sex through money or force. In South Africa, for example, a national youth survey reported that 33% of young girls are afraid to say no to sex, and 55% have sex when they do not want to because their partner insists.[63]

In many parts of the world, poverty leads girls into dangerous sexual activity. In Asia and Eastern Europe, for example, they may find themselves in sexually risky jobs, including forced prostitution. In East Africa, as mentioned in the preceding chapter, "sugar daddies" and coercive male teachers prey on young women trying to find money for school fees. In Southern Africa, "transactional sex," through which young women receive gifts of cash or goods from their boyfriends, is on the increase. Many women living in poverty rely on such relationships for economic sustenance. The rise in transactional sex is apparently correlated to the economic crises of the 1970s. Before that time, marriage involved a system in which cattle were exchanged as a price for brides. Now that few young men can afford cattle, marriage

WOMEN'S COURAGE: OUAGADOUGOU, BURKINA FASO. L'Association Burkinabé pour la Promotion de la Jeune Fille (The Burkinabé Association for the
Advancement of Young Girls) promotes young women's status by encouraging a sense of community cohesion among them. Working with young women
who are orphaned, unemployed, or school dropouts, the Association has created a safe and supportive working environment where girls come to produce
shea butter cosmetic products. The idea behind the program is to empower
and instill self-reliance in the young women with their own income. At the
same time, girls learn about health issues, such as HIV/AIDS and the practice
of female genital cutting. In Burkina Faso, making products out of shea butter
is traditionally women's work. By incorporating traditional practices into its
program, the Association is able to encourage education and skills training in
the context of local culture.

rates in Southern Africa have decreased significantly, and short term unions
involving transactional sex have increased.[64] In Zambia and Uganda, in 2000,
about a third of unmarried women aged fifteen to nineteen reported that
they had received money or gifts in exchange for sex.[65]

The intersection of trafficking in women and girls and HIV/AIDS is
particularly devastating. UNICEF reported in 2004 that "girls as young as
thirteen (mainly from Asia and Eastern Europe) are trafficked as 'mail-order brides.' In most cases these girls and women are powerless and isolated
and at great risk of violence."[66] In some Asian countries, up to 30% of sex
workers between the ages of thirteen and nineteen are living with HIV.[67]
Girls trafficked from Nepal into brothels in Calcutta, India, for example, are
dumped after they contract HIV, left to find their own way home to Nepal.
Women's groups in both India and Nepal have collaborated by lobbying with
the Nepali Government to allow these girls—who are, after all, citizens of
Nepal—to return to Kathmandu. In 2001, I visited a residential house for
girls in Kathmandu, set up by Agroforestry, Basic Health, and Cooperatives
(ABC), and met the fifteen or twenty teenage girls housed there. Unable to
return to their villages, where their families will reject them, they languish.
They were supposed to send money home; they were supposed to succeed
in adding to the family income beyond the price that was originally paid for
them through a broker; now they can bring only shame. Groups of women

set up the home, which offers some literacy and skills training (mostly sew-ing), in the hope that the girls will be able to put together productive lives. Increasingly, medications are also available for such girls, affording some hope of their continuing to live with HIV.

HOPEFUL SIGNS

The influence of HIV/AIDS on the unhealthy and unjust situation of women is beginning to be more widely understood and recognized as a threat to all of humanity. Women's groups, like those that are highlighted through-out this text, have emerged around the world, with a focus on recognizing the devastation of HIV and AIDS and doing something about it. Most are overly occupied simply by dealing with the aftermath of infection—setting up homes like the one in Nepal, for example. In other words, they may focus on treatment rather than on prevention. International agencies and major donors have begun to emphasize the development of vaccines, which is promising.

Khunying Kanitha, the Thai woman who attended the Singapore meeting in 1992, left quite rested, as it turned out. More importantly, she had joined a network of women throughout Southeast Asia who committed themselves to actively empowering women to confront HIV/AIDS and trafficking. Although the issues are horrifying and complex, positive change can happen when people come together with the commitment to address the structural problems that cause both women and men to be less than human.

Increasing numbers of local non-governmental organizations, especially in Africa, are providing health education and medications to people at the grassroots, working at community levels. What is needed now, however, is much more emphasis on providing health education and medications to people at the grassroots levels through local groups. Local community out-reach workers, midwives, and nurses can deliver education and medications that can make a difference at the time of childbirth, and teen counselors and other local workers can make available other medications and, perhaps more important, information, which will allow HIV positive people to live rea-sonably healthy and full lives. The Community Health Information Centers (CHICs) and Voluntary Counseling and Testing Centers (VCTs) created in Kenya and other countries hold promise for change. Centers that I visited in Kenya were filled with young people, many of them adolescent girls, who

WOMEN'S COURAGE: MEXICO CITY, MEXICO. Elige, Red de Jóvenes por los Derechos Sexuales y Reproductivos (Choose, Youth Network for Reproductive and Sexual Rights), as its name explains, focuses on youth sexuality, birth control, and reproductive rights. The organization attains its goals by collaborating with young people and other Mexican youth networks. Since the group's inception in 1997, youth group members have promoted women's sexual and reproductive rights issues at conferences and on the radio. Furthermore, the group works with other youth organizations to sponsor awareness campaigns such as the "Love is Non-Violent" campaign, and the "Women's Access to Justice" campaign. The Network has held meetings and conferences to generate discussion among young women on the topic of abortion, a taboo subject in Mexico and other Latin American countries. The group's work empowers Mexico's youth by helping them build a society that values gender equity and responsible sexual practices.

were eager for information, open to being tested and learning to live with HIV, and hopeful about the future.

At the same time, while medication and health education are sorely needed, along with other services for the HIV positive, the real solutions to the epidemic lie in changing the power relations between women and men. Those most affected by problems can be the appropriate people to address and solve them. Young people are not only at very high risk of experiencing poverty, violence, and unequal access to education, paid employment, and health care, they are also eager, resilient, and open to change. Young people embody our hopes for change. In a speech given at Zhejiang University in China in October 2002, Kofi Annan, the former United Nations Secretary General, stated: "Young people are the key in the fight against AIDS. By giving them the support they need, we can empower them to protect themselves against the virus. By giving them honest and straightforward information, we can break the circle of silence across all society. By creating effective campaigns for education and prevention, we can turn young people's enthusiasm, drive, and dreams for the future into powerful tools for attacking the epidemic."[68]

I wholeheartedly agree with Annan that the strength for change in tomorrow's world is the strength of the hopes and ambitions of today's youth. However, I would go further, and say that the key to the fight against AIDS—beyond health care and information—is to recognize that women themselves need to be at the forefront of providing solutions to the ongoing crisis. A permanent solution to this and other health and human rights issues requires challenging and changing women's roles in their societies, empowering them economically and socially to resist forced marriages and trafficking, and have access to education, equality, and jobs for a better life. The courageous women's groups highlighted throughout this book are part of the solution. So are young people who deserve to know that change is possible.

I am sick today,
sick in my body,
eyes wide open, silent,
I lie on the bed of childbirth.
Why do I,
so used to the nearness of death,
to pain and blood and screaming,
now uncontrollably tremble with dread?
A nice young doctor tried to comfort me,
and talked about the joy of giving birth.
Since I know better than he about this matter,
what good purpose can his prattle serve?
Knowledge is not reality.
Experience belongs to the past.
Let those who lack immediacy be silent.
Let observers be content to observe.
I am all alone,
totally, utterly, entirely on my own,
gnawing my lips, holding my body rigid,
waiting on inexorable fate.
There is only one truth.
I shall give birth to a child,
truth driving outward from my inwardness.
Neither good nor bad; real, no sham about it.
With the first labour pains,
suddenly the sun goes pale.
The indifferent world goes strangely calm.
I am alone.
It is alone I am.

—Yosano Akiko, "Labour Pains," Japan, 1878-1942[1]

5

The Maternity Death Road:
Reproductive and Sexual Health

FEILANI, AN OUTREACH OFFICER working on reproductive health in Togo, West Africa, was describing her work with all of its attendant problems to a group of American visitors: women dying in childbirth, women giving birth to nine or ten children in the space of as many years; very young women giving birth too soon. A young American in her audience asked: "Don't you feel hopeless? Isn't it all too much?" Feilani answered, "I do get discouraged, sometimes. My work is like a road, with lots of pot holes and huge boulders blocking my way. I must struggle to go around them or move them. But when just one woman can come to me and say 'Thank you. Last year you visited and told me that I didn't have to be pregnant every year, that there were things that I could do to not have more children, and this year, as you see, I am not pregnant. I have strength to look after my other children.' When even one woman tells me this, I know that struggling against the obstacles is worth it. I have made a difference in that woman's life and in the life of her village."[2]

Every year, around the world, about 600,000 women die of almost completely preventable illnesses and injuries related to pregnancy and childbirth.[3] And yet: "Maternity is not a disease. It is the means by which the human species is propagated. Society has more of an obligation to prevent maternal deaths than to prevent deaths from diseases. . . . Maternal mortality should not be lumped together with and ranked against other disease problems."[4] So writes Mahmoud Fathalla, an Egyptian physician who has been responsible for saving thousands of women's lives.

The woman that Feilani helped in Togo could have been one of the hundreds of thousands of women who die needlessly each year when they are pregnant or are giving birth, especially given that in Togo, only 7% of married women use modern contraception, only 51% of births are attended by a skilled person, and maternal deaths are more than double the world average (980 per 100,000 live births in Togo, 400 worldwide, and 440 in developing countries).[5]

Motherhood has been glorified for centuries as a noble goal, and yet the means to ensure that women can be healthy mothers continues to be denied to the majority of women around the world. Of the 120 million women who give birth every year, half experience complications, with fifteen to twenty million developing long-term disabilities. In richer countries, some, though certainly not all, receive appropriate services and help, but in poorer countries, women continue to die at alarming rates. The World Health Organization (WHO) estimated in 1997 that of the "585,000 maternal deaths each year, all but 4,000 take place in developing countries," a proportion that has remained about the same over the years.[6]

Perhaps because of the mystery and importance of women's reproductive capacities, women have been studied primarily in terms of their reproductive roles, as producers and caregivers of children. As a result, much has been written on these aspects of reproductive health. Until recently "women's health" meant maternal and child health, including family planning, issues that have been studied and debated for years. This chapter focuses on these issues of reproductive health, including maternity, and also takes up issues of sexuality, which do not have the same long history of attention.

Mahmoud Fathalla thinks of maternal mortality in terms of a "maternity death road" which leads from poverty, illiteracy, and lack of access to nutrition and family planning, through the denial of access to appropriate health and maternal care, ending in death.[7] The immediate causes of 80% of the more than half a million preventable maternal deaths each year are reported to be obstetric complications such as severe bleeding (25%), infection (15%), hypertensive disorders (12%), obstructed labor (8%), and unsafe abortion (13%). Malaria, diabetes, hepatitis, and anemia, which are aggravated by pregnancy, also kill women.[8] However, the underlying causes of maternal mortality start in the mothers' childhood, with poverty; unequal access to education, nutrition, and health care; and discrimination against girls.

"The tragedy of maternal mortality in developing countries has been neglected," writes Fathalla. "One reason is that. . . . its importance is not always evident from official statistics. In areas where the problem is most severe, the majority of maternal deaths simply go unrecorded, or the cause of death is not specified: hence the tendency to underestimate the gravity of the situation. Only 75 of the WHO's 192 member states were able to provide information on maternal mortality. Of the 117 developing countries, 73 were unable to give a rate; and many figures provided were grossly underestimated. It was only recently that systematic efforts have been made to collect valid data." Another reason, Fathalla suggests, might be "that people have lived with the problem of maternal death for so long that an attitude of fatalism has developed." Moreover, "The health service also shares some of the guilt for this neglect. [Traditional maternal and child health services] have tended to be oriented towards the child." Finally, he concludes that "The basic reason, however, why maternal mortality has been neglected is that it is a woman's problem in regions where women do not enjoy a high social status. It is a question of how much mothers are worth."[9]

The difficulty of obtaining accurate statistics about maternal mortality is complicated by problems of definition. According to most definitions, maternal mortality is "the death of a woman while pregnant or within forty-two days of termination of pregnancy," but in the late 1990s the WHO specified an additional disease classification, "late maternal death" which "occurs more than forty-two days but less than a year after the outcome of pregnancy and is attributable to direct and indirect obstetric causes." Unfortunately, as Pradhan et al. point out, "Few population-based data exist on the length of time during which the risk of mortality remains elevated following pregnancy outcome."[10] In other words, the figures currently used for maternal deaths are very likely to be underestimates.

So many factors can send a woman down the road to maternal death. Lack of education leads to low levels of awareness about the possible complications of childbirth and the importance of trained birth attendants. Problems of

WOMEN'S COURAGE: SAN CRISTOBAL, CHIAPAS, MEXICO. El Centro de Partos de San Cristobal (The San Cristobal Birth Center) is dedicated to improving the health of mothers and children. It runs a weekly radio program that informs women of reproductive health services available to them. Through another program, the Center provides training for peer health educators to raise awareness about safe birthing practices. In a city like Chiapas, where the maternal mortality rate is the highest in the country, the group's services to train midwives and provide sexual and reproductive education are highly valued. Established in 2004 "to bring Mexican families a pre-natal, intra- and post-partum experience under the midwifery model of care," the group plans to open a birthing center—the Luna Maya project—to train more professional midwives and provide safe healthcare for mothers-to-be all over San Cristobal.

WOMEN'S COURAGE: QUETZALTENANGO, GUATEMALA. The Coordinadora Departamental de Comadronas Tradicionales de Quetzaltenango (The Departmental Network of Traditional Midwives of Quetzaltenango) was begun in 2002 by a group of midwives concerned with the rights of poor indigenous Mayan women in Guatemala. The Network convenes workshops focusing on cultural training about Mayan customs, such as natural healthcare techniques. Its training sessions for group members, local government officials, and healthcare providers address the triple discrimination that some women face by being poor, indigenous, and female. Among other activities, the group lobbies for policies that address indigenous women's rights to safe and professional births. Ultimately, the group aspires to create an entire healthcare system that is sensitive to the reproductive health needs of indigenous women.

logistics like transportation and social or cultural barriers may also result in women delaying or failing to seek treatment. Even with medical care, according to many studies, poor patient management, carelessness, indifference, and inappropriate or delayed action by health staff contribute to preventable maternal deaths.[11] A lack of trained personnel at hospitals and clinics and of equipment and facilities adds to the dangers for women, and lack of antenatal care and quality health services ensure that "women at greatest risk of maternal death have the least resources to seek medical help."[12] Most people would surely agree that motherhood is a noble goal; indeed it is the

WOMEN'S COURAGE: KPEVE, GHANA. Formed in 1996, the Logba Mother and Child Health Group is an association of traditional birth attendants who came together in the village of Logba to provide basic health services to women there. They wanted to reduce the hardships women in labor and sick people face in the village. Travel to and from the nearest village is difficult in Logba, which is situated on the top of a mountain. Sick people, including pregnant women who are finding it very difficult to have babies, are carried by two men in a cloth that is hung on a stick from the village to the main road ten kilometers away, where a lorry is boarded to the hospital. More often than not, these people die from lack of medical attention.

In response to this need, the group built a mud and thatch building to serve as a clinic. However, before long it proved inadequate, with chipping of mud falling into boxes of medicines and sometimes on the new born babies and their mothers, especially in the rainy season. At this point, the group sought financial help to buy aluminum roofing (while the community provided all other supplies to build a sturdy building). Since having created a clinic, the small village may now qualify for an occasional visit from a government health worker.

In the meantime, the group continues its work, providing health services to expectant and nursing mothers, and educating the community on family planning and reproductive health. To sustain the clinic financially, the group charges a small user fee. Although they look forward to the government's staff contribution, the group will also rely on members who are familiar with local herbal remedies.

only goal for many women. Yet being female puts every woman at risk of being one of the many who die while giving life.

The neglect that women's health and nutrition can suffer in comparison to men's becomes evident when the body is taxed to it's limits during pregnancy. Poor nutrition throughout a lifetime results in anemia in half of all pregnancies worldwide.[13] Young women and women who have been pregnant many times are particularly at risk. More than seventeen million adolescent girls give birth each year, many as a result of coerced sex or unwanted pregnancies.[14] Their young bodies are more vulnerable and more unfamiliar with the pressures of pregnancy than the bodies of older women. As noted in the preceding chapter, in poorer countries, maternal mortality among girls under eighteen is between two and five times higher than among those over twenty.[15]

WOMEN'S COURAGE: CALABAR, NIGERIA. Helping women to have access to surgery to repair fistulae and return to normal lives, Bloom and Glow also works to prevent fistula occurrence by providing advocacy and public education. The group's outreach focuses on reducing early marriage, early motherhood, female genital cutting, unattended births, and other practices that increase the risk of fistulae. The group was part of a successful advocacy effort that resulted in legislation banning female genital cutting in Cross River State.

WOMEN'S COURAGE: LA PAZ, MEXICO. Centro Mujeres (Women's Center) is a community health organization dedicated to fostering the empowerment and well-being of women and adolescents. The group works to influence public policy and promote social change, particularly relating to women's health issues. Established in 1994, the Center was founded by three health professionals in response to women's and adolescents' unmet health needs in the La Paz region. A survey of community health showed that caesarean deliveries, tubal ligation rates, and teenage pregnancies were reaching epidemic proportions, and that incest, rape, and domestic violence were widespread. Apart from a drug prevention center, there were no preventive health services, health education, psychological, or legal services for women and youth in the state before the creation of the Center.

In addition, because only about half of the pregnant women in poorer countries receive care before or even during birth, complications and high-risk situations may go unrecognized. Fewer than 30% of women in poorer countries receive postpartum care, as opposed to 90% of women in richer countries. Poor women, particularly those in rural areas, may lack access to medical assistance even when it becomes obvious that such assistance is needed. All too often, they suffer from pregnancies that occur "too early, too often, too closely spaced, and too late in their reproductive lives."[16]

Non-fatal complications can have life-altering effects on women. For example, about two million women worldwide suffer from obstetric fistulae, an opening between the vagina and the bladder or rectum that results from tissue damage during prolonged labor.[17] Obstetric fistula is particularly common among young women, who have more difficult labor and more often lack access to proper care. In addition to pain, the fistula causes urine and/or feces to pass through the vagina, which results in odor and infection. Women so afflicted are frequently deserted by their partners and exiled from their villages.[18] A relatively simple surgical intervention can treat this problem, but access to appropriate facilities is beyond the reach of many women, particularly in rural areas.

Women clearly suffer from a lack of reproductive rights worldwide. They lack the right to knowledge and control over their own reproduction. This deprivation begins with the lack of education and empowerment explored in earlier chapters, and it continues through adolescence and womanhood. In many cultures, girls are denied knowledge of their bodies and reproductive systems because of traditionally conservative ideas of modesty and virginity. Women also lack full access to modern methods of contraception, either because the materials, means, and knowledge to distribute such methods are not available or because they do not have the ability to exercise power over sexuality and contraception within their relationships.

Mahmoud Fathalla writes that "When our forefathers drafted the Constitution of the World Health Organization in 1946, they were careful to condemn all types of discrimination in health, on the basis 'of race, religion, political belief, economic or social condition.' They forgot, however, about gender discrimination. Maternal mortality is a glaring case in point and deserves the designation of the health scandal of our time."[19] Endemic, yet almost completely preventable, maternal mortality is one of the starkest examples of gender discrimination in our world.

Reproductive Choice: Women's Access to Contraception

The problem of maternal mortality is intertwined with issues of fertility, contraception, abortion, and the prevention of sexually transmitted diseases. Women's control over their own reproductive lives can mean control over their own destinies. Worldwide, women's access to the means to control their own fertility is decidedly mixed.

Feilani helped at least one woman in Togo to control her reproductive life, and many others around the world have learned ways to avoid being pregnant every year. Fertility rates[20] have dropped dramatically in some of the world's poorest and most populous countries in recent years. In India, for example, the total fertility rate dropped from seven births per woman in 1960 to three births per woman in 2002. China's fertility rates have fallen

WOMEN'S COURAGE: BUENOS AIRES, ARGENTINA. Católicas por el Derecho a Decidir—Buenos Aires (Catholics for the Right to Decide) was organized in 1996 to promote Catholic women's sexual and reproductive rights. The group provides information to Argentinean women from low-income backgrounds and, using all forms of media, educates them in "free and voluntary motherhood, birth control, abortion, and sexuality." The group runs a weekly radio program to raise awareness for women's rights and advocate for the decriminalization of abortions. It also produces flyers and newsletters on the importance of the empowerment of women and the need to eliminate institutional restrictions of Argentinean women's reproductive rights. Other activities include workshops to familiarize women with the importance of access to abortion and the prevention of domestic violence. A broad goal of the group is to provide information that will inspire women to become advocates for the women's movement in Argentina's Catholic communities.

from eight births per woman in 1962 to two births per woman in 2002.[21] A combination of factors has led to the decline in birth rates around the world, including aggressive family planning programs, increased education for women, delayed marriage, urbanization, increased participation of women in the paid labor force, and, perhaps, decreases in male fertility (lower sperm counts, possibly as a result of environmental pollution). The dramatic decline in fertility rates in China has also been influenced by the country's "one-child-per-couple" norm, which China's government has encouraged since 1979, and turned into law in 2002 (the Law on Population and Family Planning).[22]

Despite the drop in worldwide fertility, however, fertility rates in some developing countries remain high, particularly in parts of Africa,[23] and worldwide there are an estimated 150 million women with an unmet need for contraception.[24] Women and men want to be able to plan their families. Unequal access to contraception and ineffective use of available methods has meant that almost half of the 200 million pregnancies that occur each year "are unwanted or ill-timed."[25] More than a quarter of pregnancies worldwide (about 52 million annually) end in abortion, split about equally between legal and illegal abortions.[26] Of the approximately 125 million births each year, more than one quarter are unwanted—16% are not wanted at the time and

11% are not wanted at all.[27] Women's lack of knowledge about and access to contraceptives has enormous consequences in terms of the situation of individual families as well as the demographics of societies and the prosperity or poverty of the next generation.

On a very personal level, a woman's ability to plan how many children she wants and when she wants them is central to the quality of her life. Furthermore, in places where emergency obstetric care is not available, access to contraception may literally be a matter of a woman's life or death. Each pregnancy multiplies a woman's chance of dying from complications of pregnancy or childbirth. Meeting the existing demand for family planning services would reduce pregnancies in developing countries by 20% and maternal deaths and injuries to a similar extent or more.[28]

Jamaica offers an example of the importance and complexity of issues of contraception. In that country, nearly a quarter of all babies are born to teenage girls. The result has been "collective worry, sermons, finger-pointing and, occasionally, over-the-top demands by anxious politicians," according to an article by Trudy Simpson, a journalist writing for the Panos Institute, a network of non-governmental organizations that provide information about international development issues with a developing world perspective. Simpson notes: "Concerned over the number of young women who seemingly shun contraceptives and whose education and life prospects have been permanently interrupted by the first of multiple pregnancies, [a member of parliament] called for introducing compulsory sterilization (tubal ligation) of young women with more than three children, arguing that 'the state cannot cope with the responsibility of so many unwanted childbirths.' [Another MP] suggested 'mandatory medical examinations of schoolgirls aged 16'—the age of consent—and under, 'to determine if their virginity is still intact.' The calls for forced sterilization and virginity tests—made amidst fiery exchanges over a damning report on sexual and other forms of abuse in several children's homes and places of safety—provoked a public and media outcry." A local human rights group spokesperson in Jamaica countered by saying: "These are really ridiculous proposals. . . . Such proposals . . . would interfere with women's and girls' rights to privacy—including the right to decide on their family size—security of person and equality before the law." Other women's rights advocates argued that women should be able to choose sterilization, but should not be forced into it by the state. One such advocate offered the following example: "While objecting to state control of women's reproductive lives, a thirty-one-year-old mother of six wishes she had known about contraception as a teenager and planned her family. 'I would have stopped at three [children]. I would have my first at twenty [instead of seventeen],' she says. [She] and her unemployed husband struggle to provide adequate food, lunch money and books for three school age children, good health care for a sick son as well as coping with a toddler and an infant."[29]

This story accords with reports from the United Nations Population Fund on low contraceptive use among Jamaican teens. Furthermore, data from Jamaica's National Family Planning Board show two thirds of all births are not planned, and that among women under age twenty, 40% of whom have been pregnant at least once, 85% of the pregnancies are unplanned.[30] Many Jamaicans become sexually active as early as fourteen or younger. Such early sex, according to the Board, is associated with factors such as poverty, absence of male role models at home—nearly half of the households are headed by single women—and cultural approval of early childbearing, particularly in poor communities. (Women in poor neighborhoods who haven't had a child by their twenties risk being taunted and labeled "mules"—or sterile.) Despite existing contraceptive distribution projects, many women and girls cannot get access to contraceptives at the right place, time, and price. Young people may be embarrassed to ask and are often prevented from getting them by providers in clinics or pharmacies who can be judgmental, especially with regard to sexually active young women. Furthermore, many teens become pregnant involuntarily through rape or incest, while others have confused sex for love, especially economically dependent girls involved with persuasive older men.

Professor Barbara Bailey, of the Centre for Gender and Development Studies at the University of the West Indies in Kingston, takes issue with the cultural implication that women should be solely responsible for contraception. "It takes two to tango. Why put the onus on the female? Why not look at the thing in terms of a partnership between two people and what is the responsibility of these two people?"[31]

The Jamaican report highlights the continuing need for comprehensive education and contraceptive programs, even though in many countries the use of modern contraceptive methods, including voluntary sterilization, has increased rapidly over the past thirty years. "Almost all of the increase

WOMEN'S COURAGE: WARSAW, POLAND. Birth in a Dignified Way is a group that was created to improve the birthing experience of Polish women. Founded in 1996, these women came together in reaction to strict Polish legislation against women's choice in abortion and contraceptive use. They expanded their concerns in recognition of reports that women were being subjected to frightening conditions and treatment in the maternity wards; there had been reports of women being tied down and experiencing other forms of hospital abuse during childbirth.

The group's overall goal is to build the community's trust in improved obstetric care by providing information and programs to expectant mothers and midwives. Its programs include practical support for women through birthing courses, information about contraception and abortion, and other types of counseling. In addition, representatives of the group work together with midwives to increase their awareness of and advocacy for women's reproductive rights. National Consultant on Midwifery is one of the group's collaborators, and together they hope to put trust back into the Polish healthcare system and help women enter motherhood in a safe and dignified manner.

reflects greater use by women rather than their partners," reports the UN Population Fund. "Fewer than 5% of couples in the majority of developing countries rely on male methods (the condom, withdrawal or vasectomy)." Still, an estimated 228 million women worldwide who want to delay or cease childbearing are in need of effective contraceptive methods. Substantial proportions of women in every country—more than 50% in some—say their last birth was unwanted or mis-timed, and, as has been noted, the more than fifty million abortions worldwide each year confirm a continuing unmet need for contraception.

Differing patterns of contraceptive use may not reflect women's personal preferences as much as political and economic decisions made by governments to promote certain methods, the attitudes of medical professionals, relative costs, the limited range of methods offered in some countries, or an uneven availability of contraceptive supplies. In fact, high-quality family planning services are often not available, as the UN Population Fund notes: "One evaluation of family planning programs in eighty-eight developing countries concludes that family planning services are routinely made available to women at reasonable cost in only fourteen countries. In many developing countries, at least a third of women need contraceptive services: Some women, like many of the young women in Jamaica, do not know about modern methods, are unable to obtain or afford them, or distrust or dislike the methods that are available. Single women and teenagers may be barred from obtaining contraceptive services. Many women are ambivalent about whether they want a child or are unsure about their ability to become pregnant. Still others live with a partner who does not approve of contraception or who wants them to become pregnant."[32]

The most commonly used type of contraception in developing countries is female sterilization, which 22% of married women have undergone, more than male sterilization (4%), condom use (3%), and the pill (6%) combined.[33] Even when sterilization is not medically indicated, many women consider it the best among a limited number of contraceptive options. In the developed world where more flexible options are available, sterilization is only half as prevalent.[34] However, it remains one of the most commonly used methods of contraception for women in the United States, where in 2002, female surgical sterilization had a prevalence rate of 23.8%, in comparison with 15.6% pill use and 13.3% condom use.[35] Sterilization is a popular contraceptive option among aging American Baby Boom women who choose to have no children or have completed their families. As an effective method, it answers women's concerns about high contraceptive failure rates; it is also safe.[36] However, because it is not reversible, sterilization is likely to be inappropriate for younger women and adolescents.

Originally, the development of the birth control pill was the answer to many women's objections that most contraceptive methods, such as the condom, were male-controlled. Although the pill is quite effective in controlling pregnancy, it offers no protection against sexually transmitted infections (STIs). Women's demands for female-controlled contraception have led to some progress, most notably to the development of the female condom, which can offer some security of blocking unintended pregnancy and preventing disease.[37] Research and development is also underway on microbicides—products that do not prevent conception but instead kill infectious agents in the vagina, reducing or eliminating the risk of STIs.[38] Both methods provide flexibility and control for women, in contrast to condoms, diaphragms, or intrauterine devices (IUDs), which are either male-controlled or cannot be used effectively without the knowledge of the partner. Although microbicides so far offer little or no protection from unwanted pregnancy, once developed they hold promise of reducing the risk of STIs that also undermine women's reproductive and sexual health.[39]

Safe and Legal Abortion: A Healthy Choice

Being pregnant when you want to be is a wonderful experience. Being pregnant when you have been raped or coerced into sex or are unready or unable to care for a child is one of the worst and most dangerous experiences a woman can have. Women in these circumstances feel so strongly about not wanting to be pregnant that they will take extreme measures to avoid it, often risking their lives and health by seeking illicit abortions.

Women will not have control over their health and their destinies—and maternal mortality rates in poorer countries will remain high—until universal access to inexpensive, safe abortion is available around the globe. Abortion is sometimes avoided as an issue because of its controversial nature and because the debate so rarely changes people's minds on the issue. But the issue must be resolved because millions of lives and the quality of women's lives rest on its resolution.

Access to safe, legal, and affordable abortion is vital for the reasons outlined in the paragraphs that follow.

FIRST: More than a quarter of pregnancies worldwide, about 50 million annually, end in abortion. This is the rate in Latin America, where abortion is generally illegal, as well as in the United States and China, where the procedure is legally available, though not always easily accessible. In South and Southeast Asia, about one in five pregnancies ends in abortion, while in sub-Saharan Africa, North Africa, and the Middle East, the proportion of pregnancies terminated by abortion appears to be about one in ten. Poor access to quality contraceptive services leads to many unwanted pregnancies and abortions.

SECOND: Women vote with their lives for safe and legal abortion: about 70,000 of the half-million annual maternal deaths are the result of unsafe, illegal abortion.[40] Around the world in countries where abortion is illegal, it remains a leading cause of maternal death. Of women in the developing world (outside of China, where abortion is legal), 44% live in countries where abortion is allowed only to save the mother's life. "Another 10% live in countries where abortion is totally prohibited . . . millions of women, unable to obtain a legal abortion on the basis of life-threatening circumstances, have subsequently died from the complications of an illegal abortion. Self-induced and dangerous abortions can involve inserting objects like rubber catheters, stones, twigs, or sharp wire objects into the uterus and cervix. They can involve ingesting or directly flushing the vagina with bitter herbs or caustic substances like dye and commercial cleansers, or deliberate physical strain or harm inflicted on the body. These insertions often cause perforation of internal organs and rupture of the uterus, causing internal bleeding that can be fatal for the mother."[41]

The 1994 UN Conference on Population and Development, held in Cairo, recognized the magnitude of this issue and acted to improve care for all women suffering from the effects of unsafe abortions,[42] though it stopped short of recommending legalizing abortion more broadly. Of the forty- to fifty-million annual aborted pregnancies (about thirty million of which happen in resource-poor countries), about half are aborted in unsafe and illegal circumstances,[43] often resulting in chronic pain, infection, disease, or death.[44] Unsafe abortions occur primarily (about 90%) in poorer countries, and the risk of dying from an unsafe abortion is one in 250 in a poorer country as compared with one in 3700 in a richer country.[45]

Such statistics have prompted many nations to ban abortions altogether. Of the 190 countries in the world, only 22% allow abortion on request; of developing countries, only 6% do, including Albania, China, Cuba, the Democratic Republic of Korea, Tunisia, Vietnam, and many of the former Soviet republics.[46] With respect to allowing abortion for particular reasons, 80% of developed countries allow it in cases of rape, incest, or a pregnancy that endangers the health of the mother, whereas only 26% and 23% of developing countries allow the procedure in cases of rape or incest, or in case of fetal impairment, respectively. Despite the reality that access to the means to terminate unwanted pregnancy is a central health issue for all women, it is more than disappointing that safe and legal abortion is not much more widely available. Although legalization may not affect the actual abortion rate, it can dramatically reduce abortion-related mortality.[47]

The current worldwide abortion rate is thirty-five abortions annually per thousand women of child-bearing age (fifteen to forty-four). Given this rate, over the course of thirty years (the average span of a woman's child-bearing years), about 1,050 abortions will occur per thousand women, or about one per woman. Some women in some regions may have many abortions while others may have none. In the Soviet Union, for example, where contraception was rarely available, women limited their family size by using abortion repeatedly, with many individual women having six or seven abortions in the course of their childbearing years. In other regions, where contraceptives and education may be widely available, some women may never have to resort to abortion.

THIRD: An often cited solution—contraceptives—cannot be substituted for universal access to safe and legal abortion. Contraceptives will reduce the incidence of abortion, but they do not eliminate the need. According to the WHO, even if contraceptives were to be used perfectly, the failure rate would result in nearly six million unwanted pregnancies each year. Given the typical imperfect use of contraceptives, that number grows to 26 million.[48] In other words, even worldwide access to and perfect use of contraceptives, which in itself is far from realistic, would not prevent unwanted pregnancies, particularly given the prevalence of forced sex.[49] Making abortion at least as safe in poorer countries as it is in some richer countries is therefore imperative, in order to save the lives of thousands of women.

FOURTH: We know that abortion will remain a central issue. "The message is loud and clear," states Silvana Paternostro, a Colombian writer, in *The Land of God and Man*. "If a woman wants to have an abortion . . . she will, regardless of its being illegal and forbidden by the Church. Nothing will stop a woman who is desperate to end an unwanted pregnancy—not the law, not her father, her husband or her God."[50] Because these words are true, providing access is vital and urgent.

Fortunately, there is a solution to this massive and critically important problem: Abortion performed by a trained professional in a hygienic setting is a very safe procedure, according to the Alan Guttmacher Institute, a New York and Washington based health research organization. The procedure is about twice as safe as having one's tonsils removed, and much safer than giving birth. In fact, it is ten times safer than giving birth if performed before the eighth week of pregnancy. Abortions after fourteen weeks are also safe, but health risks increase the longer a pregnancy goes on. Most abortions, some 90%, are performed in the first twelve weeks of pregnancy. Early abortions, with no complications, have no harmful health effects for the woman and do not increase the possibility of future miscarriages, ectopic pregnancies, birth defects, or low infant birth weight. Even if a woman has more than one early abortion, her ability to carry a later pregnancy to term is not endangered.

With a variety of inexpensive methods available, universal access to abortion could be provided. Vacuum aspiration with either manual or electrical equipment is a cost-effective method that can be performed under local anesthesia. It is easier and less complex than dilation or surgical curettage under general anesthesia. Increasingly, pharmacological agents are being made available. Misoprostol, which is a prostaglandin, can also provide safe and cost-effective abortion by impairing the growth of the fetus.[51]

Lifting legal constraints on abortion has been shown to dramatically reduce abortion-related deaths. For example, when abortion laws were made more restrictive in Romania in 1966, during the years up to 1984, abortion-related deaths increased by 600%. When the procedure was made legal again in 1990, abortion-related mortality plummeted by 67% in the first year alone. Similarly, in the United States, abortion-related mortality decreased by 85% in the five years after legalization.[52] Reasonably accurate abortion statistics exist for about twenty-five countries for the years 1975 to 1996.[53] Although arguments against legalization often point out the increase in the abortion rate following legalization in most of these countries, evidence suggests that legalization makes little difference to overall abortion levels. The increase in the abortion rate in these countries primarily derives from the scores of previously uncounted illegal abortions that are now tallied as legal procedures. In certain areas, for example Vietnam and the former Soviet Union, the rise in abortions after legalization also reflects the fact that access to contraceptive methods (such as the IUD and sterilization) remained limited.[54]

Even where abortion is legal, making it fully accessible is an ongoing struggle—a political struggle—sometimes for the very lives of women. As it is with so many issues, where abortion is outlawed, the women undergoing unsafe abortions are mainly those already disadvantaged by society. Wealthier women have always had access to abortion, whether it is illegal or not; money will buy this service, hopefully within a safe setting. But vast

WOMEN'S COURAGE: QUITO, ECUADOR. La Fundación Desafío (The Challenge
Foundation) increases awareness about sexual health and reproductive rights in
the Ecuadorian community. Since its founding in 1997, one of the group's main
programs has involved training "promotoras" who counsel women in the community and offer information and family planning services such as emergency
contraception. Young people distribute information about HIV/AIDS, condoms,
and birth-control pills to discourage too-early pregnancy. An especially important aspect of the Foundation's work is to provide safe abortions to Ecuadorian
women, the only group in the region that does so.

numbers of those who are young, impoverished, and/or caught in war or
refugee situations must rely on unsafe, illegal abortion.

Of the many women who die every day from unsafe abortion, 99% live
and die in the developing world.[55] These women die because of social structures which prevent them from learning about their own bodies and sexuality, which give power in sexual relationships to men, which deprive women
of access to the means of controlling reproduction, which criminalize safe
means of terminating pregnancy, and which surround the issue of abortion
with such shame and censure that women are isolated and desperate.

The conditions are clear: abortion must be provided by professionally
trained personnel in a clean and safe setting; it must be legal; it must be
inexpensive; it must be widely provided; and it must be socially supported
so that women do not face obstacles to using the services.

Aid to poor countries can be a force for making abortions under these ideal
conditions available. But, unfortunately, the U.S. administration's "Mexico
City policy" (so-named because it was established at the 1984 International
Conference on Population and Development, held in Mexico City) has severely
hampered several crucial efforts to provide contraception and/or to provide
safe abortion services in poorer countries around the world. Also dubbed the
"global gag rule" for its choking off of funding channels for family planning,
this rule was first established by President Reagan, then relaxed by President
Clinton, and then reinstituted by George W. Bush. The policy "restricts foreign non-governmental organizations (NGOs) that receive USAID family
planning funds from using their own, non-U.S. funds to provide legal abortion

WOMEN'S COURAGE: LIMA, PERU. El Centro de Promoción y Defensa de los
Derechos Sexuales y Reproductivos (The Center for the Promotion and Defense
of Sexual and Reproductive Rights) has as its main goal changing attitudes
in Peru about a woman's right to safely terminate an unwanted pregnancy.
Founded in 2004, the Center has been dedicated to countering the strong anti-
choice culture in Peru. As in many other Latin American countries, the Catholic
Church's influence on Peruvian society is strong. The Center conducts workshops to promote gender equality and greater access to contraceptive methods and legal abortions. The group has organized a campaign to publicize rape
victims' rights to obtain safe abortion, and it has also started using electronic
newsletters to reach the country's obstetricians, in the hope of creating more
of a pro-woman culture in the country.

services, lobby their own governments for abortion law reform, or even
provide accurate medical counseling or referrals regarding abortion."[56] As a
result, the policy is detrimental to the survival and growth of much-needed
family planning programs that may include abortion awareness and procedures among their services. Education about termination of pregnancy is
an essential part of family planning programs in many parts of the world.
The absence of U.S. funds is a blow to many well-regarded and respectable
family planning programs that serve poor women.

Among the groups disadvantaged by the U.S. administration's anti-abortion
policy, for example, was a small private program called Marie Stopes International that provided prenatal care, well-baby care, and family planning assistance to African and Asian refugees. The U.S. government decided in 2003
to cut off funds to the Reproductive Health for Refugees Consortium, the
umbrella organization under which Marie Stopes operated, on the grounds
that one of the charities listed as beneficiaries was linked to abortion-related
services in China. Consequently they cut off a lifeline for Marie Stopes, which
had to drop planned outreach programs for Somali and Rwandan refugees,
affecting the health of thousands of African women and children.[57]

The current U.S. administration under George W. Bush has also withdrawn funds from the World Health Organization and the United Nations
Population Fund for programs offering reproductive health care and certain HIV/AIDS interventions.[58] By not financing the availability of abortion

services, the U.S. misses the opportunity to save lives. By punishing those organizations that do support these services through the withdrawal of funds meant for other services, women around the globe who need other services, such as contraception, may be forced to go without. Ironically, this policy has the reverse of its intended effect: by restricting funding for non-abortion related family planning, more women may have unwanted pregnancies because they lack access to contraception. This in turn can heighten the recourse to abortion—exactly the opposite of what the Bush and Reagan administrations say they intended.

Government policy—whether foreign aid or governments focused on their own domestic populations—can be a powerful force for making life-saving services universal. To be a positive agent for change, it is not enough to stop punishing organizations that provide abortion services. Instead, we must actively support the development of those organizations *because* they provide contraceptive help as well as access to life-saving services.

Regardless of government policy, activists and others must move the debate about abortion from the myriad objections of morality and safety toward the argument of making it universally available as a means of saving human life and increasing women's opportunities and empowerment.

Sexually Transmitted Infections[59]

The same social structures that limit access to contraception also deny women the right to knowledge and treatment of sexually transmitted infections (STIs), which are, along with violence against women, one of the two leading causes of female morbidity.

The range of disorders associated with sex and reproduction is astounding, and since many are preventable or curable, they disproportionately affect women in developing countries who lack access to medical care. Many of these infections are asymptomatic or difficult to identify, particularly in women, but they have serious consequences, including infertility and death.[60]

In the preceding chapter, we discussed the current HIV/AIDS scourge. But there are many other STIs, once known as "venereal diseases," that can cause serious health problems for women and their offspring. Some STIs can spread into the uterus and fallopian tubes to cause pelvic inflammatory disease (PID), which in turn is a major cause of both infertility and sometimes fatal ectopic (tubal) pregnancy. STIs in women may also be associated

WOMEN'S COURAGE: RUSTAVI, GEORGIA. Women and Health, a group based in rural southern Georgia, educates women in family planning, reproductive rights, and HIV/AIDS prevention. The group serves the community by providing health information and services to girls and women between the ages of sixteen and sixty-five, many of whom are sex workers or unemployed. In addition to providing medical, legal, and psychological services to women who have been sexually abused, Woman and Health contributes to the community in other ways. For example, it has established a school to teach women skills in prenatal care and awareness of women's and children's rights. For unemployed women, the organization offers workshops in professional training to help them improve their economic status. Woman and Health's dedication to improving women's status in society has also reached the Parliament, where the group has encouraged elected officials to consider bills to include more women in politics and to protect the rights of sex workers.

with cervical cancer. One STI, human papillomavirus virus (HPV), causes genital warts as well as cervical and other genital cancers. STIs can be passed from a mother to her baby before, during, or immediately after birth; some of these infections of the newborn can be cured easily, but others may cause a baby to be permanently disabled or even die. An estimated 333 million new cases of curable STIs occur each year.[61]

The range of common sexually transmitted diseases, listed below, include those that only affect women and those to which women are more susceptible to infection than men: bacterial vaginosis, chlamydia, cytomegalovirus (CMV), genital warts, gonorrhea, hepatitis, herpes, human immunodeficiency virus (HIV), human papillomavirus (HPV), molluscum contagiosum, pelvic inflammatory disease (PID), pubic lice, scabies, syphilis, trichomoniasis, and urinary tract infections. The effects of these infections range from abnormal vaginal discharges, bleeding, blisters, and itching, to pain, fatigue, general weakness, headaches, hearing loss, and so on. STIs can weaken a person's immune system and provide fertile ground for other illnesses, some life-threatening.

Denied a knowledge of the normal functioning of their own bodies, millions of women live with, and many die of, diseases related to reproduction, because such suffering is considered a "normal" part of a woman's life, not something for which a woman should seek medical treatment.[62] Of the 3.4 million deaths each year related to sexual health, nearly two hundred thousand are a direct result of STIs,[63] and of the 585,000 annual deaths during pregnancy and childbirth, about 15% result from complications related to STIs. An additional 237,000 deaths each year are the result of cervical cancer, a disease of the human papillomavirus, which can be treated successfully if identified early and also vaccinated against before a woman becomes sexually active. The vast majority (98%) of deaths from reproductive health problems occur in poorer countries,[64] which reveals the tremendous disparities in our world and the extent to which lack of knowledge and education and the inability to negotiate sexual behavior can lead women to disease and death.

The Evolving Field of Reproductive and Sexual Health and Rights

A brief overview of the field of reproductive health and rights illustrates how recently women's health and sexual rights have been recognized as worth studying or including on international policy agendas. During the 1970s, reproductive health issues were part of discussions of "population control," in the context of economic development. In the 1980s, the discussion focused on family planning, still with an emphasis on population control, but people in the field also began to use the term "reproductive health" in the context of health care. The term "reproductive rights" was not commonly used until the late 1980s.

A crucial moment in this shift from a development approach to a human rights approach happened at the United Nations Conference on Population and Development, held in Cairo in 1994. Previous conferences—in Bucharest in 1974 and in Mexico City in 1984—had focused on the importance of population control through the use of family planning (in Bucharest) and on development variables (in Mexico City). At the 1994 conference, however, women's groups made a concerted effort to highlight the central role of women in "population issues" and succeeded in making the point that reproductive health and women's rights are central parts of any discussion of population and fertility rates. For the first time—at the 1994 meeting—the belief that women have the right to determine their own reproduction was clearly stated in international documents.

The International Plan of Action that was issued in Cairo stated that "Reproductive rights are a certain set of human rights already recognized in many national laws, international documents about human rights, and other important documents of the United Nations. These rights exist in the basic right of all partners and people to freely and responsibly decide the number and spacing of their children, the frequency at which they have children, and to have information and means available to do so, all of which are parts of the right to reach the highest level of sexual and reproductive health. They include the rights of all to make decisions relative to reproduction free of discrimination, coercion and violence."[65]

This idea of reproductive rights was further refined at the Fourth United Nations Conference on Women, held in 1995 in Beijing, China. The Platform for Action drawn up in Beijing included the following paragraph: "The human rights of women include their right to have control over and decide freely and responsibly on matters related to their sexuality, including sexual and reproductive health, free of coercion, discrimination, and violence. Equal relationships between women and men in matters of sexual relations and reproduction, including full respect for the integrity of the person, require mutual respect, consent, and shared responsibility for sexual behavior and its consequences."[66]

The Beijing Declaration and Platform for Action, which emerged from the Beijing conference, by confirming women's equal rights in sexual relationships, became the first instance in a UN document to mention women as sexual as well as reproductive beings. Because of age-old fears and taboos, it has been difficult to broaden the idea of rights from reproductive rights to the more encompassing concept of sexual rights. The Beijing delegates advanced into new territory by validating and claiming sexual rights that include aspects of sexuality from childhood through old age. The concept of sexual rights regards women as human beings, recognizing that the female of the species is not limited in her roles to childbearing and mothering.

On the one hand, these important policy decisions recognizing women's rights to health and choice were very long in coming. On the other hand, recognizing women as human beings not defined narrowly by their childbearing and mothering roles was a revolution in women's empowerment.

Though this book often focuses on illness and injury because they are daily realities for many women, the integrity of women's bodies is central to women's health and rights. The importance of women claiming their own

WOMEN'S COURAGE: PESHAWAR, PAKISTAN. Blue Veins (Women Welfare and Relief Services) Breast Cancer Awareness Crusade was founded in 1999 by a group of women concerned about the lack of health information and resources available to women in Pakistan. They dedicate their efforts to breast cancer victims, who often face severe discrimination and oppression due to misunderstandings about the illness in Pakistan society. Today Blue Veins is a growing national group of volunteers who embrace the motto "Awareness, Action, and Advocacy." Their goal is to "increase public awareness about breast cancer and ensure that people from all socioeconomic backgrounds have rapid access to current relevant education, support and information about this disease." Blue Veins has launched many information campaigns within Pakistan, including conferences, presentations at universities, colleges, schools, and health fairs, and lobbying federal and provincial departments. They also provide psychological and social services to breast cancer patients and their families.

WOMEN'S COURAGE: QUEZON CITY, PHILIPPINES. The Asia-Pacific Rainbow Support Center works with organizations throughout the Asia-Pacific region to ensure the rights of individuals who identify themselves as lesbian, gay, bisexual, transgender, inter-sexual, and queer (LGBTIQ). The main aim of the Center is to involve this community in the movement to prevent HIV/AIDS. Led by a group of lesbian women, the Center disseminates health information that addresses issues specific to lesbians' reproductive rights. The group's outreach program strives to prevent discrimination based on gender and sexual orientation. Since its founding in 1999, the Center has also planned workshops to bring together women's rights activists to share their visions of the LGBTIQ movement in the Asia-Pacific area.

WOMEN'S COURAGE: QUITO, ECUADOR. Fundación de Desarrollo Humano Integral (Foundation for Holistic Development) promotes women's rights in the traditionally conservative Ecuadorian population by supporting and creating awareness about lesbian, gay, bisexual, and transgender issues. The Foundation has organized events and celebrations on International Women's Day and the Day of No Violence Against Women, among others. Its radio shows and websites, which spread messages of tolerance and respect for marginalized sexual minority groups, are directed particularly to younger people. Since its founding in 2000, the Foundation has become part of a movement to build a more harmonious and inclusive community in Ecuador.

WOMEN'S COURAGE: MANAGUA, NICARAGUA. Colectivo Entreamigas (Collective Between Friends) defends Nicaraguan women against the violation of their rights, particularly focusing on the rights of lesbians, in a country where homosexuality is outlawed. Since its establishment in 1996, the Collective has worked with women in Managua, providing them with educational programs about sexual and reproductive rights as well as discussions and reflections on gender stereotypes in their communities. Through panel discussions, seminars, and training session, the Collective encourages community leadership and provides help and guidance to women who have suffered sexual violence. Similar sensitivity training is offered to officials and to the general public.

bodies as autonomous and unique entities—not battlefields, territories, or instruments—underlies every critical issue that is discussed in this book.

Most of the UN conventions and declarations are exclusively concerned with the protection of women's bodies. Although this concern is important, it also represents women as objects to defend and shelter, rather than as independent human beings who seek expression and empowerment. The Beijing Declaration and Platform for Action was an important step toward empowerment and sexual expression, particularly in provision number thirty, which declared: "We are determined to . . . Ensure equal access to and equal treatment of women and men in education and health care and enhance women's sexual and reproductive health as well as education."[67] These and other provisions of the Declaration acknowledged the right of individual people relating to sexuality, including reproductive rights, and at the same time recognized the right to self-determined sexual experience, the right to pleasure, and the right to a lesbian existence.

Acknowledging and acting on behalf of lesbian rights and health is an important aspect of sexual rights that discussions of women's health usually overlook.[68] Lesbian health has not had a place on the international health agenda. Similarly, human rights advocates have shied away from including the rights to lesbianism and lesbian health in international treaties. And even in everyday interaction, for example at the doctor's office, lesbian women may feel uncomfortable asking about lesbian-specific health problems, for fear that they will be ostracized or that the physician will condemn them or will not be able to help them.

Increasingly, however, lesbian women and their allies are making the case that they have special health and human rights needs having to do with such issues as access to care, preventing substance abuse, and freedom from violence.[69] Very little has been written on the topic of lesbian health, particularly relating to women in poorer countries. In traditional cultures, where women may be undervalued, lesbian women, marginalized within the already marginalized population of women, may be invisible or be condemned and disparaged specifically because they define their sexuality as being outside "the norm." The conspicuous lack of any mention of lesbianism in international treaties and human rights documents is significant. Our world is only beginning to accept the equality of women, much less to respect the right of women to love other women openly.

The Reading of the Names

Of the many assaults on women's health and abrogations of women's rights, maternal death is particularly outrageous. It is preventable, almost entirely without recourse to fancy drugs or exotic facilities or huge sums of money. Fathalla describes maternal deaths as women being "killed in physiological duty," and he sees the tragedy of such deaths as a "chronic holocaust and a final blow in an incessant drama of inequity and social injustice."[70]

It has become popular to list the names of the dead who died at war on memorials, most famously on the Vietnam War Memorial, and, during the war in Iraq, to read them out on news programs.

If we viewed the preventable maternal deaths as casualties in a war against women, we might find, recognize, and honor these women by reading out their names. Each minute, a woman somewhere dies from complications related to pregnancy and childbirth: 1,400 deaths every day, more than half a million deaths each year—they add up relentlessly. To read out all their names would take a newscaster two hours a day, 365 days a year.

A free woman. At last free!
Free from slavery in the kitchen
where I walked back and forth stained
and squalid among cooking pots.
My brutal husband ranked me lower
than the shade he sat in.
Purged of anger and the body's hunger,
I live in meditation
in my own shade from a broad tree.
I am at ease.

—Sumangala's Mother, India, Pali language, 13th century[1]

6

Violence against Women: Abuse or Terrorism?

THE FIRST-EVER GLOBAL STUDY on domestic violence was released in November 2005 by the World Health Organization (WHO).[2] Based on extensive research done by the London School of Hygiene and Tropical Medicine, the report shows that violence against women is widespread, with far-reaching health consequences. The report includes data from more than 24,000 women interviewed in fifteen sites in ten countries: Bangladesh, Brazil, Ethiopia, Japan, Peru, Namibia, Samoa, Serbia and Montenegro, Thailand, and the United Republic of Tanzania. Women who are physically abused by partners are likely to experience health problems, regardless of whether they live in a modern industrialized city or a rural area in a developing nation.

The Center for Gender Equity describes violence against women as "the most pervasive yet least recognized human rights abuse in the world," as well as "a profound health problem, sapping women's energy, compromising their physical health, and eroding their self-esteem."[3] It "occurs in all countries," according to the Center for Gender Equity's report, which continues, "Although women can also be violent and abuse exists in some same-sex relationships [at about the same rate as in the rest of the population], the vast majority of partner abuse is perpetrated by men against their female partners."[4] Women are shoved, slapped, punched, beaten, burned, kicked, and killed every day in every country around the world.

Violence against women is apparently universal and, as we will review in a moment, prevalent across many different cultures and countries.

About one-third of women around the world have suffered violence from an intimate partner.[5] One in five women will be sexually assaulted during her lifetime, with at least half of such attacks occurring before she is eighteen years old.[6] If domestic abuse, dowry deaths, honor killings, and rape—violent acts committed against women around the world primarily by family members and acquaintances—were infectious diseases, we would declare an epidemic. Yet many governments persist in treating these acts as private matters, distinct from crimes requiring state intervention. While violence against women encompasses violations taken up in other chapters, from infanticide and female genital mutilation to extreme brutality in conflict and refugee situations, this chapter focuses on the types of violence that are most dominant in the lives of women worldwide—violence within marriage and other intimate relationships.

Because the outcomes of domestic violence are so-wide ranging and psychologically as well as physically damaging, some question the very words used to describe domestic violence. One domestic violence counselor has developed an important insight from the situations women have described to her: "In my opinion the term 'domestic violence' sugarcoats the severity of the assaults these women endure. . . . Take, for example, the all-too-common situation . . . where a husband must approve his wife's grocery list, then wait in the parking lot while she shops, and, when she's done, check her receipt against the list to make sure she did not buy anything extra. Consider how a husband might keep track of his wife's phone calls, threatening her or beating her if she contacts her friends or family. Think of the husband who slammed his wife's face into a mirror one day, breaking her nose, her jaw. . . . Think about a woman who called me once and had a hard time hearing because her boyfriend had whacked the side of her head so hard that her ear was internally damaged. Think about how a batterer can threaten a woman's family, her children, and her pets, in addition to her own body. Think of how much detachment a woman must undergo to cope with the daily reality of being a victim, how some women consciously relax their muscles when being beaten to minimize bruising. . . . Think of the health implications. . . . There should be a better name for that kind of abuse. Maybe 'domestic terror.' Maybe 'torture in the home'?"[7]

What we call this "abuse" is important, and the term "domestic abuse" is a soft euphemism for what is in fact going on. Perhaps it *is* "domestic terror." What we call this abrogation of human rights defines our understanding of the problem. The term "abuse" implies "misuse," as when we "use," "misuse," or "abuse" alcohol or drugs. We might say that we "abuse" a car by driving it fast down rough roads. By extension, then, the "abuse" of women implies that they are being misused and, by extension, that there is a proper "use" for them. The current phrase—"domestic abuse"—is common and appears in many of the quotations included in this book. For my part, I am calling it "violence," unless I am quoting directly, and I suggest that we consider using the term "terror," since this is exactly what it is, on a global scale.

Almost every woman has a story to tell of a friend who has experienced domestic violence. I know a woman who, years ago and recently arrived in California from Sudan, was locked by her professor husband in an apartment for two years; her release only came when neighbors called to report disturbing sounds. At Stanford University, more than half of the students in my classes had experienced violence or knew a close friend or family member who had. Another woman I know told me that her husband (now her ex-) held a gun to her head because she "talked back." Stories of violence by intimate partners abound when women come to know and trust each other, or when health workers probe to try to understand the causes of bruises, broken bones, chronic pain, and persistent headaches, all illnesses associated with domestic violence.

The Nature and Prevalence of Domestic Violence against Women

The essence of domestic violence is that it is "a pattern of assaultive and coercive behaviors, including physical, sexual, and psychological attacks, as well as economic coercion, that adults or adolescents use against their intimate partners."[8] It frequently includes "controlling behaviors such as isolating a woman from family and friends, monitoring her movements, and restricting her access to resources,"[9] as was the case with my Sudanese friend and her professor husband.

Although domestic violence is hard to measure, those who work in the area of prevention of family violence consider such injuries to have reached shocking levels. "In nearly fifty population-based surveys from around the world, 10% to 50% of women report being hit or otherwise physically harmed by an intimate male partner at some point in their lives."[10] Hundreds of women's groups in countries as different and distant as India, Kenya, Mexico, New Zealand, Peru, and the United States identify violence against women as a crucial issue affecting women's development and a "constant in women's lives." Roxanna Carrillo, formerly with the UN Women's Fund (UNIFEM), writes that "Official statistics and survey data in the United States, for example, dramatically convey the endemic nature of gender violence. A rape occurs somewhere in the United States every six minutes, most often perpetrated by someone known to the victim. Domestic battery is the single most significant cause of injury to women, more than car accidents, rapes and muggings combined. Yet a 1985 FBI report estimates that wife assault is under-reported by a factor of at least ten to one. . . . Statistics from other industrialized countries are equally disconcerting. Reports from France indicate that 95% of all victims of violence are women, 51% of these at the hands of their husbands. In Denmark, 25% of women cite violence as the reason for divorce, and a 1984 study of urban victimization in seven major Canadian cities found that 90% of the victims were women."[11]

Until the WHO study, released in 2005 and mentioned above, studies of violence against women in poorer countries have been few, but the pattern is very similar, as Carrillo notes: "Its manifestations may be culturally specific, but gender-specific violence cuts across national boundaries, ideologies, classes, races and ethnic groups."[12] The Center for Health and Gender Equity reported in 1999 on various regional and local studies on physical violence, which showed the following percentages of adult women physically assaulted by intimate partners: in Ethiopia 45%, Nigeria 31%, South Africa 29%, Bangladesh 47%, India 40%, New Zealand 35%, Papua New Guinea 67%, Netherlands 21%, Turkey 58%, United Kingdom 30%, Barbados 30%, Mexico 27%, Egypt 34%, and Canada 29%.[13]

Physical violence in intimate relationships is almost always "accompanied by psychological abuse and, in one-third to over one-half of cases, by sexual abuse. . . . For example, among 613 abused women in Japan, 57% had suffered all three types of abuse—physical, psychological, and sexual. . . . In Monterey, Mexico, 52% of physically abused women had also been sexually abused. . . . In Leon, Nicaragua, among 188 women who were physically abused by their partners, only five were not also abused sexually, psychologically, or both."[14]

WOMEN'S COURAGE: DURBAN, SOUTH AFRICA. Founded in 1992, the Wings of Love Care Centre of South Africa is dedicated to supporting women in domestic violence situations. As in many cities, in Durban, where crime and unemployment rates are high, domestic violence cases often go overlooked by law enforcement agencies. Among several programs to combat the results of domestic violence, the Centre runs a shelter for women who run away from their abusers, and provides psychological and legal counseling, education sessions on victim empowerment, child abuse, and parenting skills for women in the region. To change the attitude of indifference among law enforcement officers and raise awareness for domestic violence issues, the Centre provides sensitivity training to police officers and to others in community organizations.

Shocking as these statistics are, most people agree that estimates of prevalence are almost always undercounted because of the shame and under-reporting associated with violence between intimate partners. Studies of the prevalence of intimate partner violence are usually based on police or hospital admissions reports, thereby leaving out experiences of the many women who are too afraid or ashamed to approach authorities.

Just how prevalent is this abuse? The Population Information Program and the Center for Gender Equity, two respected research institutions based in Washington, D.C., studied numerous local research projects and produced findings in 1999 that echo the consensus of numerous public health and human rights authorities: "Around the world, at least one woman in every three has been beaten, coerced into sex, or otherwise abused in her lifetime."[15]

Partner violence cuts across societies, affecting women of all classes, ethnicities, and levels of education. Poverty and lack of education often exacerbate the situation because of a lack of resources and therefore of alternatives, but women of all social strata find it difficult and dangerous to escape violence. Indeed, in some countries, women whose incomes or educational levels are higher than those of their husbands are at higher risk than others. In a series of studies carried out by the International Center for Research on Women in collaboration with independent Indian colleagues, researchers found that, especially in India, "a woman's risk of being beaten, kicked or hit rose along with her level of education." The study found that 45% of Indian women suffer violence by their husbands. Kumud Sharma of the

Centre for Women's Development Studies in New Delhi noted: "Educated women are aware of their rights. . . . They are no longer willing to follow commands blindly. When they ask questions, it causes conflicts, which, in turn, leads to violence." The Indian researchers surmised that women who challenge their husband's right to control their behavior—perhaps by asking for household money or stepping out of the house without permission—are questioning men's ideas of manhood, i.e., the extent to which they can control their wives. "Although men's preoccupation with controlling their wives declines with age . . . researchers found that the highest rates of sexual violence were among highly educated men. Thirty-two percent of men with zero years of education and 42% of men with one to five years of education reported engaging in sexual violence. Among men with six to ten years of education—as well as those with high-school educations and higher—this figure increased to 57%. . . . A similar pattern was seen when the problem was analyzed according to income and socioeconomic standing. Those at the lowest rungs of the socio-economic ladder—migrant labor, cobblers, carpenters, and barbers—showed a sexual violence rate of 35%. The rate almost doubled, to 61%, among the highest income groups."[16] It is not known whether this pattern of abuse is more prevalent in some societies than in others.

HEALTH EFFECTS

The researchers who produced the 2005 WHO study, for which 24,000 women in ten countries were interviewed, found that "victims are about twice as likely as non-victims to suffer from poor health, and that such effects persist long after the violence has stopped. This health impact of domestic violence went beyond injuries, as women who had experienced physical or sexual violence by a partner were more likely to have pain, dizziness, and mental health problems. Victims were also more likely to have considered suicide and to have suffered miscarriages."[17]

Violence costs society in numerous ways. The most immediate cost is the injury and disability, and sometimes death, that result from both physical and psychological violence. Of murders attributed to intimate partners, nearly three out of four have a female victim.[18] Short of that final outcome, women who are the targets of domestic violence may suffer the following health problems:

WOMEN'S COURAGE: GURJAANSK, KAHETINSK, GEORGIA. Since its establishment in 2001, the Kahetinsk Regional Committee of the National Network for Protection Against Violence has been an important resource for women in the impoverished region of Kahetinsk in Georgia. In Georgia, abused women receive little protection from the law, and many are dependent on men for income because they tend to hold lesser-paid jobs. The Committee strives to defend women's rights against violence by providing direct support to them. It has created a domestic abuse crisis center and a telephone hotline for women survivors who seek psychological and legal support.

When the Committee learned of an increasing trend of sexual abuse of girls between the ages of twelve and seventeen, it quickly acted to establish a support group tailored specifically for adolescent girls. In an attempt to reach and help more women, the Committee has trained and involved associates in rural regions of Kahetinsk to provide direct support to survivors of domestic abuse.

- Serious pain, injuries, and permanent disabilities, such as broken bones, burns, black eyes, cuts, and bruises, as well as headaches, asthma, stomach pain, and muscle pains that may go on for years after the abuse. Of women seeking care in hospital emergency rooms in the United States in 2000 for violence related injuries, 37% were injured by an intimate partner.[19]

- Mental health problems, such as persistent fear, depression, lack of motivation, lack of a sense of self-worth, isolation, shame, self-blame, and problems eating and sleeping. Domestic violence is strongly associated with depression, post traumatic stress disorder, and suicide. Over half of battered women (56%) manifest symptoms of psychiatric disorders; 29% of all women who attempt suicide were battered; 37% of battered women have symptoms of depression; 46% have symptoms of anxiety disorder; 45% experience post-traumatic stress disorder.[20]

- Sexual health problems: as a way to cope with the violence, women may begin harmful or reckless behavior, such as using drugs or alcohol, or having many sex partners. Others may suffer unwanted pregnancies, or contract sexually transmitted infections, including HIV/AIDS, as a result of sexual abuse. Sexual abuse can also lead to a fear of having sex, pain during sex, and a lack of desire.[21]

Women who have suffered domestic violence have little control over their own reproduction and thus may have more children than women in non-violent relationships. Reports issued in 2002 based on data in the United Kingdom and the United States—few, if any, studies on the relationship between pregnancy and domestic abuse have been done in poorer countries—report on research that "has shown that domestic violence toward a woman might begin or escalate during her pregnancy. . . . One U.S. study showed that 37% of obstetric patients were suffering violence, and that 30% of domestic violence actually started during pregnancy. Domestic abuse was identified as a major health issue for pregnant women: a Yale study revealed that abused women were fifteen times more likely to suffer a miscarriage. Studies have shown that . . . about 23% of pregnant women suffer violence by intimate partners."[22] Wife battering is correlated with miscarriages, low birth weight, poor natal care, and higher infant mortality.[23] Studies are few on this issue, particularly those that would provide cross-cultural comparisons and get at the question of why violence seems to escalate during pregnancy.

THE SILENCE SURROUNDING

The endless outrage of intimate partner violence unfolds in silence and invisibility. A variety of forces stifle the revelation of such violence. To a great extent, the silence can be explained by distinctions that have been made between the public and private spheres. International human rights norms have applied, until very recently, only to activities in the public sphere (violence and torture in wartime camps, for example), not in the privacy of a home. Moreover, the axiom that "a man's home is his castle," where he is lord and master and his wife and children are "subjects" over whom he can wield power as he wishes, has been widely accepted.

In cultures where women's subordination is particularly pronounced, as in Bangladesh, Cambodia, India, Mexico, Nigeria, Pakistan, Papua New Guinea, Tanzania, and Zimbabwe, for example, studies have shown that violence is frequently viewed as physical "chastisement—the husband's right to 'correct' an erring wife. . . . As one husband said in a focus-group discussion in Tamil Nadu, India, 'If it is a great mistake, then the husband is justified in beating his wife. Why not? A cow will not be obedient without beatings.'"[24]

Women sometimes agree; a counselor shared with me her experience of counseling a Chinese woman: "She asks me again and again, 'How can I make

WOMEN'S COURAGE: NIZHNIY TAGIL, RUSSIA. In May of 1995, women in the rural town of Nizhniy Tagil decided to take a stance against the problem of domestic violence in their community. Together, they formed the Center Lana, the first and still the only organization in Nizhniy Tagil to provide services and raise awareness about violence against women. The Center provides medical, psychological and other support services to more than 5,500 women. Legal consultations and careful documentation led to Lana's successful campaign for a government-sponsored shelter, which opened its doors to victims of violence in 2000. Lana has spread its message, with over thirty seminars on domestic violence for police, social workers, psychologists, and school teachers.

Domestic violence has long been viewed as a socially accepted practice in the region. Center Lana is dramatically changing this attitude in women themselves and in the community as a whole. In 1997, of their clients only twelve women reported cases of violence to the police; in 2000, 600 reports were submitted. Women began to find their voices.

him stop? What can I do? I want to be a good wife.' She tells me that she deserved a beating for not taking out the trash. She wavers between blaming her husband and blaming herself."[25] "Why did I feel such shame? . . .I had told myself a thousand times that what happened to me was not my fault, but I did not really believe it," writes Nancy Raine, a U.S. rape victim, similarly conflicted.[26]

In addition, though resources to support women who have experienced violence are increasing in both richer and poorer countries, many women cannot disclose domestic violence because they have nowhere to go to escape it and no resources to draw upon. Others remain silent because of the pain of remembering, and therefore reliving, the violence. "Too terrible to utter aloud: this is the meaning of the word 'unspeakable,'" Raine says.[27]

In a study of American women, 92% of women who were physically injured by their partners did not discuss the incidents with their physicians, and 57% did not discuss the incidents with anyone.[28] At the same time, four different studies of survivors of violence reported that 70% to 81% of patients studied reported that they would have liked their healthcare providers to ask them privately about intimate partner violence.[29] Changing laws, developing policies, and ending the private violence of domestic violence and rape requires ending the silence that reigns and providing women with safe opportunities to talk about these issues.

TRIGGERS AND CAUSES

Worldwide, studies identify a consistent list of events that are said to "trigger" domestic violence. These include situations in which the intimate partner, usually the man, perceives that his partner is disobeying him, talking back, not having food ready on time, failing to care adequately for the children or the home, questioning him about money or girlfriends, going somewhere without his permission, refusing him sex, or expressing suspicions of infidelity. A more prevalent trigger for violence is the man's suspicion of his wife's infidelity. All of these situations, particularly when they describe male-female relationships, constitute transgression of gender norms in many countries.

Those who study intimate partner violence have concluded that the general causes of such violence are:

- unequal distribution of power within the family and community

- the belief that women and children are possessions a man can control

- the belief that women should be economically dependent on men, even though many women earn some money

- lack of skill in communicating and resolving problems without recourse to violence

- lack of action by the community, witnesses, friends, and neighbors to prevent or stop violence being perpetrated in their communities and routinely depicted in the media[30]

Violence is central to discussions of women's health and human rights, not only because it is one of the two major causes of morbidity in women (the other being sexually transmitted infections) but also because it is a major strategy for maintaining power in societies organized in terms of hierarchies. In our hierarchically structured societies, we not only categorize people but we also make the mistake of assigning values to various categories. We learn that strong is "better" than weak; bigger is "better" than smaller; rich is "better" than poor; white is "better" than black; and male is "better" than female.

WOMEN'S COURAGE: KANPUR, INDIA. In March of 1981, a group of women activists organized a two-day march against dowry and rape in Kanpur, India. After some discussion, the activists formed Sakhi Kendra, a group where problems could be discussed fearlessly and where collective social action could be encouraged. Sakhi Kendra provides housing, legal services, and medical assistance to survivors of dowry abuse, rape, forced prostitution, domestic violence, and other forms of violence against women.

Over half of the women in Uttar Pradesh, where Kanpur is located, have reported physical assault by an intimate partner. Many women are killed and others driven to suicide in increasing incidents of domestic violence. In the face of institutional and intimate-partner violence, Sakhi Kendra publishes women's rights newsletters in Hindi, runs micro-funding and employment workshops, and offers training to emerging women's groups in vulnerable and poor areas. In conjunction with its gender sensitivity training for girls, boys, couples, media, and the police, the group also coordinates festivals and street dramas to raise public awareness of gender issues, dowry, and violence against women. Sakhi Kendra provides its services to women throughout Kanpur, regardless of caste, creed, or social standing.

Those higher in the structure expect to wield power and/or feel they must maintain their positions by retaining control. Those lower in the structure my see themselves as the inevitable victims. Or worse, as we have seen above, they sometimes see themselves as responsible for their own fate. When some who are lower in the hierarchy begin to be restless and want to exert independence, those in power feel compelled to respond to maintain the status quo in power relationships. Sometimes they even feel that tradition expects them to maintain control—and if people lack tools to peacefully negotiate differences, they resort to violence. If someone is becoming "uppity," hit her/him. If a child disobeys, spank her/him. Violence requires very little imagination as a strategy of those in power to maintain their position.

SOCIETAL COSTS

The health consequences of domestic violence extend beyond the individual costs discussed above, to the realm of public health. A study on "The Economic

WOMEN'S COURAGE: PRAGUE, CZECH REPUBLIC. In 1993, two Czech social workers established ROSA—Center for Women Victims of Domestic Violence as the country's first information and counseling center for women survivors of domestic violence. ROSA is one of the few groups in the area that combats systematic violence against women and provides direct help to victims. ROSA operates an information and counseling center that offers low-cost legal aid and psychological support.

In 2002, the center provided thirteen legal consultations and 443 psychological counseling sessions. In 1998, the group opened its own shelter that has twelve beds and is managed by the clients themselves. The shelters are now open to women without children, migrant women, and elderly women. ROSA's work does not end with these women; it also conducts trainings with law enforcement staff, medical professionals, and social workers. ROSA staff have launched a website and circulated "I Survived," a brochure on legislative barriers encountered by women seeking help, to members of Parliament, police, and judges.

WOMEN'S COURAGE: SULAYMANIYAH, IRAQ. Asuda for Combating Violence Against Women was formed in 2000 to address the problem of violence against women in the region of Sulaymaniyah. Asuda works to directly assist and empower women. It has organized a shelter where women fleeing their abusers can seek refuge and psychological counseling. In addition, it provides family counseling and legal assistance to attempt to create safe environments for women.

Asuda also runs a radio program that encourages women to share their problems and to seek advice. In a 2001 photography exhibit, Asuda invited women survivors of violence to contribute their works; it was a venue that empowered women by showcasing their talents; at the same time, the event raised public awareness about the issue of violence against women in the community.

Dimensions of Interpersonal Violence," released by the World Health Organization (WHO) in July 2004, noted that in addition to devastating individual families, interpersonal violence also results in major economic costs to societies. "Some nations spend more than 4% of their Gross Domestic Product (GDP) on violence-related injuries, and low-income nations may be hardest hit. . . . Colombia and El Salvador [for example] spend 4.3% of their GDP on violence-related expenditures—the highest of any nation. The United States spends 3.3% of GDP on violence-related matters[31]. . . . 'Responding to violence diverts billions of dollars away from education, social security, housing and recreation, into the essential but seemingly never-ending tasks of providing care for victims and criminal justice interventions against per-petrators,' said the Assistant Director of WHO. . . . A major challenge in the years ahead will be to strengthen and support developing country research into the costs of interpersonal violence, and to feed the findings into policy making and advocacy where it can reinforce arguments for prevention."[32]

The cost to society of this morbidity is enormous, yet it is only the beginning of the cycle. Children who witness domestic violence experience behavioral and physical health problems, including depression, anxiety, and violence toward peers as they enter adolescence. Further, they are more likely to batter or to be battered as adults. They are also more likely to attempt suicide, abuse drugs and alcohol, run away from home, engage in teenage prostitution, and commit sexual assault crimes.[33]

More Family Violence: "Honor" Killing and Dowry Death

In regions where women in general have especially low economic and social status—South Asia and the Middle East, for example—violence against women takes other extreme forms. The murder of young women by family members, usually a father or brother, because of perceived flirting or adul-tery—known as "honor killing"—continues to the present day. According to the UN Commission on Human Rights, "Honor killing is one of his-tory's oldest gender-based crimes. It assumes that a woman's behavior casts a reflection on the family and the community. If women fall in love, seek a divorce even from a [violent] husband, or enter into a relationship outside marriage, they are seen as violating the honor of the community."[34] The prac-tice is mostly centered in the Middle East, but it has also been documented in Bangladesh, Brazil, Ecuador, Egypt, Uganda, and Turkey. In 1999, an estimated two-thirds of all murders in the Gaza Strip and West Bank were likely honor killings,[35] and more than one thousand women were reported killed in Pakistan alone.[36] Norma Khouri cannot return to her homeland of Jordan because she has publicized the murder of her best friend Dalia, stabbed by her father for walking in public with a man.[37] Although such

WOMEN'S COURAGE: NEW DELHI, INDIA. The Recovering and Healing From Incest Foundation (RAHI) was founded in 1996 by a survivor of childhood sexual assault. The organization raises awareness about issues of incest and sexual abuse against women and girls. RAHI, which was the first organization to conduct research on the prevalence of incest in India, shared its findings widely, raising the visibility of this serious issue in India. In addition to doing research, RAHI has created peer centers where education and training to prevent sexual abuse is provided. In a 2001 national workshop, RAHI collaborated with other women's groups in India to train counselors to help survivors heal emotionally by encouraging them to speak up and share their experiences in a safe environment. To improve the future of women's rights in India, RAHI favors stricter laws to protect women and girls against incest and sexual abuse. Taking the position that no woman deserves abuse, RAHI makes its services available to all Indian women regardless of their caste, religion, or sexuality.

WOMEN'S COURAGE: RANJPUR, PAKISTAN. In 1996, a group of women activists formed the Women's Rural Development Organization in reaction to honor killings and the trafficking of young girls, which have persisted in the populous region of Ranjpur. In this area, many Pakistani women are compelled to live under very difficult conditions and often meet with violence when they try to change their situations. Since its founding in 1996, the Organization has created girls' schools and has provided legal aid and health services. The group has also conducted two in-depth, district-wide research studies. In 2000 and 2001, the group interviewed local people about the issue of honor killing in Rajanpur and later presented its findings in seminars to police, government officials, media professionals, and NGO representatives. In 2003 and 2004, some 1,800 women attended the group's rights awareness seminars, and hundreds of people throughout the region hear its weekly radio programs.

murders often go unrecorded, the U.N. Population Fund estimates that as many as five thousand honor killings take place each year.[38]

In Western Europe, governments in Great Britain and Sweden have become increasingly concerned about honor killings among immigrants. Police are investigating murder cases involving Middle Eastern, Asian, Arabic, and Eastern European immigrants, suspecting that young girls have

WOMEN'S COURAGE: SANTIAGO, CHILE. In the past three decades, the women's movement has spread across Chile. In an attempt to strengthen and link the movement, women's groups formed the Red Chilena Contra la Violencia Domestica y Sexual (Chilean Network Against Domestic and Sexual Violence) in 1991. The Network created visibility, expanded public awareness, and provided community education on violence against women from a feminist perspective.

The Network has successfully lobbied for legislation against domestic violence. It has also spearheaded national women's movement campaigns, such as the International Day Against Violence Against Women and "Democracy in The Nation and in The Home." The Network has established permanent lobbying, information campaigns, and marches, and has played a very important role in enacting the law penalizing domestic violence in Chile. The group is very active in promoting the straightforward message that no one should have to endure violence.

been killed by their families for carrying on unsanctioned relationships. As of June 2004, authorities in England and Wales were investigating one hundred murders they suspected to be honor killings.[39]

Dowry death, which occurs in parts of South Asia, is another practice of murdering women in one's family. In India, an estimated six thousand women were killed in 1997, mostly by their in-laws, often through burning, in family disputes over dowries and wifely duties. Dowry death occurs when the bride does not bring a sufficient dowry to the marriage or the family and/or the groom does not approve of the bride.[40] More than a dozen women die each day in supposed "kitchen fires," often a cover-up for dowry killings. Acid attacks are much more common in Bangladesh, where, in 2002, 315 were reported. Many women's groups in India are working to eliminate the practice of dowry death. They are working to amend the 1961 Dowry Prohibition Act to include "dowry prohibition officers" and other reinforcements. Unfortunately, such laws have not been universally enforced and dowry deaths remain a reality.[41]

Both dowry deaths and honor killings have been characterized by the United Nations Development Fund for Women (UNIFEM) as "harmful traditional practices." These practices, along with female genital mutilation, "refer to the types of violence that have been committed against women for so long that they are considered to be part of accepted cultural practice."[42] It is very important to note, however, that this characterization does not take into account the fact that in most countries both perpetrators of and witnesses to these practices are conscious that they are crimes; hence the cover-ups. Though measures to counter these and other criminal activities may not be strong enough, particularly in poor countries, they are not necessarily "accepted cultural practice," even in remote rural areas.[43]

Countercurrents against the Tide of Domestic Violence

Refugees and immigrants to the United States can seek asylum from persecution that results from race, religion, nationality, political opinion, or membership in a particular social group—but not yet from persecution based on gender. Despite the negative effects on society that extend far beyond the realm of the family, gender-based violence is not yet fully recognized as a human rights violation.[44]

Women fleeing female genital mutilation or domestic violence must attempt to prove their cases in indirect ways. And although rape as a war crime, honor killings, and dowry deaths are beginning to be talked about as human rights violations, both in the laws of individual countries and at the international level, "ordinary rape and domestic violence" has not yet been so recognized. However, thanks to strong lobbying efforts on the part of women's groups, the issue of violence against women is coming out in the open. The United Nations did not officially recognize violence against women until 1993, when it was discussed and defined in the Declaration on the Elimination of Violence against Women as "any act of gender-based violence that results in, or is likely to result in, physical, sexual, or psychological harm or suffering to women, including threats of such acts, coercion or arbitrary deprivations of liberty, whether occurring in public or private life."[45]

That violence against women is being seen as a problem worthy of attention at the UN level is heartening. But this awareness is quite new. It is an important step that the issue of violence against women has been taken up by international organizations. Human rights advocates at local, regional, and national levels gain strength by aligning themselves with international standards of behavior, even though more often than not, many of the conventions and declarations of the UN are non-binding on member states.

WOMEN'S COURAGE: ULAANBAATAR, MONGOLIA. The National Center Against Violence is Mongolia's first organization to provide shelter for survivors of domestic violence. It was created by three women who joined forces in 1995. In addition to providing support to women survivors, the group works to prevent domestic violence in the region. In the Center's shelter, women can receive psychological and legal counseling and participate in support groups. The shelter also operates a hotline for victims of domestic violence to call in and seek help. Among the Center's programs is one that promotes counseling for men to change their behavior and attitudes toward women. On a broader scale, the Center lobbies for national laws that promote gender equality and equal spousal rights.

WOMEN'S COURAGE: SAN RAMON, ALAJUELA, COSTA RICA. Mujeres Unidas en Salud y Desarrollo (Women United in Health and Development) focuses on increasing awareness of and preventing domestic violence in Costa Rica. Since its establishment in 1986, the group has operated on the basis of income generated from the community services it has offered, including training for women and daycare for their children. From teaching management skills to women with entrepreneurial aspirations, to offering school programs to prevent interfamilial violence, to providing legal assistance and moral support for violence victims, Mujeres Unidas offers its services to Costa Rican women from all walks of life. Because of women's hesitance to testify in court against their own family members, many acts of violence go uninvestigated or unpunished. This group works not only to support such women but to create a culture where women are confident to make their voices heard.

Still, women are feeling more empowered, and men are wanting to feel more fully human. Hundreds of groups have formed to prevent domestic and other forms of violence against women. Studies are being done to document the violence, and there is a movement against domestic violence that is growing around the world, even as such violence persists at shocking and depressing levels.[46]

With regard to domestic violence and rape, hundreds of women's and human rights groups have developed around the world to prevent these practices and

WOMEN'S COURAGE: DILI, EAST TIMOR. The Communication Forum for East Timorese Women was established to address issues of women's rights, and in particular, issues of sexual and domestic violence. Established in 1997, the group focuses on providing support for women to attempt to increase the standards of living for women in East Timor. Given civil conflict, the condition of women has steadily declined in recent years. Women are often violated and lack necessities such as food, adequate healthcare, and even water. Over the years, the Forum has built a shelter and offered counseling for survivors of violence. More recently, firmly believing that the creation of a vocal women's group to advocate for change is essential, the Forum has lobbied for legislation to provide for women's basic necessities, and trained women community leaders to actively participate in the women's movement in East Timor.

WOMEN'S COURAGE: ULAANBAATAR, CHINGELTEI DISTRICT, MONGOLIA. The Mongolian Gender Equality Center is the only non-governmental organization that focuses on the prevention of sexual violence in Mongolia. The Center was created in 2001 to provide different social sectors with information and direct training to reduce the prevalence sexual violence. The Center works with and serves the needs of a wide range of people, primarily woman and girl survivors of domestic and sexual violence.

In addition, representatives of the Center travel to correctional facilities to provide sensitivity training to prison guards and support services to inmates who are faced with sexual violence. To promote public awareness of the problems of sexual violence, the Center publishes handbooks for professionals on issues of healthcare, social work, and law enforcement. On a national level, the Center lobbies for stricter policies against sexual violence, harassment, and discrimination against Mongolian women.

establish ways of supporting women in culturally appropriate ways. In South India, for example, women's groups have developed a process of "shaming" a man who has abused his wife, either by surrounding him in a marketplace or by surrounding the house until the wife indicates that she is safe. Such community-based approaches to dealing with violence are more appropriate in some countries than an approach that encourages the wife to leave (to go where?) and/or seek formal legal help (from whom? with what resources?).

WOMEN'S COURAGE: MAZAR-I-SHARIF, BALKH, AFGHANISTAN. The Association for Defense of Women's Rights of Balkh works to foster safe and inclusive environments for women in their homes. Not only does the group provide direct assistance to women victims of domestic violence, such as legal advice, but it also empowers women through education and other types of vocational training to decrease their financial dependence on men. Through a program for men, the Association provides awareness seminars for males, works to decrease future occurrences of gender-based violence, and advocates for gender sensitivity within Afghanistan's Islamic society.

WOMEN'S COURAGE: PRAGUE, CZECH REPUBLIC. The end of Communist rule in the Czech Republic brought many changes; in particular, women were creating new non-governmental organizations, to a great extent in response to the effects of poverty and violence against women. In 1999, AdvoCats for Women, a program of ProFem, was created because increasing numbers of women were seeking help for domestic abuse and rape. AdvoCats for Women trains women lawyers to advise and help women experiencing violence by intimate partners or acquaintances. The group offers a legal aid telephone helpline and conducts trainings with social workers to better identify and address domestic violence. The program also manages a legal aid fund for women survivors of violence to defray some of their court costs.

Perhaps the most extraordinary aspect of this worldwide problem today is the courage of the endangered women who are speaking out and challenging traditions and legal systems. Violence against women has become a central issue for women's organizations around the world in the last decade, as women respond to the brutality they face in daily life simply because of their sex. Until fifteen or twenty years ago, the issue of domestic violence was largely invisible even in the United States. Now, because medical and legal officials and others are increasingly recognizing the extent of the problem, agencies that offer services to women who have suffered domestic violence exist in virtually all U.S. communities and in many other countries.

Although family violence against women is often taken as a given or ranked low on the list of priorities that poorer nations must address, in

WOMEN'S COURAGE: BAMENDA, CAMEROON. Women in Action against Gender-Based Violence was founded in 2005 to promote a "culture of peace, social justice, and legal empowerment for women and girls." The group participates in radio programs on women's issues and provides outreach to women's groups. It also raises scholarship money to send poor girls to school. Its main emphases are on educational equity, domestic violence, HIV/AIDS prevention, and public sanitation. The group started as a social group, known as "amicable ladies," where women could meet and share some of their problems. They expanded their activities after learning that 90% of women in their communities faced domestic violence. As a result, the group developed sensitization campaigns in villages and began to meet with government officials and traditional leaders to educate them about the importance of developing laws to protect women. Recently the group initiated a research project designed to learn more about discriminatory behaviors and attitudes in five villages.

WOMEN'S COURAGE: ACCRA, GHANA. Women in Law and Development in Africa (WILDAF) is a pan-African network of six hundred organizations and activists that implement strategies which link law and development with the aim of expanding women's rights. Through a legal awareness program, WILDAF educates communities on human rights, particularly women's legal rights. Through legal literacy and youth peer volunteers, thousands of women have benefited from pro-bono legal services and mediation. WILDAF also has done research on women's property rights; carried out training programs for judges, doctors, traditional leaders, and others on laws relating to women; and played a central role in advocacy campaigns to pass the Domestic Violence bill and petition for action by municipal authorities to end domestic violence.

WOMEN'S COURAGE: RIO DE JANEIRO, BRAZIL. CEPIA, a research and policy group, is dedicated to implementing projects that promote human rights, especially among groups historically excluded from exercising their full rights. For this purpose, since 1990, CEPIA has conducted studies, as well as educational and social intervention projects, that are shared widely with civil society organizations and government agencies. Working from a gender perspective and within a human rights framework, CEPIA focuses on issues of violence and access to justice, health, sexual and reproductive rights, and poverty. Advocacy is also an important part of CEPIA's agenda. The group published a definitive study on "violence against women in the international context" in June 2007.

country after country, non-governmental groups, particularly groups led by women, are emerging to address violence and other health and human rights issues affecting women. Some of them are highlighted throughout this chapter. These groups subscribe to the statement in the Universal Declaration of Human Rights that: "All human beings are born free and equal in dignity and rights. . . . Everyone has the right to life, liberty, and security of person. . . . No one shall be subjected to torture or to cruel, inhuman, or degrading treatment or punishment."[47]

I tell you simply: we just would like to survive. We don't want to perish in this senseless mess. We hope somehow to raise our children and to find jobs and a place somewhere in this world. . . . Where are we going to find a place where they will take us in? A place that we can once again really feel and call home?

> —Ilona, a refugee woman from Voivodina, Serbia. August 1993[1]

Warfare is just an invention known to the majority of human societies by which they permit their young men either to accumulate prestige or avenge their honor or acquire loot or wives or slaves or grab lands or cattle or appease the blood lust, their gods, or the restless souls of the recently dead. It is just an invention, older and more widespread than the jury system, but nonetheless an invention of men. It has been women's task throughout history to go on believing in life when there was almost no hope. If we are united, we may be able to produce a world in which our children and other people's children can be safe.

> —Margaret Mead, "Warfare is Only an Invention," 1940[2]

7

Women Caught in Conflict and Refugee Situations

A Rwandan widow, Mukandoli, describes her ambivalence and agony about keeping the baby of her rapist thus: "After the genocide, I went for an HIV test and found that I was negative but I had conceived due to the killers. The child was born, but most of the time I am not happy about him, especially because he reminds me of the bad images of the people who raped me. I lost seven children [in the war] and I am now bringing up a child of bad luck; he can't substitute [for] the seven children that I lost. It is very hard for me because all the time I hear my [other] children's voices asking for food. The pain never goes away, and it feels like yesterday. I cannot love this child. Knowing that he is the only one I have, I can't say that I am living. It's hell on earth and the genocide continues to live with me."[3]

War affects women intensely and disastrously. In addition to the complications of caring for a family during wartime, women may face displacement from home, separation from loved ones, and extreme abuse, including rape, torture, and death. The gender bias that fuels violence against women during periods of peace boils over and intensifies in conflict situations as military officials ignore or sanction gross violations of human rights. Though war is perceived as a male activity, and indeed those involved in militaristic actions are overwhelmingly men,[4] it is largely civilian women and children who bear the costs in the many civil wars that characterize our time.

The Nature of Present-Day War

The majority of the conflicts occurring now around the world are civil wars fought within the borders of countries, often among and supported by multiple actors and fueled by religious, ethnic and tribal, economic, and political differences. These conflicts precipitate humanitarian crises, like those in regions around Afghanistan, Liberia, and Sudan, where thousands of people have been displaced, affecting the social and economic situations of neighboring, often resource-poor, countries. These conflicts are sometimes known as "complex emergencies" for their seemingly intractable character, long durations, and disastrous consequences.

Since 1991, such conflicts have become more numerous and more deadly, and the nature of warfare has changed. Nowadays war often involves the deliberate targeting of civilians, noncombatants, and their livelihoods. The "goal of modern civil wars usually is not so much to eliminate the opponents as to destroy their culture and the very fabric of society," according to a 2002 Save the Children report called *The State of the World's Mothers*.[5] For example, in Darfur, Sudan, thousands of civilians, many of them women and children—those who weren't killed—have been forced from their homes, often raped, and left to wander or to try to find help in neighboring countries. Similarly, in Afghanistan in 1999, the Taliban employed a "scorched-earth" policy in the Shomali plains south of Kabul, whereby they burned homes, killed livestock, uprooted orchards and vineyards, poisoned wells, destroyed irrigation systems, and forbade the people to return. Human Rights Watch quotes the Secretary-General of the United Nations, Kofi Annan, making the point that Taliban forces essentially "made no distinction between combatants and non-combatants."[6]

This deliberate targeting of civilians, as well as the "collateral damage" caused by modern weapons of destruction, means that civilians are now dying at higher rates than in any other period in the last hundred years. Casualties as a result of conflict have risen from 5% at the turn of the last century, to 65% during World War II, to 90% in some recent conflicts.[7] A fact sheet on how women have fared during armed conflict, prepared for the UN in 2002, reported that approximately forty million people worldwide had fled their homes because of armed conflict and human rights violations.[8] Currently, there are an estimated twenty million refugees and other persons of concern to the United Nations High Commission for Refugees (UNHCR) around the world.[9]

Clearly, "the war to end all wars," as World War I was known, didn't turn out that way. Today there are approximately thirty "major" conflicts (those with more than a thousand casualties, both military and civilian) happening in nineteen countries, including: Afghanistan, Algeria, Burundi, Colombia, the Democratic Republic of Congo, India, Indonesia, Iraq, Israel, Pakistan, the People's Republic of China, Peru, the Philippines, Liberia, Nigeria, Russia, Somalia, Sudan, and Uganda.[10] The list of recent post-conflict countries is also extensive, including: Bosnia and Herzegovina, the Central African Republic, Cyprus, East Timor, Eritrea, Ethiopia, Georgia, Guatemala, Guinea Bissau, Haiti, the Ivory Coast, Kosovo, Nepal, Nigeria, Rwanda, Sierra Leone, Somalia, Sri Lanka, Tajikistan, and Western Sahara.[11] Permanent peace, worldwide, seems more unlikely than ever.

Women and children comprise the majority of civilians killed and injured in wars, and they make up 80% of those who have fled their homes because of conflict and human rights violations. Likewise, women and children make up 80% of the caseload of the UNHCR.[12] As Vesna Nikolic-Ristanovic writes in *Women, Violence, and War*, "Women are non-combatant victims in all forms of warfare—international and internal, religious, ethnic or nationalistic, and from both enemy and 'friendly fire.' Women suffer numerous and diverse violent acts—the majority of which remain invisible."[13]

Only recently has it been publicly recognized that war and conflict affects women differently. The first UN Security Council resolution ever to specifically recognize the issue (Resolution 1325) was adopted in October 2000. It advocated increased participation by women in peace-keeping and conflict management activities, and recognized the special vulnerability of women in times of conflict.[14] Two years later, the first UN study on The Impact of Violent Conflict on Women and Girls was issued. Also in 2002, Secretary General Annan issued a report to the Security Council in which he acknowledged that "Women and children are disproportionately targeted in contemporary armed conflict and constitute the majority of all victims," and that "During conflict, women and girls are vulnerable to all forms of violence, in particular sexual violence and exploitation, including torture,

WOMEN'S COURAGE: PORT-AU-PRINCE, HAITI. As Haiti rebuilds after extreme political turbulence, organizations such as the Collectif Féminin Haïtien Contre l'Exclusion de la Femme (Haitian Women's Collective Against the Exclusion of Women) have come to recognize the need for women to actively participate in national policymaking. The Collective set a goal of educating women about national and international issues and encouraging female participation in policymaking. The Collective is made up of women from all walks of Haitian society. Participants from more than fifty professions come together to develop their debating skills, such as note-taking and argument construction. To make the women's skills directly related to political participation, the Collective hosts discussion events where participants learn about issues in the national government, as well as contemporary international events.

WOMEN'S COURAGE: KABUL, AFGHANISTAN. The Afghan Women Council works within the cultural context of Afghanistan to bring political, social, and economic security to women in the country. The group provides direct aid to women in this post-war society, and also promotes women's political participation while working respectfully with the religious principles of Islam. Since its establishment in 1986, the group has served the women and children of Afghanistan in a variety of ways. It provides them with psychological and grief counseling as they recover from war. Widows and children also benefit from health care, food, and education programs funded by this group. To encourage gender equality, women learn vocational, business management, and leadership skills. It is estimated that more than ten thousand women and children have participated in the Council's work.

rape, mass rape, forced pregnancy, sexual slavery, enforced prostitution, and trafficking. They face numerous health threats grounded in biological differences, and the high rate of infection and death increases women's workload in maintaining their households and community and providing care to orphaned children."[15]

Women's health, already under siege during times of peace, is profoundly affected in times of war: rape, forced marriages, domestic violence, widowhood, and sudden responsibility for heading households without the necessary resources intensify the already catastrophic effects of conflict.

The Devastating Effects of War on Women

The disparate effects of war on women arise from the social and cultural context preceding the onset of conflict. Another UN report from 2002 underscores their essential disadvantage: "The economic, social, political, legal and cultural structures that perpetuate gender inequality are still in place throughout the world, and in no nation do women have complete equality within these structures to participate as fully as men."[16] These hierarchical structures resulting in discrimination against women and their second-class status in society during peacetime limit women's ability to cope with the consequences of war, especially in countries with a fundamentalist interpretation of religion which is repressive of women's rights. For example, in 1996 the Taliban rulers of Afghanistan both forbade women and girls to be examined by male physicians and prohibited female doctors and nurses from practicing. This decree was later modified to state that women could be examined only if a male relative was nearby. The Taliban also closed to women all but one of Kabul's 22 hospitals.[17] The effects of the Taliban's gender apartheid have compounded those of extensive bombing by American and other forces; at present Afghanistan has the highest maternal mortality rate in the world, 1,600 deaths per 100,000 live births, according to UNICEF and the Centers for Disease Control.[18]

Women face additional vulnerabilities when they are associated with nationalist and cultural ideologies that define their bodies as a battleground. One of the most important constructs of many ethnic groups and nations, writes Nina Yurval-Davis, is the "imagined community," in which "people feel that their membership is 'natural,' not chosen"; in other words, one can only be born into the group,[19] born, that is, through its women, who become symbolically identified as the "reproducers" of its people. Hence, the mother who symbolizes the collectivity—Mother Russia, Mother Ireland, Mother India, La Patrie in the French Revolution.[20] In conflict, men violate and brutalize women's bodies in order to control, subjugate, and destroy the opposing community. Therefore, it is perhaps not surprising that sex-specific violence is prevalent in war, especially the use of systematic rape and forced impregnation or sterilization to advance political and nationalistic goals.

Underlying rape and other types of assault aimed at women during conflict are peacetime inequalities of power between men and women, including the objectification of women and male control over women's bodies, whereby they are considered the "property" of fathers or husbands. Vesna Nicolic-Ristanovic explains: "Patriarchy means that women are regarded as men's property, a pure addition to the territory and other things that men possess. Rape is to male-female relations what conquering troops are to occupied territories, and imperial authority is to colonialism."[21]

Ultimately, clearly women experience war differently than do men. The inequities that women around the world face during peacetime and the health risks of their reproductive function are compounded by the enacting of nationalist, social, and cultural notions of gender and state. These conditions render them especially vulnerable to stress, trauma, and disease at every state of war—during conflict, flight, displacement, and the aftermath.

The Breakout of Conflict

During the initial breakout of fighting, general health risks such as disease and malnutrition become more prevalent when agriculture and farming are disrupted. Physical territory becomes highly contested and inaccessible because of the presence of landmines and combatants; the quantity, quality, and availability of food become limited; health care providers flee; and facilities are closed or destroyed.

Unfortunately, disease, malnutrition, and a breakdown in health services affect women more severely than men. According to a 2001 report by the International Committee for the Red Cross, "The reproductive role of women increases their vulnerability to food shortages or inadequacies. Women of childbearing age may need more vitamins and minerals, e.g., iron, proteins and iodine. Similarly, pregnant and lactating mothers have specific nutritional requirements in order to bear and raise healthy children while maintaining their own health."[22] And, as Elizabeth Rehn and Ellen Sirleaf remind us in the 2002 UNIFEM *Report on Women, War, and Peace*, "The exposure of trauma and violence itself may have an effect on pregnancy."[23] The UNIFEM Report notes that research findings in Southern Sudan corroborate those from an earlier study in Santiago, Chile, on the relationship between complications of pregnancy and the sociopolitical violence of 1985-86. The Chilean study found that "women who lived in neighbourhoods with high levels of violence, including bomb threats, military presence and demonstrations, were five times more likely than women in other neighborhoods

WOMEN'S COURAGE: ERBIL, IRAQ. The Women Empowerment Organization was formed in 2004 in Erbil, Iraq, to promote women's rights by encouraging more female political participation. With training sessions and workshops, the group mobilizes women to take active roles in the reconstruction of Iraq. The situation of women living under occupation in Iraq is extremely difficult. Women face increasing physical threats, and many women are afraid to leave their homes. In addition, violent traditional practices, such as honor killings, persist in Iraq. The Women Empowerment Organization believes that increasing women's roles in politics will help to solve some of these problems. Since its establishment in 2004, the organization has hosted many events to raise awareness of the importance of women's participation, including trainings to instruct more than four hundred women on how to become involved in the drafting of the new Iraqi constitution.

to experience pregnancy complications such as preterm contractions, rupture and haemorrhage."[24]

Furthermore, women's reproductive role places them in the position of being targets for special kinds of violence in conflict. "Forced impregnation, forced maternity, and forced termination of pregnancy are specific violations that uniquely affect women and girls. Women may also be forcibly sterilized."[25] Sexual violence during conflict also increases exposure to HIV/AIDS and other sexually transmitted infections. "Sexually transmitted infections can have grave consequences for women, including infertility, pelvic inflammatory disease, abortion, puerperal (post childbirth) infection, ectopic pregnancy, and cervical cancer."[26]

WOMEN'S BODIES AS SYMBOLS

In many parts of the world, men carry out religious and ethnic struggles through violence to the bodies of women. To cite some recent cases: the Burmese military's ongoing raping of women from ethnic minorities as a weapon of war; the Hindu fundamentalists raping Muslim Indian women as a form of attack against the Muslim population; and the raping, forced pregnancy, and forced infection of Tutsi women in 2000, as part of the state-sponsored genocide against Tutsi minorities.[27] According to the *New*

York Times, in 1996, "by conservative estimates there [were] 2,000 to 5,000 unwanted children in Rwanda whose mothers were raped during the civil war and mass killings. These children . . . are known in Rwanda as "enfants de mauvais souvenir," children of bad memories. . . . Women were raped by individuals, gang-raped, raped with sharpened stakes and gun barrels, and held in sexual slavery."[28]

The centrality of women's reproductive role in nationalist conflicts and how it can disastrously affect women's lives was also present in the Bosnian conflict. Militarized rape, "particularly the version that uses forced pregnancy as a kind of biological warfare,"[29] was used widely by the Yugoslav Army, the Bosnian Serb forces, and the irregular Serb militia as part of the Serbian genocidal policy of "ethnic cleansing" and "cultural cleansing" during the conflict. An estimated twenty to fifty thousand Bosnian women were raped.[30]

Three major goals of rape as warfare have been identified by analysts:

- to terrorize women and their families out of a contested territory, rendering it "ethnically clean"

- to humiliate men and induce a breakdown in the social fabric

- to effect pregnancy in order to "purge" the "inferior" race and propagate a "new" race[31]

"You are going to have our children. You are going to have our little Chetniks," a twenty-six-year-old woman recalls Serb soldiers yelling at the Muslim women in a Gracko rape camp.[32]

The Darfur region of Western Sudan is another site of such atrocities on a mass scale. In 2004, Marc Lacey, a reporter for the *New York Times,* wrote: "Amnesty International accused pro-government militias in the Darfur region of Sudan of using rape and other forms of sexual violence 'as a weapon of war,' to humiliate black African women and girls as well as the rebels fighting the government in Khartoum." Calling for the creation of a commission to investigate and bring to justice those responsible for sexual violence against the women of Darfur and noting that rape is a particular cultural taboo in Sudan, Amnesty stated that: "The suffering and abuse endured by these women goes far beyond the actual rape. . . . Rape has a devastating and ongoing impact on the health of women and girls, and survivors now face a lifetime of stigma and marginalization from their own families and communities." One woman from Silaya, near the town of Kulbus in western Sudan, was five months pregnant when abducted with eight other women in 2003. "'Five to six men would rape us in rounds, one after the other, for hours, during six days, every night,' the woman . . . told Amnesty researchers. 'My husband could not forgive me after this; he disowned me.'"[33]

The outbreak of hostilities can also have an impact on the frequency and severity of domestic violence that women experience, as weapons end up in the hands of men who may be "frustrated, nervous, intolerant, and usually very aggressive"[34]—and as violence becomes not only an acceptable way of resolving conflict, but the norm. In the former Yugoslavia, the Belgrade SOS Hotline (a women's group) reported that the number of violent acts committed by sons increased from 6.4% in 1991 at the beginning of the war to 11.4% in 1993. Also, the use of weapons in domestic violence increased over the duration of the war; some 40% of women who called said their "partners were threatening them with pistols, grenades, and similar weapons." A similar situation was documented in Croatia, where the majority of offenders were husbands and intimate partners or former partners.[35]

Flight and Forced Migration

The flight and forced migration of refugees take place under a wide range of conditions, from women fleeing with their families to women being kidnapped by rebel forces. And the journeys themselves have a remarkable variety of dangers, from robbers preying upon the travelers to landmines blowing them up.

Particularly in wartime, women who flee from home, community, and sometimes country are beset by forces beyond their control. "We headed for the unknown, overwhelmed by fear," recalls a woman from Sarajevo, Bosnia, of her flight. "We passed through the part of the city where all the houses were burned, destroyed, and deserted. I left behind all the comfort I had, which I experienced as major violence."[36] Often, women are not even consulted about the decision to leave. An Afghani woman remembers that "My husband came in and said, 'We're leaving. Women, prepare our things. We are taking as little as possible. All the rest will be left behind . . . ' Deaf to our protests, he had made up his mind."[37] In other cases, the uprooting may be precipitated by extreme gendered violence: forced eviction through

WOMEN'S COURAGE: IXCÁN, QUICHE, GUATEMALA. Puente de Paz (Bridge of Peace) was established in 1998 by a group of feminist activists to counter the violence against indigenous women of Guatemala. In addition to the problem of domestic violence, Mayan women in Guatemala also face genocide directed toward minority indigenous populations. Puente works to empower woman survivors of violence and help them rebuild their lives. The group provides various kinds of support to women survivors: economic guidance for those who seek reparations from the government for genocidal acts against women and their families; general information about indigenous culture and issues of health, reproduction, and politics; and emotional support from trained mental health counselors.

rape, sexual assault, and deliberate targeting of women of a particular eth-nicity in order to intimidate others of that group into leaving. In these cir-cumstances, eviction may be compounded by "physical injuries, death of family members, relatives and friends, homelessness/landlessness, extreme poverty, lack of resources, the destruction of family life and community, the eradication of social support mechanisms, living in a new country, and the fear of continued physical violence."[38]

Forced migration affects everyone, but for most of the world's women, the home is the most important place in the world, providing shelter, a space to nurture children, possible respite from violence in the streets, and, for some women, their only locus of social activities. Thus, women may be dis-proportionately affected psychologically and physically by being forced out of their homes and having those dwellings destroyed. During the tumult of flight and displacement, women may become separated from family, friends, and other social support. Separation from male family members may render women even more vulnerable to threats against their physical security, such as abduction, rape, assault, harassment, and extortion from people they meet on their way to refuge, including army and militia units, peacekeepers (UN-mandated or otherwise), humanitarian aid providers, pirates, highwaymen, border guards, and male refugees.

A Vietnamese friend who at age six fled with her family, heading for Malaysia, told me the following story: "In the middle of the sea, pirates suddenly appeared and took over our boat. They killed my uncle and my father, they raped my mother, and they took our money. My traumatized mother was unable to function for many years. We children had to find our way into the future by ourselves. The pirates gave us water. Without it, we would have died."[39]

For women who have young children or are pregnant, forced migration is especially perilous because they may be hampered by the additional burden of caring for others during the journey, or may even be left unattended while giving birth.

SEX FOR SURVIVAL

Moreover, on the road, women may be forced to trade sex for food, sustenance, or protection. A woman from Monrovia, Liberia, recalls that during the civil war that began in 1989 when the National Patriotic Front of Liberia (NPFL) invaded, "Our bodies were exchanged for food. The rebels were in charge of all the food in the country at that time. Some women that had pride, high esteem, they would rather die from hunger. But if you wanted to live, you had to have some connection with a rebel."[40]

Women may also be kidnapped and pressed to serve militia groups, trafficked into prostitution rings, or sexually enslaved to particular combatants. Human Rights Watch noted in 2001 that, in Sierra Leone, "during the course of the attack, the victims were most often abducted and forced to become sexual partners or 'wives' to their rebel captors. Once captured, victims often described trying to attach themselves to one rebel so as to avoid gang rape, be given a degree of protection, and be subjected to less hardship." [41] A Liberian woman recalled, "I was abducted around 2 p.m. from my compound and taken to the rebel camp where I was left to stay in a hut [with] a man. At night he asked me for sex but I refused. We continued like this for a week; then I had to give in—there was no way I could escape. So we started living as husband and wife. At one time I told him that I wanted to go back home, but he threatened to kill me if I did such a thing. He was killed, just about the time when I left [the rebels]. When girls of about fourteen were abducted, the [rebel] leaders would want to take such a girl for a partner even if he were aged. Should [she] refuse, she would be beaten in front of everybody until [she] agreed."[42]

LANDMINES AND DISABILITY

If women and their families are able to avoid abduction, assault, or death, the road toward some safe place is still full of other dangers, notably landmines. According to a 2003 report in the Human Rights Watch *Landmine Monitor*, an estimated 110 million anti-personnel mines were laid in about sixty-eight countries around the world. In the preceding year and a half, in sixty-five of those countries, more than 11,700 landmine casualties occurred, in which 15% of the injured were military personnel. The majority were civilians fetching food or water, or engaged in agricultural farming, activities more often than not undertaken by women.[43]

The UN Fund for Women (UNIFEM) reported in 2002 that "Women and men in some eighty countries live daily with the threat of landmines; women are particularly affected as they comprise the majority of the world's farmers and gatherers of food, water and firewood. Landmines block access to farmland, food, water and shelter, and act as a major obstacle to the transport and distribution of basic relief supplies, the repair of essential infrastructure, and the rehabilitation of homes, schools and clinics. An essential component of de-mining operations should be to ensure that those conducting the operations consult with women, as they often identify priority areas for clearance, such as transportation routes to fields or markets, that may be different than those identified by military or political authorities. A second implication is that landmine awareness training, campaigns or classes are more successful when women are involved because women multiply vital information throughout their families and communities, particularly about signs of danger and preventing injury."[44]

Unfortunately, when displaced women are injured or disabled by landmines "because of cultural restrictions," they may be "less likely [than men] to receive medical care or to be interviewed and recorded by the surveillance system."[45] In addition, the high cost of prosthetics can mean that injured or disabled women do not receive equipment that might allow them some semblance of normalcy. Women also suffer more from the repercussions of such injury and disability than men. As the 2002 UNIFEM report explains, "Women who have been injured by mines are not only a burden on their families and communities but are often no longer perceived as being productive members of society. Amputated women are often perceived as less desirable as wives because they are no longer able to work in the fields, which is their traditional role in many countries."[46] The International Labor Organization (ILO) noted in 1998. "Evidence from Cambodia illustrates the gender dimension of disability as disabled men relied on their wives for support, while disabled women were abandoned by their partners or had difficulty in finding one."[47]

Women who are injured may find that they cannot marry and become mothers, which is one of the highest status roles for them in many societies. They are also hard pressed to support themselves, generate income, and pay for specialized health care. "Men who are wounded . . . are still able to marry, and when they get ill their wives and children can help. [On the other hand] I am still single and live with my mother," said Thom, a Vietnamese woman who is now barren because of a lethal fragmentation bomb dropped by a U.S. fighter jet during the Vietnam War, its shrapnel embedded in her womb.[48]

Unequal Access to Safe Haven

Despite their dire circumstances, fleeing and displaced women and girls often go unnoticed by the international community. The "Lost Boys of Sudan"—children from the Kakuma Refugee Camp in Kenya who fled the Sudanese conflict to Ethiopia in 1987 and were targeted and pursued again in 1991—have been designated since 2000 by UNHCR as a "priority caseload" for refugee resettlement in the United States. The UN Integrated Regional Information Network reported in 2002 that 3,276 Sudanese boys had been resettled in the United States, but only eighty-nine of their girl counterparts [had been], despite the similar, often more dangerous, circumstances of the girls.[49]

As with the Sudanese boys who resettled in the United States, flight during conflict for some women may include entry to other countries that are ranked higher on the UN Human Development Index and that offer a higher quality of life than the immigrant's country of origin. Offers of resettlement to Australia, Canada, the United Kingdom, and the United States are often coveted. Unfortunately, asylum laws generally discriminate against women in terms of migration to a country of choice. For example, in Britain, asylum laws do not take into consideration particular dangers to women, such as sexual violence in wartime and rape in war. Rather, the definition of "persecution" to determine asylum status has generally been based on the person's overt political activity.[50]

Women may migrate to countries closer to their own, but wherever women move to, they will often suffer forms of psychological health problems associated with the shock of living in a new environment, which may involve problems with ethnic, linguistic, social, and cultural differences. Often, there is xenophobia in the new country. A Bosnian immigrant said of her experience after migrating to Serbia, "People told me, 'You don't have any rights here, your rights are there, in Alija Izetbegovic's Bosnia.' Everything happening there becomes quickly reflected here, and me, being in a minority, I have to shut up. Thus, it happened to me several times that I was so tense that I vomited or was dehydrated. I grew terribly anxious, I began shivering. I just felt terribly unsafe and I just want to get out of here." And yet, she points out, "I really had nothing to do with the war. I did not want it, and I did not help initiate it." [51]

Life in a Refugee Camp

Although a place of refuge, either within or beyond the war torn country, offers the only hope for people fleeing the violence, when they arrive there is no guarantee that life in the camp will be a healthy one. The often crowded conditions, compounded by a lack of access to safe drinking water, poor sanitation, inadequate or nonexistent medical facilities, and the degraded health of the refugees can make the camp an unhealthy place to live. Conditions that normally would be relatively easy to treat—acute respiratory infection, diarrhea, malaria, measles, and malnutrition—are the five major causes of death among refugee communities.[52] A July 2003 report by the Women's Human Rights Net describes some of the obstacles to improvement: "While UN and international relief and humanitarian organizations continue their efforts to respond to the survival needs of most refugees and some IDPs [internally displaced persons], the continuous increase in refugee and IDP populations inevitably results in diminishing funds, goods, and services. Humanitarian efforts are also continually held back by massive looting of refugee supplies, insecurity, and violence within and around refugee camps."[53]

It is hard for IDPs to help themselves since, for the most part, they have no access to schools or sources of livelihood. The report goes on to catalogue additional gender-specific "hardships and vulnerabilities" that women face in such situations. "[W]omen carry the burden of searching for food and other means for their family or children's survival. Pregnant women and mothers and their children suffer or die due to insufficient health supplies and services.

WOMEN'S COURAGE: ACCRA, GHANA. The civil war in Liberia drove many to leave their homes and seek refuge in places such as Buduburam Refugee Camp in neighboring Ghana. In addition to the hardship of exile, women in the refugee camp faced sexual and domestic abuse. To improve the quality of female refugees' lives, women of the camp created the New Liberian Women Organization/Skills Training Center in 2003. The Organization aims to defend and promote women's rights and prevent the occurrence of domestic violence. To achieve its goals, this group provides women with professional training in the hope of liberating them from financial dependence on men. Through the training center, women learn skills in typing, carpentry, embroidery, beauty care, and masonry. Additionally, the Organization supports programs aimed at raising awareness and sensitivity to women's right to live free of violence.

Women suffer gender-specific forms of violence such as abduction, rape and enforced pregnancy, slavery, sexual trafficking, enforced sterilization, and infection with sexually transmitted diseases and AIDS . . . within refugee camps. . . . They are the 'invisible' refugees who are left out of processes to design or plan programs that affect them. They are less likely to receive a fair share of food, water and shelter allocations. In the 1980s the UNHCR admitted that assistance was generally distributed to 'able-bodied male heads of households.'" Further, "Women in camps are highly vulnerable to sexual abuse and attacks by other refugees and humanitarian workers. The UN agencies and international community have been alarmed several times by reports about the sexual abuse of refugee women and children by humanitarian workers in exchange for food and other basic needs. Some humanitarian workers have also been accused of pimping or acting as middlemen in the prostitution and sexual trafficking of refugee women."[54]

REPRODUCTIVE HEALTH ISSUES

Around the world, about one quarter of refugee women are of reproductive age (fifiteen to forty-five).[55] While the reproductive health struggles that women in camps confront are similar to those in other settings, the deprivation and dangers of camp life exacerbate the problems of pregnancy. Some 19% of pregnancy-related deaths in developing countries involve indirect causes, such as anemia and malaria, which are related, respectively, to inadequate nutrition and unclean water supplies.[56] Also, unhygienic conditions and sexually transmitted diseases can lead to sepsis, a severe illness caused by extreme infection of the bloodstream, which accounts for 15% of maternal deaths.[57] Further complicating the maternal health problems of refugees is the fact that many births are not attended by anyone, even traditional birth assistants. Various NGOs and UN agencies are now attempting to provide basic "birthing kits" to women in camps. Using the kit can save lives. But in a world of camps where tens of millions live for long periods, even decades, the provision of a kit costing about U.S. $1, consisting of a plastic sheet, a sterile razor blade to cut the baby's umbilical cord, and a string to tie the cord—life- saving as it surely can be—can hardly be seen as an adequate response.

All refugee women need access to information and contraceptive services because of the risk of rape and unprotected sexual activity. Interviews with Afghani female refugees in Peshawar, Pakistan, revealed that the birth control service, if any, given by the local NGO, Union Aid for Afghan Refugees, consisted of a few pills, not the standard thirty-day supply. Unfortunately, most refugee women have little knowledge of the correct use of birth control and so may buy only what they can afford or what is available, which obviously lowers the pills' effectiveness. Furthermore, without medical consultation, refugee women may purchase tablets and injections of dubious quality from black markets or bazaars.[58]

In other refugee settings, abortion, despite its illegality in many countries around the world, becomes emergency birth control when there is no other option. Refugee women are forced to choose between carrying a risky pregnancy to term under impoverished, unhygienic conditions, and accepting the health consequences of a medically unassisted, often self-induced, abortion. The World Health Organization estimates that complications arising from unsafe "back-alley" abortions account for an estimated 25% to 50% of maternal deaths among refugees.[59]

OTHER HEALTH ISSUES

The previous section outlined special challenges women in conflict and refugee situations have relating to reproductive health. But there are other manifestations of discrimination that women face in the camps. They get less—less medical care, less food—and face violent assault because they are women.

Women's reproductive health is closely linked to nutrition and other health issues, as noted in earlier chapters. A 1996 study on the health of

Somali refugee women in Dadaab, Kenya, found that female refugees suffered more from morbidity and malnutrition than the male refugees in the camp; the researchers realized that the "gender morbidity differences are not solely biologically related. They are strongly influenced by the social context, for example, by the position women and men occupy in society, the access each gets to services, and the kinds of care each receives."[60]

In the camp, researchers found, for instance, that women were less likely to participate in tuberculosis detection programs than men because the women had been ostracized or expelled from their families after being abused or raped. The study also found gender differentials in compliance with supplementary feeding programs. The gendered division of household chores in the camps meant that girls were more likely to stop participating in the feeding programs than boys. Moreover, gender preference within the household affected the allocation of food and resulted in measurable differences in weight gain between boys and girls.[61] Inequitable food distribution led to high rates of maternal mortality as well. The study noted that "Women are treated particularly badly when they question the size of their ration, to the point where they no longer feel it is worth inquiring and often do not have the time to waste arguing."[62]

Not surprisingly, women who have escaped military conflict are likely to suffer psychological health problems caused by the many hardships they have faced since the break-out of conflict and during flight and displacement. In the Afghan refugee camps in Pakistan, it has been observed that "many women . . . suffer from post-traumatic stress disorder, from a combination of shell shock, combat fatigue, the loss of their birth place, being uprooted to another country against their will, and being dependent on hand-outs."[63]

Women's psychological problems may be compounded by the crowded conditions of the camp, and restrictions imposed as a cultural response to the altered social situation. For example, Afghan women's mobility became more restricted inside the Pakistani refugee camps where they "faced a stricter version of *purdah* [seclusion from men] than they had experienced in the villages and cities." This seclusion was enforced both by women's family members, because of the proximity of male strangers, and by the differing conservative Islamic factions that controlled the camps.[64] The psychological needs of female refugees frequently go unmet in refugee camps, not only because funds are unavailable but also because of cultural obstacles.

WOMEN'S COURAGE: BUREIJ, GAZA, PALESTINE. The Palestinian-Child Support Society was founded in 2000 by a group of women who had become concerned about the deteriorating quality of life that women and children refugees experienced in the Bureij Refugee Camp. Refugees displaced by the conflict between Palestine and Israel gathered in Gaza, making it one of the most densely populated regions in the world. Many women and children there have witnessed violent events and suffered physical abuse as well as psychological trauma.

To help this vulnerable population, the Support Society conducts outreach projects that aim to improve the well being of women and children refugees. The group provides women with access to basic education, healthcare, parenting workshops, and skills training programs. As for the children, group members have created libraries and extracurricular clubs for them, such that they can better cope with the experience of living under occupation. The group also offers psychological services and other outreach for people with disabilities, including awareness programs of the dangers and consequences of landmines.

Women suffering from psychological trauma may not even seek help at all if mental illness is stigmatized. Others are afraid that asking for help will limit their chances of migrating out of the camp.

In many African refugee camps, female genital mutilation (FGM) has escalated as families try to resurrect what they believe is an important component of their culture in the new and unfamiliar environment. In other cases, they adopt the practice as a means of assimilating into the local population. For example, a survey published by the Program for Appropriate Technology in Health found that many Southern Sudanese, who do not traditionally practice FGM, were beginning to do so after moving to camps in Khartoum, where the procedure was common among the Northern Sudanese refugees.[65] As discussed in the chapter on childhood, FGM poses significant health risks for girls and women, including blood-borne infections transmitted through the use of dirty and unsanitary instruments, along with a high risk of infection, followed by increased pain during urination and sexual intercourse, and complications during childbirth.

Unfortunately, gender discrimination in implementing humanitarian programs is not unusual. The failure to consult refugee women when setting up camps and food distribution programs has often resulted in the inappropriate, sometimes dangerous, placement of essential facilities, such as wells and defecation areas for women. Zamzam, a woman from Somaliland, relates a typical example: "It is the women's job to collect water for the family, so UNICEF should have consulted the women. But they didn't. They went straight to the men, the ones they called the elders. The elders wanted the pipes installed near the mosques. So women were forced to collect their water in front of the mosque where the men go to pray. They have to watch their modesty in front of a mosque full of men preparing for their prayers, while dealing with the problem of collecting water. Agencies look at what they have been told is the 'culture' and conclude, 'In this country, we must listen to the men.'"[66] Having habitually overlooked the particular needs of women, humanitarian agencies have only recently begun including sanitary supplies along with relief packages, despite the importance to women's dignity and mobility of a hygienic method of dealing with menstruation.[67]

Humanitarian aid itself is also sometimes associated with sexual violence and exploitation. One Bosnian woman said, "In refuge, I have been insulted, unfortunately, by the activists of [an aid group]. There was the abuse of official position and there were some humiliating sexual offers."[68] An April UN Development Fund for Women (UNIFEM) publication reported widespread exploitation committed by peacekeepers and humanitarian workers in Guinea, Liberia, and Sierra Leone refugee camps. In the report, refugees have testified: "If [a girl] refuse[s] [to have sex], when the time comes for the supply of food items, you will be told that your name is not on the list," and "If you do not have a wife or a sister or a daughter to offer the NGO workers, it is hard to have access to aid."[69] These and other testimonies from refugees suggest that, in many cases, the people to whom the international community has delegated the care of refugees are among those who commit humanitarian offenses against them.

Domestic violence is also widespread in many refugee camps because "there is evidence the psychological strains for husbands unable to assume normal cultural, social and economic roles can result in aggressive behavior towards wives and children. The enforced idleness, boredom and despair that permeate many camps are natural breeding grounds for such violence."[70] This situation, reinforced by norms that tolerate violence against women, results in domestic violence in refugee camps all over the world.[71]

WOMEN'S COURAGE: BOGOTÁ, CUNDINAMARCA, COLOMBIA. Fundación Indígena Jitomagaro Gente del Sol (Foundation of the Jitomagaro Indigenous People of the Sun) is an organization formed by a group of indigenous women who migrated to the city of Bogotá in search of better opportunities. Indigenous people from all over the Amazon region have been forced to leave their native lands because of the expansion of industrialization and armed conflicts in the country. The female founders come from various tribes who hope to preserve their unique culture and raise awareness for minority women's rights.

The Foundation provides basic support for women to help them survive in the city—education, legal advice, and social skills. The group has developed programs to raise awareness of the difficult situation of displaced indigenous women in the city, and members of the group have collected information about indigenous women's experience. The group hopes that by compiling a report for government bodies, people and officials will recognize and increase support for the needs of minority women.

While refugee women face many health struggles, the women who cannot cross internationally-recognized borders for refuge are often more vulnerable than women who have been accorded refugee status. Refugees are eligible to receive protection and help from the United Nations High Commission for Refugees (UNHCR). However, the international community is not under the same legal obligation to protect and assist internally displaced people (IDP). In these cases, national governments have the primary responsibility for the security and well being of IDPs in their territory. Unfortunately, as in Western Sudan, the legally responsible body is often the same government that is persecuting its displaced nationals. In any case, remaining within a war torn country may negate the possibility of receiving any assistance from aid agencies, which, in fact, may have little or no access to the area because of security threats or government bans.

The Aftermath of Conflict

The assault on women's health during times of conflict does not end when the fighting stops. Anu Pillay, a gender and development specialist writing about the aftermath of conflict in South Africa, states that "violence during war escalated into the most atrocious and heinous acts of brutality and torture,

WOMEN'S COURAGE: BUJUMBURA, BURUNDI.   L'Association des Femmes Repatriées (The Association for Repatriated Women) was founded in 2002 by three Burundian women who, like many other people, had fled to neighboring countries to escape the violent ethnic conflict in the region. Upon their return to their country, they found women's rights to be violated in many ways; rapes and beatings against women had increased dramatically because of unstable social conditions. The founders created the group to defend and empower women in society by providing education and psychological support. The Association has pooled their resources and raised funds to send young girls to school, offered awareness programs about HIV/AIDS prevention to the community, and provided leadership training, rights education, and technology tutorials through the group's outreach workshops to women.

and intensified in the aftermath of conflict. Mass rapes became gang rapes, mass murders turned into serial killings. [Conflicts that legitimize] violence as a means of ending war effectively legitimize the use of violence to solve conflicts at home."[72]

The effect on women of postwar social, demographic, economic, and political upheavals can hardly be overestimated. Communal support networks and systems of law and order, which may have protected women from abuse, disintegrate. The economy breaks down, and men who had been socially valued according to their work become unemployed. The combination of poverty, stress, altered circumstances, and a martial atmosphere creates a situation terribly conducive to increased violence against women.

The World Health Organization noted in 2002 that "in many countries that have suffered violent conflict, the rates of interpersonal violence remain high even after the cessation of hostilities," citing as reasons "the way violence has become more socially acceptable and the availability of weapons."[73] The aftermath of conflict can increase violence toward women when soldiers go home to countries where the war did not take place. According to Amnesty International, in the United States, "domestic violence and murder by soldiers returning from combat is emerging as a serious issue." They cite a study conducted by the US Army that found the incidence of "severe aggression" against spouses to be three times as high in army families as in civilian ones.[74] An example of such aggression occurred at Fort Bragg, North Carolina, where

WOMEN'S COURAGE: GJAKOVA, KOSOVA (SERBIA AND MONTENEGRO). After years of violence in Kosovo, the Kosovo Woman Initiative was created to improve the status of women in the region. Founded in 2001, the Initiative works to rebuild civil society in Kosovo and to empower women by increasing their political and economic status. With literacy and job skills courses, this group has served over a thousand women in fifty villages in Kosova. Through education, the group encourages women to assert their views in local and national politics. The Initiative also works to decrease domestic violence against women and girls in the region through the construction of counseling centers, advocacy campaigns, and political lobbying. In 2004, the National Action Plan on Gender Equality, a bill which the Kosovo Woman Initiative co-drafted, was approved by the national government.

in 2002, four soldiers killed their wives over a six-week period. Three of the four men had recently returned from active combat in Afghanistan and were presumed to be under stress from having engaged in combat.[75]

Organized violence against women, such as forced prostitution and trafficking, also increases in post-conflict societies. Porous borders and the collapse of a criminal justice and police system offer excellent conditions for the sex-slave trade. Traffickers "operate boldly across sovereign borders . . . and have exploited regional conflict, such as [in] Kosovo."[76] Unfortunately, the presence of peace-keeping forces and even international humanitarian aid personnel in post-conflict countries has increased the demand. One twelve-year-old Albanian girl told Amnesty International representatives: "Even in cold weather I had to wear thin dresses. . . . I was forced by the boss to serve international soldiers and police officers."[77] In 2004, Amnesty reported that "Women from neighbouring countries have been trafficked into Kosovo for forced prostitution since the deployment of the international peacekeeping force, KFOR [the NATO-led Kosovo Force], and the establishment of the UN civilian administration, UNMIK [United Nations Interim Administration Mission in Kosovo], in July 1999."[78] Between 1999 and 2000, international personnel comprised 80% of the clients of trafficked women in Kosovo; they have also been implicated in the trafficking itself.[79]

Aside from the problem of violence against women in the aftermath of conflict, there are also countless numbers of women whose wartime experience results in psychological conditions such as "anxiety, post-traumatic

WOMEN'S COURAGE: CHIANG MAI, THAILAND. In 1999, a group of displaced Kachin women in Thailand founded the Kachin Women Association Thailand (KWAT). Women living in the border regions between Thailand, China, and Burma have experienced violent conflicts since the early 1960s. One of the consequences of the political turmoil was the neglect of women's rights. In the region, young women are especially vulnerable to forced sex. The Association sets out to promote women's rights and restore their status in the post-war society. To do so, KWAT offers awareness programs to bring women's attention to the reality and threat of trafficking. The group also offers leadership and skills training to help women become politically aware and economically independent. One of the goals of the group is to train young women to become women's rights advocates to carry on the cause and to set a tone of gender equality in the community.

stress disorders, depression and suicide" that will continue much longer than the period of conflict itself.[80]

The 2002 UNIFEM *Women, War, and Peace Report* notes that "little attention has been paid to the effects of conflict on the psychosocial status of women or on how women process and cope with their experiences."[81] However, we do know that coping mechanisms such as alcoholism and drug abuse become prevalent in post-conflict societies, affecting both women and men. In an interview recorded by Olivia Bennett of PANOS, an international communications organization, Agnes, a woman from Liberia, describes how war has contributed to her alcoholism: "My personal behavior has changed . . . I drank only occasionally before the war. But now I drink any kind of alcohol, in any form, without anybody to tell me what to do. It's a habit that developed during the war because we saw all sorts of things going on. You had to drink alcohol to be able to sleep, so that you won't suffer nightmares or see terrible things, even day visions. You would drink alcohol and smoke a lot of cigarettes because of the smell of the bodies in the streets."[82]

Psychological and physical health problems are intensified when the women have been attacked sexually. According to a 2002 study by the International Red Cross, "Survivors of rape or sexual violence may have further problems such as ostracism or retribution . . . in some societies [they] may also risk being accused of adultery, prostitution and/or bringing dishonour upon the family—and these are seen as crimes which may be punishable by imprisonment and/or the death penalty."[83] Women may find that they cannot return to, or will not be accepted by, their families and communities after they have been raped. Faced with abuse and threats on their lives, women may be left to fend for themselves with few skills and no education, which renders them particularly vulnerable to trafficking and forced prostitution.

Yet another set of problems in the aftermath of war concerns the births that result from sexual aggression. In the Rwandan genocide, survivors of rape have given birth to between two and five thousand children.[84] As mentioned earlier, in Rwanda, the children of women raped in war are called *enfants non-desirés* or *enfants de mauvais souvenir*, "unwanted children" or "children of bad memories."[85] A child so regarded is likely to face rejection from others, and the mother may be forced to care for that child without assistance from her community.

Women like Mukandoli, the Rwandan widow who become pregnant as a result of rape in ethnic warfare, cannot forget the assault or hide the fact of it from their community. The woman may suffer trauma and depression, especially if she has internalized the notion that her child's ethnicity is determined by the man who raped her because woman is only a "vessel" for man's seed. In any case, she is faced with the awful decision of either undergoing a potentially dangerous abortion or bearing and raising a child who may be a lifelong reminder to both her and her community of what she has suffered during conflict. Another woman from Rwanda, who decided to continue her pregnancy, said, "Almost all my family members have refused to accept the baby—it is a child of an Interahamwe [enemy militia]. They have told me that they do not want a child of wicked people. They always tell me that when my baby grows up that they will not give him a parcel of land. I don't know what is going to happen to him. The only help I have received is from Réseau des Femmes [a local women's rights organization]."[86]

Other long-term consequences of war include various effects of military pollution on reproductive health, which may only become known decades later. In both the United States and Russia, releases of radioactive materials from nuclear weapons production and testing are associated with sterility, cancer, genetic abnormalities, and the birth of so-called "jellyfish babies."[87] In Vietnam, the herbicide Agent Orange sprayed by the U.S. military to destroy the jungles that provided cover for the Viet Cong, has caused birth defects, abnormal births, miscarriages, and reproductive cancers more than twenty-five years after the conflict. Nam, a Vietnamese woman, bluntly tells of the effect "Orange" has had on her family: "My eldest daughter died

WOMEN'S COURAGE: UZICE, SERBIA, SERBIA AND MONTENEGRO. The Women's Center in Uzice was formed in 1997 by fifteen women from various professions who had been providing social and psychological support to refugees in the camps located near Uzice. The group provides local and refugee women with various kinds of support to promote economic independence and to link them with other women's groups in the region. A major component of the work relates to the three breast cancer centers that the Center established after a surge in cancer rates subsequent to stress and chemical warfare during the conflict in the early 1990s and during later bombings in 1999. The three centers offer lectures on women's health, causes and problems related to breast cancer, and workshops on treatment and coping with cancer. In response to the rise of nationalism, militarism, war, and economic crisis which has intensified the violence against women in Serbia and Montenegro, the group has expanded its programs to reach many more women and has increased its advocacy for women's right to live without violence.

in 1986, the third [daughter] in 1987. The second child went blind and her muscles shrunk, and then she died. My husband's health was getting worse and worse. It was so painful. . . . When my children had all died, my friends advised me to have another child."[88] Nam eventually gave birth to two boys, both of whom cannot see and hear properly. In other cases, the effects of war persist even longer, as later-generation girls grow up to find that they too are suffering reproductive health problems presumably caused by the conflicts of those long dead. Reports are emerging from Iraq about increases in birth deformities and child cancer rates among Iraqi infants exposed to depleted uranium munitions used by U.S. and British forces in the 1991 Gulf War. Although it is generally accepted that there was a relationship between the herbicide used in Vietnam and some birth defects, studies on the long term effects of chemicals used in Iraq have not been conclusive.

After conflict and flight, women attempt to gather the pieces of their lives together. Even now, many are hard at work, trying to make the world safe for their children and the children of others. All this they do in conditions of extreme inequality.

Become aware
of who pays what
for you to live the way you do.
Remember,
cheap labor is never cheap
for the person who performs it.

  —Audre Lorde, U.S.A., 1989[1]

The next exhibit lies flat on her back
while eighty men a night
move through her, ten an hour.
She looks at the ceiling, listens
to the door open and close.
A bell keeps ringing.
Nobody knows how she got there.

  —Margaret Atwood, "A Women's Issue," Canada, 1981[2]

8

Laboring in a Globalized World

ONE DAY IN 1975 in Iceland, society ceased to function. The amount of labor performed, both in and out of the home, dropped precipitously. The reason? Every woman in the country took a day off of all types of work, paid or unpaid. As a result, the people of Iceland at least would not forget the value of women's work.[3] If every woman in the world similarly ceased work for a single day, the results would be staggering. Most unpaid labor would go undone, including many tasks essential for survival. Water would go uncollected, meals unprepared. Crops and animals would go untended, clothes unwashed, children unwatched, and the old and the sick uncared-for. In addition, millions of family businesses would be unable to operate, thousands of service and manufacturing industries would suffer from a lack of employees, hundreds of corporations would lack managers, and a handful of countries would be paralyzed without the heads of state. The boards of directors of many international agencies and corporations would be minimally affected, however, since they have few or no female members. And the recorded economic impact of such a day would be less severe than the crippling effects experienced by everyone on the planet, simply because of the way "work" is measured.

Women's Work: Unrecognized and Undervalued

A woman's labor includes whatever she is expected to do for no money as well as what she may choose or be coerced into doing in order to have money to care for her family and herself. More than a third of the world's households depend solely upon women for all income and necessities.[4]

"Women work longer hours than men in nearly every country. Of the total burden of work, women carry an average of 53% in developing countries and 51% in industrial countries." Furthermore, "of men's total work time in industrial countries, about two-thirds is spent on paid activities and one-third on unpaid activities. For women these shares are reversed." In poorer countries the gaps are greater. "So, men receive the lion's share of income and recognition for their economic contribution—while most of women's work remains unpaid, unrecognized, and undervalued."[5] These are the findings of the United Nations Development Programme (UNDP) in its *Human Development Report* of 1995, one of the first global studies of women's work and time spent on labor. In short, "Women's work is greatly undervalued in economic terms."

Gita Sen and Caren Grown state the situation clearly: "Women's work, underremunerated and undervalued as it is, is vital to the survival and ongoing reproduction of human beings in all societies. In food production and processing, in responsibility for fuel, water, health care, child-rearing, sanitation, and the entire range of so-called basic needs, women's labor is dominant."[6]

But for all their hard work, "the majority of the 1.5 billion people living on U.S.$1 a day or less are women. In addition, the gap between women and men caught in the cycle of poverty has continued to widen in the past decade, a phenomenon commonly referred to as 'the feminization of poverty.' Worldwide, women earn on average slightly more than 50% of what men earn. . . . [Discriminatory laws result in many poor women being denied] access to critical resources such as credit, land, and inheritance. Their labour goes unrewarded and unrecognized. Their health care and nutritional needs are not given priority, they lack sufficient access to education and support services, and their participation in decision-making at home and in the community are minimal. Caught in the cycle of poverty, women lack access to resources and services to change their situation."[7]

WOMEN'S COURAGE: ACCRA, GHANA. The Network for Women's Rights in Ghana was formed to increase awareness about the impacts of national policies on the economic welfare of women. Recognizing the need for more female political participation as a means to promote equal treatment of women in economic policy, the group has organized demonstrations and seminars to raise visibility about women's poverty in Ghana. The Network's programs include activities relating to domestic violence and discrimination in property ownership, acknowledging the close relationship of these issues to women's poverty. Working at both local and national levels, the Network collaborates with small groups and national associations to advocate for effective distribution of resources and other strategies to promote economic justice.

Given this extremely difficult economic situation, women must seek paid employment of all kinds, and they may be coerced or trafficked with relative ease into vulnerable situations through promises of a better life and some income to feed themselves and their families. In this chapter we look at this situation as it pertains to women in poorer countries, particularly focusing on the effects of globalization and the issue of trafficking.

Measuring Work: Not!

Measurements of countries' economic progress for the most part ignore the contributions of women in households because women's domestic labor is not recognized as wage work. If such unpaid labor were included in statistics measuring economic transactions, the world's economy would increase by about $11 trillion. This more accurate measurement could help create a shift in valuing the unpaid work done by women, at least in official circles. [8] But this hard labor is missing: official statistics show men contributing much more to the family than do women. The consequences are more than perceptual. In many countries, even today, women may have little or no access to social security or other benefit programs because they are calculated on the basis of paid labor. In much of sub-Saharan Africa, for example, customary laws have greater influence than statutory law when it comes to women's property rights, and if a marriage dissolves, the husband usually receives everything of monetary value.

Marilyn Waring, a political economist, author, and feminist activist from New Zealand, provides examples of this unpaid labor. She writes of women in richer countries who spend their days in such "unproductive" activities as cleaning house, tending children, providing healthcare, doing laundry, and so on. She also describes girls and women like Tendai, a young girl in the Lowveld, in Zimbabwe, thus:

> Her day starts at 4 a.m., when, to fetch water, she carries a thirty-litre tin to a borehole about eleven kilometers from her home. She walks barefoot and is home by 9 a.m. She eats a little and proceeds to fetch firewood until midday. She cleans the utensils from the family's morning meal and sits preparing a lunch of sadza for the family. After lunch and the cleaning of the dishes, she wanders in the hot sun until early evening, fetching wild vegetables for supper before making the evening trip for water. Her day ends at 9 p.m., after she has prepared supper and put her younger brothers and sisters to sleep. Tendai [like other women working in households] is considered unproductive, unoccupied, and economically inactive. According to the international economic system, Tendai does not work and is not part of the labor force.[9]

Proponents of gender equality, including Waring, argue that measuring women's work is straightforward and should be accounted for in the System of National Accounts (SNA), an international system which measures output, income, and expenditures. Currently, the SNA only incorporates common economic indicators, such as labor in services and agriculture. If non-waged work were to be taken into consideration, however, activities like work in the home could be given equal weight with work in industry. Such work could be measured, either by market cost, in which the cost to perform domestic chores, for example, would be taken to the marketplace, or as a replacement cost, in which the cost to get someone else to perform the household jobs would be determined.[10]

Informal "Paid" Work[11]

Many women do get paid for domestic work—cleaning homes, babysitting, and doing other tasks for wealthier families. But even this work (in what is known as the "informal sector") falls outside of official statistics because it is often "under the table." The vast majority of these paid domestics are women

WOMEN'S COURAGE: LISAKOVSK, KOSTANIA OBLAST, KAZAKHSTAN. Women comprise more than 70% of the unemployed population in Kazakhstan. The Lisakovsk Businesswomen's Association was formed in response to female economic dependence in Kazakhstan and in recognition of high levels of domestic violence against women. Since its creation in 1999, the group has provided unemployed women with technical training, mentorship, and other social support. One project of the group provided women with the wherewithal to start small gardening businesses; they received loans and skills training to establish gardens and sell herbs and other vegetables for profit. A strategy of the Association involves giving younger women the opportunity to shadow other women in business and learn about the business world.

lacking benefits or security in their jobs. This kind of work can provide women with some income, but such unregulated jobs are usually low paying and can trap women in situations that provide neither benefits nor means of advancement. Jobs outside of the structured relationships with employers that characterize the formal economy have increased. From self-employed persons to sub-contracted workers, workers in the informal economy lack benefits or security in their jobs. The majority of these workers are women.[12]

Many women are also self-employed in small businesses that fare poorly as vehicles for economic security. Women accept such jobs because they offer flexibility (for example, street vendors can keep their children with them as they work), or, because of a lack of other opportunities, they cannot afford to turn down work, even if it involves a badly paid job with poor and sometimes dangerous working conditions.

The lack of official recognition of the informal sector has two main effects: On a local level, it exempts such jobs from health and labor standards, which may result in unsafe conditions. And on a global level, like the invisibility of domestic work, it contributes to the continued marginalization of women in the global economy, through international policies that disadvantage or overlook such work and therefore the women who perform it.

International agencies, such as the World Bank and the regional development banks, and economic analysts have introduced built-in biases to their approaches. For example, it has been assumed by analysts that the distribution of resources within households is equal and that women's unpaid work is irrelevant to any economic analysis. Second, they have assumed that women's capacity for labor could expand indefinitely. Increasing women's participation in the formal or informal labor system was not seen as detrimental to women's unpaid work, since such unpaid work was never recognized or measured. Diane Elson, formerly with the the Bard College Levy Institute's program on gender equality and the economy, writes on structural adjustment programs. She describes the inherent bias in them, which results from formal sector employment being dominated by men and the increase in informal sector labor adding work outside the home to women's already heavy labor within the home.[13] Though this change constitutes an economic gain from the standpoint of international commerce, it can degrade the quality of life and well-being of those caught in such situations. Women who, through poverty and gender discrimination, lack external resources to change their lives attempt to maximize their economic situations by working outside of the home, sometimes to the detriment of their own health and their families' well being.

Women seeking to support themselves and their dependents and to improve their lives are denied access to crucial resources through widespread discrimination. For example, women lack access to tangible resources like land, about 90% of which worldwide is owned by men,[14] and credit, only 10% of which goes to women, as well as to other resources such as education, technology to ease the burden of manual labor, and leaders who consider their needs.[15]

Women are also constrained by the unequal burdens of domestic labor. For example, women in southern Asia who work in paid jobs outside the home also perform approximately twenty-four hours more unpaid work than men do each week.[16] Women's and girls' access to education is hampered by the demands of domestic labor. Nor does young girls' labor only include domestic tasks: worldwide, 110 million girls age five to fourteen years old do non-domestic work in addition to domestic work.[17] Throughout their lives and around the world, women face formidable barriers in their efforts to control the way they work and live.

Globalization: Boon or Bane for Women?

Globalization has resulted in a climate where low-level and low-paid employment has become increasingly feminized.[18] Indeed, female labor has

WOMEN'S COURAGE: GORI, GEORGIA. A violent conflict between Ossetia and Georgia left the local economy of Gori in a devastated state. Recognizing that the failing economy put women into a particularly vulnerable situation, four women university students created the Intellectual Women's Association Kartlis Deda in 1997. The Association started out by lobbying for greater assurance of women's rights. More recently, however, the group has worked directly with women to help them become financially secure and self-sufficient; the group provides women with the social and career skills necessary to improve their lives. Specifically, the Association is providing training in practical income-generating work such as gardening and sewing and, more recently, in business and computer skills.

become a commodity in export-oriented economies in Asia, Central America, and Eastern Europe because it is cheap, flexible, and easily controlled. Women, not men, are filling the assembly-line jobs opening up in the textile and electronic industries and in data processing. Furthermore, women's alternatives—jobs as temporary workers, part-time employees, and home-based workers—have grown tremendously in comparison with their numbers prior to the onset of globalization.[19]

Clearly the rapid development of communication, transportation, and business technologies that have encouraged the spread of Western and neoliberal economic policies—i.e., globalization—is here to stay. Large transnational corporations (TNCs) have emerged, encouraging the globalization of commerce and operating without accountability to any democratically elected group. The result of this widespread development is a world in which international trade takes precedence over local cultural or economic concerns. According to the Washington-based Center for Strategic and International Studies, globalization may be seen as "a force for economic growth, prosperity, and greater freedom of choice. . . . [It may also be seen as] a force for environmental devastation, exploitation of the developing world, and suppression of human rights."[20] And evidence is mounting that globalization hurts wealthy countries as well.[21] Indeed, even some proponents of the benefits of globalization are expressing doubts.[22]

Globalization has opened opportunities for women—for paid employment and a way out of very restricted lives. At the same time, many believe that work in the new global economy is exploitative, and in some sense makes life even more difficult than it was before the surge of globalization. A report from Emory University states:

> Many critics fear that globalization, in the sense of integration of a country into world society, will exacerbate gender inequality. It may harm women— especially in [developing countries]—in several ways:
>
> - Economically, through discrimination in favor of male workers, marginal- ization of women in unpaid or informal labor, exploitation of women in low-wage sweatshop settings, and/or impoverishment though loss of traditional sources of income.
>
> - Politically, through exclusion from the domestic political process and loss of control to global pressures.
>
> - Culturally, through loss of identity and autonomy to a hegemonic global culture.
>
> At the same time, many women's advocates recognize that globalization affects different groups of women in different ways, creates new standards for the treatment of women, and helps women's groups to mobilize. In situations where women have been historically repressed or discriminated against under a patriarchal division of labor, some features of globaliza- tion may have liberating consequences. While in many countries women remain at a significant disadvantage, the precise role of globalization in causing or perpetuating that condition is in dispute.[23]

With globalization, in addition to bringing home money, women still bear the responsibility of raising a family. Moreover, they are still subject to gender inequities, now under different guises. Women migrate from rural villages to urban centers and give up subsistence agriculture to sell cheap plastic products made on another side of the globe. Though they may have made a transition from subsistence farming to participating in a cash economy, women's labor remains discounted and undervalued, often not even considered part of the formal economy. Moving from a rural area to a larger city does not necessarily increase women's quality of life. Likewise, women's migra- tion from a poorer country to a wealthier one does not ensure them higher standards of health or human rights. Many find themselves still domestic servants, now in different countries where they may be unable to speak the language and are denied legal protection by either their home country or the country where they work.

Perhaps the worst fate: many women are trafficked by organized crime rings and/or coerced into modern-day forms of slavery. These processes are not new, but ease of communication and transportation, as well as porous borders, has increased their scale tremendously. This chapter will address the ways that globalization impacts women's work and health, with specific attention paid to domestic labor, trafficking, and sex work. Now, however, we will offer a discussion of globalization and raised expectations.

Globalization is upheld by the belief that capitalism, applied everywhere so that rich and poor countries become economically intertwined, is the most effective way of alleviating the world's poverty. Proponents argue that as global economic output increases, productivity and efficiency levels rise, thereby creating millions of jobs. In the 1990s, foreign entities invested $1 trillion in developing economies.[24] According to prevailing notions of economics, this money would reduce poverty and the social ailments that arise from it. Some take the view that economic integration is not only good for the poor but is absolutely necessary: "To embrace self-sufficiency or to deride growth . . . is to glamorize poverty," writes Tina Rosenberg, a *New York Times* writer.[25] With all the promises globalization offers, it is not surprising that an ever-increasing number of countries want to become part of the World Trade Organization (WTO) and to have the International Monetary Fund (IMF) and World Bank underwrite their economic revitalization.

At the same time, the downsides of globalization, particularly as they affect poor people, are evident. For example, in a study on health inequity produced by the Rockefeller Foundation, the authors state: "The globalization of trade and finance are giving rise to ever greater economic and social disparities between those with money—plus access to information, education, and the power to act on what they know—and those without."[26] Transnational corporations (TNCs) are also increasing the economic gaps between rich and poor regions of the world. The world's TNCs, composed of 40,000 parent firms and 250,000 foreign affiliates, are responsible for two-thirds of world trade in goods and services.[27] Moreover, they generated $5.2 trillion in 1992, eclipsing the $4.9 trillion of world exports of goods and non-factor services.[28] Most of the transnational corporations, not surprisingly, are based in industrialized countries—the United States, Japan, England, Germany, and Switzerland—while most of the factories are in poorer regions in Asia, Eastern Europe, and Central America. The industrialized countries—or, more to the point, the corporations of these industrialized countries—by investing the money are garnering profits, while the developing countries provide cheap labor. Yet even the borders of sovereign states do not limit transnational corporations. By operating in multiple countries, especially in "export processing zones," and extending their networks deep into many countries' infrastructures, TNCs are able to control not only the output of material goods but also the flow of information. Indeed, as Chakravarthi Raghavan, editor of *Third World Economics* and representative of the Third World Network in Geneva, writes, "their power far exceeds that of any government on earth."[29]

The Rockefeller Foundation study further points out that "such globalization is likely to enhance health opportunities for the fortunate and empowered while imposing further obstacles to health among the poor and excluded. . . . In addition to heightened social polarization . . . [rapid global change] has resulted in retrenchment of the public sector, and the concomitant growth of the private sector in the provision of health care."[30] As the public sector is weakened with regard to the provision of health care, more care-giving burdens fall on the shoulders of poor women.

There is growing awareness by those concerned with women's health of the many ways in which globalization and international policies have exacerbated the poverty many women encounter. The Association for Women's Rights and Development, an international policy organization based in Toronto, Canada, for example, has made the point that women's rights to food, housing, heath care, and political participation continue to be violated either directly or indirectly by trade liberalization and investment policies.[31]

Admittedly, globalization involves beneficial processes: faster communications and transportation as well as sharing of knowledge and culture, including information about life-saving technologies. At the same time, globalization has expanded corporate power to the point that some calculate that about half of the world's one hundred largest economies are corporations. The governments of nation-states have grown weaker and less relevant while transnational corporations have increased their scope and power, concentrating more wealth in the hands of a few. Together with governments of their home countries in Europe, North America, and Japan, as well as

WOMEN'S COURAGE: DHAKA, BANGLADESH. After suffering unjust corporate practices, three female garment workers founded the Bangladesh Centre
for Workers' Solidarity to inform other women of their labor rights. Originally,
the group served only the garment industry, but it has now expanded to serve
women workers of other trades as well. Globalization has led to a proliferation
of factories and the presence of large corporations in Dhaka. In the face of these
developments, the Centre is working hard for women's rights to attain reasonable
wages, maternity leave, and safe work environments for women workers.

   The group has approached government officials such as the Chief Factory
Inspector of Bangladesh to mandate maternity leave for female workers. It also
offers direct assistance by helping women seek unpaid wages, explaining their
work contracts, and creating a generally safe work environment for women
workers. The Centre sees its role as encouraging women's economic and social
growth while at the same time creating a united and trustworthy organization
working against the abuse of female workers.

international institutions such as the WTO, the World Bank, and the IMF,
these corporations are part of an international system in which they can
trade and invest more freely than ever, a system where they are accountable
to no democratically elected entity.[32]

   Nevertheless, globalization is a pervasive and dominating part of the
global infrastructure. While recognizing the possible benefits and costs of
globalization, it is important to be aware of its effects on individual lives. The
current plight of women working in poorer countries stems from a combination of age-old discrimination and a recent history of economic policies gone
awry, which has widened gender disparities. As debts in developed countries
became increasingly unmanageable in the 1980s, investors become wary of
lending money to developing countries. With nowhere else to turn, poorer
countries have been forced to adopt economic packages—dubbed "structural
adjustment programs" (SAPs)—developed by the World Bank and the IMF.
The SAPs originally constituted a lending policy that focused on gradual
growth through investment in export commodities and participation in the
free market. Less governmental control and more free flow of capital, the
World Bank and IMF believed, would naturally lead to improved incomes
and standards of living in the long term.[33]

WOMEN'S COURAGE: KHUJAND, TAJIKISTAN.   As a response to the high unemployment rate in Tajikistan, five women created Farohdasti (meaning "the giving hand") to help women learn about their human rights and about basic business management skills. Prior to running Farohdasti, the founders themselves suffered the hardships of unemployment when they were all laid off from the same company. Reacting to that experience, the founders set out to empower themselves and other Tajikistani women. Farohdasti provides women with small loans and training to start and maintain their own small businesses. The group also supports women through its psychological counseling and legal assistance services. Farohdasti's outreach programs include a concern with the issue of domestic violence and with women's full participation in society. In other words, along with improving women's economic condition, helping women find and assert their voices in society is another of Farohdasti's main objectives.

Sadly, especially for many women, this assumption could not be further from the truth. Reductions in government expenditures on health and education, for example, place heavier burdens on women, who are the primary caregivers for their children, the ill, and the elderly. And even though economic liberalization has increased the number of jobs, many of these jobs, owing to the severity of free-market competition, offer insufficient income and poor working conditions.[34] Although some of these policies have been modified in very recent years, with some debts being "forgiven," the result of SAPs in many countries has been to increase the gap between the rich and the poor and to reduce social services, placing a burden particularly on women.

The situation in sub-Saharan Africa is a prime example of how globalization can undermine the poor. SAPs have required thirty-six countries in Southern Africa to reduce domestic consumption and shift resources into cash crops for export—even though half the population in the region lives in poverty and needs crops that they can eat.[35] Between 1990 and 1993, countries in sub-Saharan Africa were forced to pay $13.4 billion to creditors linked to World Bank and the IMF, and their debt continued to rise to $312 billion.[36] At the same time, many social services in the region were slashed, especially in the realm of health care. Maternal and infant mortality rates continue to remain high in these countries, even increasing in Zimbabwe.[37] Despite nationalization of health services, the general quality of health care declined, and health care services and personnel have continued to be under-funded.[38]

Structural adjustment programs also make life more difficult for women engaged in other types of unwaged work, particularly in households. As the gap between prices and incomes continues to increase and governmental systems weaken, women travel longer distances, wait for longer periods of time, and devote more time to finding cheaper food and goods for their families.[39]

Despite its exacerbation of gender inequalities, globalization also offers a number of opportunities to some women. Many are now the main breadwinners in their households, and may even be the sole income earners.[40] As a result, young women are entering the public sphere and filling roles that benefit their families and the wider society. In the process, they are reversing the stereotypes of the patriarchal family model.[41] In some countries, women are no longer dependent housewives, being helpmates to their husbands by fulfilling their duties in the domestic sphere. Instead, they actively contribute to the family income. Even if their social status is not on a par with their husband's, the level of respect they can attain may rise. In the process, women may gain greater autonomy and independence, so that they have greater leverage in asking men to help with domestic chores.[42]

As the world moves toward cultural homogeneity through mass entertainment, women in poorer countries can now see a romanticized version of what life is like in richer parts of the world. This knowledge leads some to migrate to richer countries to improve their lives: from Southeast Asia to the Middle and Far East; from the former Soviet bloc to western Europe; from south to north in the Americas; and from Africa to various parts of Europe.[43] Even though globalization brings ambitious women together from disparate parts of the globe, their convergence is not the kind of strengthening coalition that feminists may have envisioned, of women working together within a context of common goals and principles for the betterment and empowerment of an entire gender. Instead, as Barbara Ehrenreich explains, "they come together as mistress and maid, employer and employee, across a great divide of privilege and opportunity."[44]

Lucy, for example, is a woman from the Philippines working in Hong Kong. As a housekeeper, she works fourteen hours a day shopping, cooking, and cleaning. The conditions that she works under, however, are stifling.

She rarely receives enough to eat, and she is treated like a child. Her employer—the woman of the household—sets her work hours, tells her what to wear, and does not give her overtime pay. She must ask permission to use the telephone, and her contract can be terminated at her employer's whim. Lucy bears it, hoping to earn money quickly so she can go home with resources for her family.

Back in the Philippines, women like Lucy may be vilified for leaving their responsibilities at home in search of better economic opportunities. The media may denounce them for abandoning their families, whereas migrating men are often lauded for taking a chance abroad.[45] Nevertheless, domestic work abroad was the Philippines' primary export in 1999, totaling $7 billion.[46] As opportunities for paid employment at home become limited or disappear, women emigrate, leaving their children with relatives; they face a potential situation of caring for other people's children while being unable to tend to their own. Although their children sometimes experience emotional distress, they eventually come to terms with the fact that their mothers have to go abroad in order to support the family.[47] Thus, globalization forces many Filipino women to choose between better economic prospects, no matter how harsh the labor, and their families.

Moving to the City for Pay

Globalization also accelerates technological innovation, which, along with streamlining the production of goods, may displace women and/or eliminate their jobs. As agricultural production in many countries is increasingly dominated by corporate interests, farmers, many of them women, in Africa, Asia, and Latin America are forced to become dependent upon informal wage work to make a living. In Mexico, to meet their needs, women are going into the informal labor sector to support their families. Although their husbands may have steady incomes, lower-class women in Mexico City are still offering informal domestic services, including baking, dishwashing, and crafts work, to other women in exchange for money. Indeed, most elderly, divorced, and widowed women depend entirely on their domestic abilities to feed themselves.[48] Even in Brazil, which has shown moderate growth in jobs overall, employment spurred by industrialization has been unable to counteract the loss of agricultural jobs.[49]

In many poorer countries, women, displaced from agricultural jobs, also head to urban areas in search of economic opportunities. Indeed, women are now migrating to cities in greater numbers than men.[50] If they cannot sell their domestic skills, they turn to work intimately related to their sexual and care-giving roles. The nature of much of women's work means that their jobs have little or no growth potential.[51] Because the job market—and, indeed, many facets of society—is still male dominated, it is not surprising that women have consistently lower salaries than men.[52] So, despite the technological innovations that globalization produces, many women in developing countries still only have access to jobs that have existed for years and certainly long before the growth of globalization.

Even when women fill a new job niche opened up through globalization, they may suffer negative economic and health consequences—as Mexican women's experiences in maquiladoras (export zone assembly plants) illustrate. After joining the General Agreement on Tariffs and Trade (GATT) in 1986, Mexico continued the march toward economic liberalization that it undertook in subscribing to the North American Free Trade Agreement (NAFTA) in 1994.[53] American companies, eager to take advantage of cheap labor in Mexico, rapidly moved their factories across the border, to the dismay of U.S. labor unions. At the same time, Mexican grain farmers, overwhelmed by competition from an influx of attractive American food products, suffered a punishing series of financial blows.[54] As a result, maquiladoras quickly grew along the U.S.–Mexican border as corporate owners sought cheap labor and displaced workers sought jobs. Not surprisingly, Mexican women, particularly young women, migrated from the countryside to the border cities, hoping for a better life.

For instance, a seventeen-year-old named Ana from a village in northern Mexico obtained work in the export-processing zone along the border. She works at least ten hours a day, doing meticulous, repetitive work, living in a tiny apartment with six other young women workers, earning more money than she has ever seen before, yet not enough to pay her bills and send some money back to her mother in the village. She worries a little because some of the female workers who try to lobby for higher wages are being harassed and threatened by the managers. They are afraid that they will be fired.[55] Asked why young rural women are the group that factory owners focus on

WOMEN'S COURAGE: TIJUANA, MEXICO. "Women workers: human and with rights" declares the slogan of Casa de la Mujer - Grupo Factor X (Woman's House -Factor X) in Tijuana. The group vigorously defends women's reproductive and labor rights along the Mexico-U.S. border, where many women work in maquiladoras, or factories. Since 1992, the network has mobilized maquiladora women and activists for social change and has convened regional workshops with maquiladora women in Chihuahua and Coahuila at the northern border of Mexico. The workshops brought together workers and representatives from small collectives that have never had the opportunity to exchange experiences and collaborate to effect positive changes for women workers.

WOMEN'S COURAGE: BEIRUT, LEBANON. The Machreq/Maghreb Gender Linking and Information Project trains women in leadership skills, with the broader purpose of strengthening the women's movement in the Arab region of the world. The Project was created in 1999 to address issues of gender equality at local levels and in the region in general. In Lebanon, most women are literate but not well educated. Many women work as unskilled laborers and receive little pay, benefits, or labor-law protection. The group believes that altering societal expectations of gender roles will improve women's economic situation, and so it encourages Lebanese women to participate more actively in the political process. At the same time the Project offers education about leadership and economic alternatives for women.

recruiting, an American business owner responded, "They [the girls] are just so damned good at [the repetitive mechanical work]."[56] Others argue that young rural women are hired because their labor is cheap and because they are compliant workers. Furthermore, even though the young women are now wage earners, they suffer the same gender discrimination that undermined and jeopardized them back home. While women put together electronic parts on the assembly line or piece together shirts and blouses for export, almost all the workers offered training as technicians, supervisors, and managers are men. In this environment, men play favorites with the younger, prettier girls, even holding industry beauty contests with the requisite swimsuit competitions.[57] On the weekends, "maquila girls" may also act as casual prostitutes, offering sex in exchange for material goods that they otherwise could not afford.

The physical status of women in the maquiladoras, unfortunately, is just as dire as the social situation. With wages below the national average, women have great difficulty affording basic necessities such as rent and electricity. Moreover, they report numerous occupational hazards, including exposure to airborne chemicals and being subjected to repetitive, machine-paced work for weeks at a time.[58] The reproductive outcomes may also be negative: one study showed that women working in maquiladoras had babies with lower birth weights.[59] Probable explanations include "chemical exposures, ergonomic factors and socio-demographic variables, such as lower wages, longer hours, and lower rates of union membership among maquiladora workers."[60]

Sex Trafficking

From the devaluing of women's work within the home to the underpaying of female workers in the formal and informal economy, the labor of women is taken for granted while their desires and need for autonomy are ignored. Performing sexual services for money, because of poverty, a lack of alternatives, and/or coercion, is, unfortunately, a common form of work in the global informal economy. And at the far end of the spectrum of exploitation is modern day slavery—the worldwide trafficking of women and children, of which 65% to 95% has to do with the sex industries.[61]

The United Nations estimates that two to four million women are trafficked each year; U.S. government agencies estimate that between 600,000 and 800,000 women and children are trafficked annually for sex and labor.[62] However, neither of these estimates includes within-country trafficking, and all such statistics are, at best, educated guesses, attempts to illuminate a shadowed and well-hidden world of exploitation and abuse.

I learned of Priti from friends at ABC Nepal, a women's group in Kathmandu. Priti was twelve when her father told her that he was going to take her to a nearby town in Nepal to meet a woman who would give her a job. She was excited about traveling beyond her village, and she and her father walked for two days to reach the town. There they met a woman who told her father that she would look after Priti. The woman gave him $50, an enormous sum for a poor farmer. Priti's father seemed sad to say goodbye, and he promised his daughter that he would see her in a year or two. The woman then took Priti to a larger town, where two other girls about her age joined them for a journey across the border to India. The woman had friends who had arranged for documentation, and the girls enjoyed the novelty of riding on a train. Upon their arrival in Calcutta, the girls were taken to a crowded part of the city and sold to a brothel owner. They were indoctrinated into the sex trade, raped, and beaten when they refused to do the work. The girls had no idea of what was involved; they were taught brutally and told that they would work for the first year to pay off their "debt," the amount that had been paid for them, plus their food and clothing. Priti remained in the brothel for two years, until she became ill and was dumped on the street. Social workers helped her return to Nepal, where she now lives with fifteen other young girls, all HIV/AIDS positive, in a house in Kathmandu. She is learning to sew. She will not return to her village; her family does not want her there.

Although it is important to keep in mind that trafficking includes not only sexual exploitation but also forced labor, domestic servitude, and agricultural work, this discussion primarily focuses on coerced sexual activity.[63] Each year, millions of women are tricked or sold into prostitution—more than one million in Asia alone. According to the 2006 UN Office of Drugs and Crime report entitled "Trafficking in Persons: Global Patterns" and the 2000 UN Convention Against Transnational Organized Crime, "trafficking in persons" is "the recruitment, transportation, harbouring or receipt of persons, by means of the threat or use of force or other forms of coercion, of abduction, of fraud, of deception, of the abuse of power or of a position of vulnerability or of the giving or receiving of payments to achieve the consent of a person having control over another person, for the purpose of exploitation. Exploitation includes, at a minimum, the exploitation of the prostitution of others or other forms of sexual exploitation, forced labour or services, slavery or practices similar to slavery, servitude or removal of organs."[64] The definition includes three component parts: "the act of trafficking, the means used to commit those acts, and the goals or purpose of various types of exploitation."[65]

Emphasis on all three components of trafficking distinguishes it from both smuggling and prostitution. As defined by the Protocol Against the Smuggling

WOMEN'S COURAGE: AMERSFOORT, NETHERLANDS. The International La Strada Association, formed in 2004, is a network of nine independent organizations based in Poland, Belarus, the Czech Republic, Bosnia and Herzegovina, Moldova, Ukraine, Bulgaria, Macedonia, and the Netherlands, all dedicated to raising public awareness about trafficking of women and children. These groups lobby and inform legislators and public officials, educate women and girls, and refer survivors of trafficking to support networks. La Strada reports that "since the fall of the Berlin Wall in 1989 and the resulting political and economic instability, there has been an alarming increase in trafficking in women from Central and Eastern Europe and the New Independent States."

In a region where thousands of women are trafficked each year, the La Strada organizations conduct important advocacy to prevent trafficking, while supporting survivors of trafficking, who receive little or no support from other sources. In addition to organizing international networking, lobbying, and public relations on behalf of the whole network, the Association coordinates fundraising and national capacity building for its member organizations, and increases effective collaboration among members. Like GAATW, also described in this chapter, La Strada has greatly contributed to the international discourse on trafficking, and has helped shift focus from the nature of the work to the working conditions. This has broadened the scope of trafficking to include many forms of forced/exploitative labor, and moved away from the stereotypical view of women as meek victims.

of Migrants by Land, Sea, and Air, smuggling is the "procurement . . . of the illegal entry of a person into a country of which the person is not a national or permanent resident."[66] Though both smuggled and trafficked individuals may leave a country willingly, an element of deceit is employed in cases of trafficking, as we saw in Priti's story. Smuggled and trafficked persons may face similar dangers and discomforts in their journeys. Upon arrival however, trafficked individuals are "put in a situation of debt bondage and forced into slavery-like practices in the sex or labour market."[67] While prostitution may be the goal or purpose of trafficking, trafficking itself is a lengthy process involving recruitment or abduction, travel and transit, and ultimately exploitation upon reaching the area of destination.[68] From a human rights perspective, trafficking is a violation of the Universal Declaration of Human Rights, Articles 4, 5, and 13.[69] Indeed, many groups assert that women's trafficking, a torturous activity that is carried out with blatant disregard of sovereign boundaries, qualifies for the definition of slavery.

In an article on trafficking of women and children in the Americas, Alison Phinney, for the Inter-American Commission of Women, argues that, "Regardless of how they are recruited and transported, most women and children trafficked for sexual exploitation are denied at some point the right to liberty, the right not to be held in slavery or involuntary servitude, the right to be free from cruel and inhumane treatment, the right to be free from violence, and the right to health. . . . It is also an issue which speaks clearly to global injustices of wealth and power—the most trafficked people worldwide are women and children of low economic status. . . ."[70] (The practice was mentioned briefly in Chapter 3, particularly as it relates to children.) Facing persistent poverty, families in many regions around the globe make whatever use they can of their women and girls. Many young women, including 86% of Nepali prostitutes in one survey, are tricked into prostitution, often through the offer of jobs,[71] while others are sold by their families or neighbors. Once in the hands of the pimp, women are trapped in lives of continual rape and abuse.

The economic desperation created by globalization provides the conditions for the rapid growth in human trafficking. In some regions, globalization has made it easier for women to be smuggled across borders or even halfway around the globe, brought from poorer countries to wealthier ones. Technical innovations (cell phones and other devices) have served traffickers by providing ease of communication. Women from Vietnam, China, and Burma are shipped off to the Philippines, Taiwan, and Korea; women from Africa are brought into Europe; Indonesian women become maids in Saudi Arabia; and women from Eastern Europe find themselves in Western Europe.[72] Women from Southeast Asia and Mexico are trafficked into the U.S. in an alarmingly prevalent and largely hidden trade.[73]

HEALTH AND OTHER CONSEQUENCES

The health consequences resulting from these violations of human rights are profound, especially for younger women—and many are young; the desired age for prostitutes in Asia, for example, is thirteen to sixteen years old.[74]

WOMEN'S COURAGE: SUMY, UKRAINE. Since 1999, Sumy Local Crisis Center has worked against violent and exploitative treatment of women in Sumy, Ukraine. Many Ukrainian women have entered or been sold to the sex industry in order to support themselves and their families financially. With the increase in sex trafficking in the area, the group has tailored its programs to curb the spread of the industry through direct support to women survivors of sex work and through raising public awareness about violence against women. The Center offers psychological and social assistance to women who have been trafficked and/or have worked as sex workers. This rehabilitation process provides support to help women adjust and find alternate means of income. The group also partners with local law enforcement officials and shares insights on recognizing and handling situations of violence against women.

The poor quality of food and care most women experience results in a high incidence of preventable diseases like malaria and tuberculosis.[75] Frequent physical abuse results in broken bones, cuts, mutilation and other injury. Sex workers, particularly those who have been trafficked away from their homes and are thus most vulnerable to exploitation, can exercise little control over their clients in terms of sexual practices and condom use. Thus the women contract sexually transmitted infections and suffer other complications, such as vaginal irritation and pelvic inflammatory disease.[76]

Because of their biological vulnerability, young girls are more susceptible to all of these conditions. They are the least able to resist, and therefore face increased exploitation. And when they have medical problems, their pimps are reluctant to provide medical attention; bringing an obviously abused child to a clinic or hospital poses a risk and danger to the child's "owner."[77]

As discussed earlier, AIDS transmission is now a major source of concern with respect to trafficked women. In Bombay, for example, there were about 13,500 Nepalese women carrying the HIV virus in the mid-1990s.[78] Upon discovering that girls were HIV positive, Indian brothel owners sent them back across the border to Nepal. At home, however, they were rejected by their friends and family, and, through media exposure and enforced medical examinations, their reputations have been permanently tainted. Ultimately, these young women may turn back to sex work for lack of an alternative.

WOMEN'S COURAGE: PHNOM PENH, CAMBODIA. The Praleung Foundation, created in 2005, is "led, owned, and run by survivors of trafficking and businesswomen working toward economic justice." Because trafficking survivors are often shunned by their families and left with little means of supporting themselves financially, the foundation was established as a worker-owned and -operated business venture to help survivors of sex trafficking gain economic independence, while also advocating for increased awareness among Cambodians to reduce the stigma associated with trafficking victims. From the 1970s through the mid-1990s, the people of Cambodia suffered civil war, genocide and starvation, followed by more civil war, resulting in many deaths and the destruction of the social and political structure of the country.

A continually unstable political situation and persistent poverty has resulted in Cambodia today being one of the most active sex trafficking centers in the world. Although technically illegal, prostitution and the sex trafficking of women and children flourish, bringing in millions of dollars each year for organized crime rings and the officials that support them. Given resistance to enforcing anti-trafficking laws at the national level, increased awareness and political pressure from inside Cambodia and the international community is vital in ending the cycle of exploitation.

Praleung (meaning "soul" in Khmer) provides social rehabilitation for survivors and sex workers by establishing a network of support, providing business management training, and developing income-generating activities to help survivors earn sustainable incomes, thus reducing the likelihood that they will be forced back into sex work. Praleung staff, who are also shareholders, are involved in every step of the business design, to ensure the continued involvement of sex workers and survivors in the organization's development, while providing an opportunity for hands-on business training.

Yet back in the brothels, women still do not have the social power to negotiate condom use, so the vicious cycle is perpetuated and more people become infected with HIV.

Even more prevalent than physical illness is the psychological distress of trafficked women, with rates of depression near 80% in one cross-country study; other emotional reactions include hopelessness and rage.[79] Women trapped in prostitution must make what they can of their situation—some are able to send money home to relatives, though most will never contact their

WOMEN'S COURAGE: KATHMANDU, BAGMATI, NEPAL. In some regions of
Nepal, women and girls are sold to sex traffickers to help their families survive
financially. Formed in 2003, Mukti (Salvation) Nepal introduces women to alternate means of income generation in order to reduce the rates of sex trafficking.
Mukti's women's center provides counseling, legal assistance, education, and
vocational training for women to sustain themselves without turning to sex
trafficking or staying in abusive relationships. Working with former prostitutes
and with police groups, Mukti has also been able to arrange for the safe return
to their homes of women and girls forced into prostitution. Through its activities, Mukti strives to change the social situation of women and girls in Nepal
by encouraging them to enter the paid labor force.

families again. Some women may even assist their pimps or become traffickers
themselves, sharing somewhat in the profits of this lucrative industry. But most
of the women forced into such a violent existence struggle simply to survive,
exploited by those around them and ignored by most everyone else.

In most countries, trafficked women, if found by authorities, are classified as illegal immigrants. (This happens even in the U.S., where trafficked
women are not officially classified as illegal immigrants; unfortunately,
however, because of flaws in the process, they often are treated as illegals.)
They are then jailed and deported to their countries of origin. Back home,
however, life is still tough. Traffickers often find escapees and return them to
prostitution.[80] Even if women return to their families, they may face revenge
from criminals and punishment by their native country's law enforcement,
which may cite them again for being illegal immigrants.[81] Family and friends,
furthermore, may ostracize the woman and disown her because, as a prosti-
tute, she is unfit for marriage, or because the stigma of sex work is so strong.
In many ways the experience of being trafficked—something that a woman
has no control over—continues to shadow her at home. Trafficked women,
confronted by rejection from their communities and in despair over a lack
of alternative ways to earn money, sometimes return to the sex industry.

In addition to facilitating the flow of trafficking victims, globalization
has contributed to the expansion of trafficking in other ways. Dennis Altman, in his book *Global Sex*, argues that "changes in our understandings of
and attitudes toward sexuality are both affected by and reflect the larger

changes of globalization. Moreover, as with globalization itself, the changes are simultaneously leading to greater homogeneity and greater inequality. As all but insignificant pockets of the world's peoples are brought within the scope of global capitalism, a consumer culture is developing which cuts across borders and cultures and is universalized through advertising, mass media, and the enormous flows of capital and people in the contemporary world." These days, he continues, "The provision of male sexual pleasure is part of sexual regimes in societies marked by the imperative to produce—namely those in the early stages of industrialization—as much as in those dominated by the imperative to consume. Prostitution and pornography flourish in both, and are largely created as means of satisfying male 'desire' through the services, in both the corporeal and fantasy realms, of women."[82] Moreover, this worldwide business of supplying the globally inflated demand for sexual services is enabled by other negative effects of globalization, such as "increased inequalities between countries and between social classes within countries; increased landlessness and debt in rural areas; development-related environmental degradation which increases rural poverty and displacement; and growing concentration of land ownership due to expansion of agribusiness and reliance on export crops."[83]

However, as Swedish Deputy Prime Minister Margareta Winberg states: "The true problem lies with the buyers. Far too many men . . . see women as objects, as something that can be bought and sold. . . . A woman's body is not the same as a glass of brandy or an ice cream after a good dinner. There is a difference between shoelaces and girls' bodies."[84]

AGENTS OF TRAFFICKING

No longer able to rely on agriculture or other sources of income to sustain themselves, women are often forced to migrate to a city where they may be drawn into prostitution through an employment agency that may seem legitimate. Such agencies are often fronts for organized crime rings, sophisticated networks of recruiters, document forgers, and people who smuggle victims across borders and work in tandem with strip clubs, massage parlors, and prostitution rings.[85] In the process, organized crime rings that facilitate trafficking exploit borders made porous through the process of globalization, garnering profits of between $5 and $20 billion a year.[86]

Trafficking is lucrative because it yields "steady profits from forced labor and sexual exploitation over a long period of time," and "humans may be sold repeatedly and continue to work and earn money for their owners."[87] At the same time, traffickers keep their costs low by forcing women to live in dilapidated conditions and giving their victims little food and medical attention. The women are kept in bondage until they pay off their debt—although even then, they are often never released, their "owners" maintaining that ongoing costs continually add to the debt. Thus the crime rings carry out a modern-day form of slavery, one in which women are forced to obey traffickers down to the smallest detail or face severe injury, and, in many cases, even death.

The way Mexican trafficking networks (which are often family businesses) operate is typical of how such enterprises work.[88] For example, the Los Lenones, a group based in Tenancingo, near Mexico City, troll rural and suburban towns throughout Mexico, targeting their victims. Boy apprentices, who drop out of school at age twelve, begin their training by raping and then pimping out a couple of girls.[89] When the boys are deemed experienced enough, they attend school dances and stake out bus stations and factories, where young girls gather and socialize. They then seduce the girls by buying them material goods and heaping them with affection. Once a girl is alone, however, a Lenone will drug and beat her, and take her to a far-away location. Then her "training" ensues. Girls in Santo Tomas, for example, are broken in by being forced to have sex with twenty to thirty men a day, seven days a week, for months on end, before they are sent to the United States as prostitutes.[90] If they refuse or try to escape, they will be beaten or killed.

Worldwide, traffickers employ a variety of methods to ensnare their victims. Some persuade the parents, relatives, or husband of a woman to sell her. More ruthless traffickers kidnap women, or plan a rape, after which the woman, ostracized from her social network, is obliged to enter prostitution.[91] Others trick women with false prospects of marriage, vacations, student grants, political asylum, and visas.[92] The victims of these scams, aspiring to higher standards of living like those glamorized in the media, are enticed to leave their homes in search of better lives—sometimes by answering an obscure ad.

According to UNIFEM, "Women and girls may be pushed toward trafficking as an alternative to the drudgery, danger and exploitation inherent

WOMEN'S COURAGE: HAIFA, ISRAEL. Isha L'Isha, the Haifa Feminist Center, addresses the practice of sex trafficking by raising public awareness about the issue, by rescuing sex-trafficked women, and by promoting the economic empowerment of women. The women who founded the Center in 1983 had these goals: "advancing the status of all women in Israel by empowering and encouraging them to become leaders in their communities; creating solidarity and cooperation between women of different backgrounds; campaigning for full civil rights and equal opportunities for women; opposing all forms of violence against women; and promoting collaboration between women's organizations."

One of the Center's recent projects provides a variety of courses to help low-income women improve their financial status. Between 2002 and 2003, the group rescued 157 trafficked women and helped them return home. In an environment where clashing traditions exist, the Center provides working space and training to other women's groups and offers services to women of different religions and ethnicities, to demonstrate that all women deserve to be treated with respect.

in the traditional lot of women in poor countries—especially in rural areas. Young women may literally be running away from the prospects of marriage and a large family, the dangers of high maternal mortality, the trauma of high infant mortality, and the drudgery involved in fetching fuel and water, caring for their families, and contributing to the family income through labour-intensive agriculture or the other kinds of low paid and unskilled jobs available locally."[93]

The growth of the internet has fed the trafficking phenomenon. In countries of economic hardship, such as some of the states of the former Soviet Union, young people search online for better prospects abroad. Aija, a young Latvian woman, is one example. Through the internet, she learned about and was promised a job in Israel that paid $1,000 a month. After making her way from Latvia to Israel, she was greeted, robbed of her passport, and sold to a brothel owner for $15,000. She was forced to have sex with as many as thirty clients a day. Later, she was shoved from brothel to brothel, her price declining each time, until at last she was thrown out on the streets, left to find her own way back to Latvia, with limited language skills and no money.[94]

Traffickers also sometimes operate through so-called marriage agencies, which offer "mail-order bride" catalogues, to enable men to obtain a foreign sexual partner or spouse.[95] The process, however, is not regulated. The agencies do not run criminal background checks on the men; indeed some of the agencies have ties to organized crime, particularly in Russia. In addition, such agencies often advertise minors. Nonetheless, there were more than two hundred mail-order bride agencies in the United States in 1998. A search on the internet reveals hundreds—if not thousands—of such agencies. That year alone, they imported four to six thousand women, mainly from the Philippines and Eastern Europe.[96]

Traffickers also implement domestic employment schemes, by which women are brought from overseas, their documents are seized, and they are forced to work long hours. Usually their salaries are paid to the placement organization, which may in turn give the servant a nominal percentage.[97] Many are simply exploited like slaves, forbidden to leave the house. Approximately 3,800 domestic servants are smuggled into the United States each year on temporary employment visas to work for diplomats and officials at international agencies.[98]

Supik Indrawati, an Indonesian, came to the United States to work as a maid after her aunt convinced her that wages in Indonesia would never allow her to fulfill her dream of opening her own boutique.[99] Indrawati arranged for a job as a maid for a wealthy family living in a Los Angeles suburb. They treated her like an indentured servant. Indrawati had to work twelve hours a day, seven days a week, including holidays. She cleaned the dirt from her boss' toenails and emptied debris from gutters as rain poured down on her. Worse still, she was never paid a wage. Instead, her boss family sent about $1,800 to her family over two and a half years. Her "owners" were finally exposed only after Indrawati painstakingly penned a letter in English—it took her a month to write—alerting her neighbor that the husband in the household was sexually assaulting her. Although this case may seem extreme, it is not uncommon. Often women shipped to foreign countries for ostensibly legal labor are trapped, unable to speak the language, scared of their bosses, and longing for home. Having left their native countries hoping for advancement, they find themselves in a nightmare of perpetual labor and unhealthy working conditions.[100]

The United States is a major portal for trafficked people. The CIA estimated that between 18,000 and 20,000 were shipped into the United States in

WOMEN'S COURAGE: SANTIAGO, CHILE. The Fundación Margen (meaning the Margin Foundation, so named because of the marginalized position of sex workers in Santiago) works to improve the quality of life of sex workers and help child prostitutes get off the street. The Foundation has collaborated with health centers to modify their office hours to accommodate sex workers' irregular schedules. Furthermore, sex workers receive reproductive health information and treatment for HIV/AIDS. The group also provides women's rights awareness programs and psychological counseling to help sex workers discover sustainable lifestyles. Founded in 1998 to "meet the needs of those who have been sexually exploited, including children, young adults, and women," the group focuses on the growing population of sex workers in Chile. Chile has seen a rising trend in sex work. As a marginalized group, sex workers tend to develop more problems such as sexually transmitted diseases, depression, and social isolation.

2004, about 10,000 for sex.[101] In 2006, the U.S. State Department estimated 14,500 to 17,500, but NGOs continue to believe that about 45,000 to 50,000 women are trafficked into the U.S. every year, holding that recent research has not shown significant decreases in levels.[102] Such victims have traditionally arrived from Southeast Asia and Latin American, although recently more have come from Southern and Eastern European countries.[103] They are sent to work in predominantly urban areas, to about thirty major destinations, including Los Angeles and New York City. Eventually, trafficking victims may suffer from tuberculosis, hepatitis, ulcers, malnutrition, sexually transmitted diseases, and cervical cancer.[104] Mental health problems, including anxiety, mood, personality, and psychotic disorders, add even more strain to trafficked women already burdened with compromised physical health. A young trafficking victim typically remains "of use" in the United States for two to four years. Afterwards, she may be killed, dumped, or deported. The least likely outcome is that she survives to testify against her traffickers; nevertheless, this does happen occasionally.

Since forced labor and mail-order bride marriages are officially considered "trafficking," whereas the smuggling of migrant women who voluntarily leave their homes is not, some defense attorneys for traffickers have attempted to argue that because trafficked women are sometimes not physically confined, they are not technically captives.[105] But the reality is that trafficking victims are plunged into a climate of fear and extreme vulnerability, one in which women undergo psychological and physical abuse on a continuous basis. This is often the case for prostitutes who work on their home soil as well.

Sex Work by Choice

Such discussions and distinctions raise questions about whether it is possible for women ever to undertake sex work "voluntarily," in the sense that they choose to do it for money when offered real alternatives, rather than being forced into it. Many women in the sex trade in richer countries and states, such as the Netherlands and Nevada, argue that it is their right to use their bodies as they choose, that they have entered into sex work voluntarily. In these places and some others, groups and authorities have worked to regulate sex work in order to ensure basic health and wage levels.

Things could be worse for these women; they have indeed made their own choices. But the question remains, how limited was this array of choices? Most women enter the sex industry out of economic necessity. Some, whom economists refer to as "floating" sex workers, fulfill traditional family roles in the daytime and earn fast cash in red-light districts at night. According to a survey by Sleightholme and Sinha of Calcutta prostitutes, 52% said they took on sex work because of financial difficulties. In the same survey, 28% reported that they turned to the sex industry as a result of spousal violence, 24% because of family problems, and 10% because they were deserted or divorced.[106] It seems that, in addition to poverty, unequal social relations between men and women play a significant role in determining a woman's entrance into the sex industry.

In some communities in Thailand, prostitution has become socially validated and women support their families through sex work.[107] Most of the young women come from the north and northeast, areas characterized by poverty, arid land, and a per capita average income of less than half that in other parts of the country. When these uneducated, unskilled women arrive in urban areas, they often first go into wage labor. However, if a woman loses her job, she may have no choice but to turn to prostitution. There are perceived advantages to going into the sex trade, especially in countries where prostitution has been legalized. Incomes are sometimes much higher than for factory labor. Moreover, the flexible working hours offer single mothers greater flexibility in their personal and sexual lives, and make them less dependent on men for material goods.[108]

In an article on "prostitution and tourism in Southeast Asia," Wendy Lee argues that sex work is a consequence of "women's lack of economic and educational opportunity, their neglect in development or land reform schemes, their subjugation within the family, their domestic burdens and family responsibilities, and their exploitation in new forms of factory work."[109] Nevertheless, some Thai prostitutes do not view themselves in this light. They maintain their dignity and emphasize their self-sufficiency. Most "voluntary" Thai sex workers also return to their home villages; for them, prostitution is a temporary means to earn money. Recently, Thailand has become an international leader in prosecuting traffickers and protecting victims, having toughened its trafficking laws in 1997. The Thai government has also created shelters and worked with neighboring governments to ensure that trafficking victims return to their home countries.[110] Indeed, the Thai program has adopted a grassroots approach that involves agencies at local as well as national levels, and includes police, immigration officers, and social workers.

In at least one village in the Yunnan province of southern China, attitudes toward the social value of daughters have become more positive because of their sex work abroad. In some villages of this region, a majority of young women are leaving to work as prostitutes in Thailand and Malaysia. Their work yields more money and more comfortable houses for their families at home. In his article entitled "A Village Grows Rich Off its Main Export: its Daughters," Howard French describes a twenty-year-old girl, Ye Xiang, who spent two years in the Thai sex trade. Ye Xiang is "eager to return to that work," on the chance that she may not only earn more money but also meet and marry a wealthy man. "'There's a guy in Malaysia, and he calls me every day,' she announced proudly, showing off the cellular phone he had bought her."[111]

It is imperative to point out that there are vast distinctions between those choosing sex work and those forced into it. A critical question that cannot easily be answered is this: How many well-off sex workers are there, compared to women and girls trapped in brothels? The latter is probably a vast sea of misery in comparison with a few islands of choice. Studies have shown overwhelmingly that women enter or are lured or forced into prostitution out of economic necessity, having few or no alternatives.

WOMEN'S COURAGE: BANGKOK, THAILAND. The Global Alliance Against Traffic in Women (GAATW) was formed at an international workshop on Migration and Traffic in Women, held in Chiangmai, Thailand, in October 1994. The aim of the Alliance is "not to stop the migration of women but to ensure the protection of the human rights of these women by authorities and agencies." Since it was founded, the group has initiated a variety of seminars and programs related to trafficking. It has also helped to facilitate the self-empowerment of sex workers in the fight for their rights, rather than the more traditional approach of "saving" women from prostitution. A staff of nine and a handful of rotating volunteers run the group's programs.

Currently, GAATW has more than 150 institutional and individual members around the world, representing activists from Latin America, Africa, Eastern Europe, and Asia. The primary activities of GAATW involve documentation and publication, reflecting its work in advocacy, research, and training, all of which has begun to affect the approach to trafficking by international agencies, including the UN. GAATW's initiative is a crucial step in the advancement of the anti-trafficking movement across regions. This is especially true in the wake of anti-trafficking policies initiated by the U.S. government that GAATW believes simultaneously victimize migrant and trafficked women and also makes impossible the delivery of legal, social, and medical services to any trafficked persons engaging in sex work.

GAATW holds that the adoption of anti-prostitution policies in organizations that receive U.S. government funding impedes feminist organizations from functioning within a rights-based framework that takes into consideration the sophisticated social and economic circumstances women face, as well as proven methods of improving the legal rights and health status of migrant women. According to the framework used by the U.S. government, activities like skills-training for women engaged in sex work to find alternative sources of income, or holding HIV/AIDS prevention seminars, violate these anti-prostitution policies. Despite these challenges in the international arena, GAATW has been a leader in addressing much of the U.S. government's work to decouple human rights work from anti-trafficking work. Its research, publications, and capacity, building programs have been used in five continents to "ensure that safe migration and protecting women's rights are at the core of anti-trafficking efforts."

Taking Action

In the face of worldwide trafficking, a problem that for the most part seems intractable, there may be some basis for optimism. New United Nations protocols and conventions hold the promise of more protection for victims. UNIFEM, under the leadership of Noeleen Heyzer, has played an important role. In December 2000, some eighty countries signed the United Nations Protocol to Prevent, Suppress, and Punish Trafficking in Persons. This legislation recognized the international scope of the problem, and, more importantly, paved the way for a comprehensive legal definition that will make trafficking a human rights violation.[112]

In the United States, the situation is less clear. The Victims of Trafficking and Violence Protection Act, passed in 2000, increased penalties for certain trafficking offenses; the bill also allocated money for victim protection and benefits and for prevention programs in countries with the largest trafficking problems. The Act calls for the implementation of economic sanctions should countries not adhere to trafficking laws. Offending states that do not meet minimum standards for the elimination of trafficking are to be denied "non-humanitarian, non-trade-related foreign assistance."[113] Some feminist groups (such as the Global Alliance Against Traffic in Women, described on the previous page) have challenged the anti-trafficking policies initiated by the U.S. government, holding that they victimize migrant and trafficked women and make it difficult for sex workers to receive health and other services.

Furthermore, many women who have been misled and abused by traffickers are not passive or helpless.[114] Some choose to leave their countries of origin because they are strong and independent and resolve to start better lives in a completely foreign locale. That same strength allows them to endure the trauma that the traffickers may inflict upon them, so that they can recover from their situation with dignity and respect. Indeed, some women act as witnesses against their traffickers in courts of law, even when threatened with retaliation.[115]

Combating trafficking, however, calls for more than just women's resilience. It requires that societies invest in women on a fundamental level and over the long term, making sure that girls and women have equal access to education and skills training, access to the paid labor force, as well as a chance to participate as full citizens in the political and social life of their communities. Although trafficking is in part a consequence of inequities stemming from capitalism and globalization, it is possible that, working together, women and men can employ some of the benefits of globalization—instantaneous communication, the uninhibited flow of knowledge and ideas, and major upgrades in the technological infrastructure—to prevent trafficking. Globalization of communications is helping women as we unite across national borders to work for human rights and justice.

She left, no cheek turned pale, no
  lip trembled.
The doors did not hear the story of
  her death . . .
The news tumbled down the
  avenue its echo not finding a
  shelter
So it stayed forgotten in some hole,
  its depression the moon
  lamenting.

  —Nazik al-Malaika, "Lament of a Worthless Woman,"
  1952, Iraq[1]

. . . already old age is wrinkling my
skin and my hair is turning from black
to grey; my knees begin to tremble
and my legs no longer carry me. . .
oh but once, once we were like young deer
. . . what can I do?. . .

  —Sappho, Greece, 6th century BC[2]

9

Aging in a Man's World

DOÑA EULOGIA HAS LIVED her sixty-five years in Esquencachi, an indigenous community in Bolivia. "I live on my own apart from two grandchildren, Lucia, eleven and Dania, six. I have four children—three girls and a boy. The girls have married and moved to other areas. My son's house is here, but he's working away. I look after my grandchildren who are orphans of one of my daughters. Their father abandoned them so I have to feed us all." Increasingly, young adults move to the cities to try to make a better living but, given Bolivia's recession, most earn only enough to keep themselves alive, and cannot afford to send money home for their children and parents.

The burden of feeding and educating the children falls on grandparents like Doña Eulogia. "We eat potatoes and wheat. It's not much. This year we don't have so many potatoes; we had a bad crop. I grow all our food myself and I keep animals. If there's no school, the girls help me with the llamas." Doña Eulogia is weary, but there is no rest in sight. "The work is the hardest thing, but how can I stop? We would have nothing to live on."[3]

Doña Eulogia's story exemplifies many challenges faced by older women throughout the world. Doña Eulogia is poor. She is tired. She lives in a rural community while her children have migrated to the city. She depends upon her own labor for her survival. Yet she also supports her grandchildren, serving as their primary care provider since their mother died.

Though she is marginalized in her own country, Doña Eulogia is a member of one of the world's fastest-growing population groups: older women. Coping with aging while struggling to survive is a challenge that eventually befalls all impoverished women (and men) who survive long enough. As with so many aspects of life, women bear a special burden. We know this because of stories and a few studies. In general, data and research on elderly women in resource-poor countries is minimal, though no doubt as this group grows in number, more information will become available. Statistics that are available paint a rather grim picture.

Demographics and the Feminization of Aging

The world has never had so many old people, and the pace of growth of the world's older population has accelerated. According to the Population Reference Bureau, the global population of people aged sixty-five or older was estimated at 461 million in 2004, an increase of 10.3 million since 2003.[4] The majority of the elderly are women, because on average women live longer than men (globally sixty-nine years versus sixty-five).[5] More than half of the world's women aged sixty years and over are living in developing regions, numbering 198 million compared with 135 million in the developed regions.[6] In some countries, notably Japan, a woman's longevity reaches over eighty years on average. This is a full 25% longer than the global average and approaching or exceeding 50% longer than the average for women in the poorest countries. In some countries in Africa (Botswana, Kenya, Lesotho, and Namibia, for example), life expectancy of women and men has dropped to between thirty-five and forty years, primarily because of the HIV/AIDS pandemic.

Nevertheless, this demographic group—women over sixty years of age—will only continue to grow as many poorer countries experience the increase in life expectancy already evident in richer countries. In twenty years, more than one billion people over the age of sixty will inhabit the world, with 70% found in poorer countries, more than half of them women.[7] In about seventy-five developing countries, there is a 150% projected growth rate for older women in the next thirty years.[8] Worldwide, women make up 54% of people aged sixty and over and 62% of elderly aged eighty and over. Experts call this growing percentage of females among the elderly the "feminization of aging."[9]

Longer life expectancy is no doubt a sign of progress, of increasing wealth and access to medical care among all people, and it is tempting to think that the problem of women in poverty is gradually ebbing. But, as discussed below, the situation is more complicated, and not nearly as rosy.

Not only are the old likely to be women, but they are also likely to be poor. Todd Peterson, chief executive of HelpAge International, explains that "the developing world faces the harsh reality that it is growing old before it is growing rich, with potentially traumatic consequences for old people, their families, and their societies."[10] The consequences of aging and poverty are not merely traumatic; they violate the human rights of the elderly. Article 22 of the Universal Declaration of Human Rights proclaims: "Everyone, as a member of society, has the right to social security and is entitled to the realization, through national effort and international cooperation . . . of the economic, social and cultural rights indispensable for his[/her] dignity and the free development of his[/her] personality." Put simply, poverty among older people, combined with social exclusion and discriminatory attitudes, is a violation of human rights.

Poverty, social exclusion, and discriminatory attitudes are generally more acute for older women than they are for older men. Women's disadvantaged status in childhood and adulthood is intensified in older age. Aging is a women's issue not only because the majority of older people are women but also because aging is a gendered experience. Throughout life "and in all societies," writes Clara Pratt, whose work is referenced in a 1999 UN International Institute on Ageing publication, "males and females play different roles, receive different rewards, and experience differing realities. . . . Many have suffered throughout their lives from poor health care, malnutrition, illiteracy and low social status simply because they were born female."[11]

These gendered experiences come together and may be magnified at the end of a woman's life.[12] The UN International Research and Training Institute for the Advancement of Women (INSTRAW) observes that "Examination of the myths and stereotypes that surround older women shows how gender bias and discrimination intensify in old age everywhere, although cultural forms may differ."[13]

WOMEN'S COURAGE: DHAKA, BANGLADESH. In 1998, a former teacher/ democracy supporter formed the Rakhaing Women's Union (RWU) with the goal of elevating the condition of women, including elderly women, living in regions along the Bangladesh–Burma–India border. Many women who lost their husbands and families in Burma's violent March 1997 coup migrated to the border region as refugees. In those areas, women's rights are often neglected and violated. The RWU sets out to provide aid to refugee women, both young and old. RWU has set up health clinics where they provide healthcare and HIV/AIDS education. Women are also taught basic language and computer skills to help them improve their status in society. The group also trains women to become educators and leaders and to spread the message of women's rights.

What Does it Mean to Be Elderly?

What does it mean to be "elderly" or "aging"? Women in West Africa live an average of fifty-two years; in South Asia the average is sixty-two. In New Zealand and in the United States women can expect to live at least to eighty.[14] In some countries, women over fifty or even younger may be considered "old." They are easily grandmothers, having been married in their teens and given birth soon after. Thus, it is common to find grandmothers who are in their forties, considering, as we did in the chapter on adolescence, that half of girls aged nineteen worldwide are already married and many of them are mothers. Women in Africa, Asia, and the Caribbean who present themselves and are treated as "old" may be in their fifties or even their forties. Ill health, hard work, and multiple births have tired them out, and they look (and, in fact, are) old. Most international statistics on aging, when they refer to "older people" and "older populations," are describing people age sixty-five or older, sometimes describing people age eighty or older as the "oldest old." For the purposes of this discussion, however, we are focusing on women who are considered or consider themselves "older."

Do the words "older" or "elderly" bring to mind someone who is no longer productive? Or someone who is living a life of leisure, enjoying the "golden years"? Does the word imply an "elder," a person who over the years has accumulated and can now share wisdom? Or does the word describe someone who is bent over, sick, and disabled, a person who is dependent on others? The "elderly" and "aging" in our world are all of these people.

Some members of the current generation of elderly persons have benefited from improved public health over the years but have suffered from being stereotyped and discriminated against. Despite the diversity of women around the world and the vast range of their experiences, both positive and negative, women who are beyond reproductive age are grouped into a homogenous mass of persons who are generally seen to lack autonomy and require support from family or society at large. As a result, older women's needs are often overlooked, and the many ways in which they can and do contribute to society may be disregarded.

How is an older woman's health affected by the consequences of a lifetime engaged in reproductive and productive labor, increased social exclusion and isolation, and the continuing role of caretaker? This chapter addresses that question.

A Lifetime of Work

Even in wealthy countries, older women's productive contributions are seldom formally recognized. Many perceptions of older women as unproductive stem from the belief that women's productive role is limited to their reproductive capacity. Women's value is believed to lie in their ability to bear children, and particularly sons. Once women pass the age of reproductive potential, they are seen as useless. It is assumed that they will no longer contribute to society and will instead become burdens, dependent upon support from their children and possibly their national government. Margaret Locke, who writes on menopause among women in Japan, explains this as "the thinly disguised assumption . . . that reproduction of the species is what female life is all about, and that the situation [in which] we now find ourselves in 'advanced' societies [i.e., that older women may be relevant irrespective of their reproductive role], is not only an anomaly but a costly superfluity."[15]

Many more people around the world are living longer lives, thanks to medical advances, according to the 1997 health report of the World Health Organization (WHO). In richer countries, however, cancers, heart attacks, strokes, and other illnesses in which diet and lack of exercise are often believed to play a part are on the rise. So, too, in poorer countries, where lifestyles

are changing and people are living longer. They are living longer but paying the price of living with chronic diseases.

Improved maternal care has added years to the lives of many women
around the world, but for the 600,000 women each year whose lack of access
results in their dying as a result of pregnancy and childbirth-related injuries
and illnesses, this is not so. As discussed in Chapter 5, 95% of deaths relating
to maternity occur in developing countries. Nevertheless, given population
growth rates, more and more women are surviving into old age. As more
women are living longer, menopause has become a subject of interest and even
a major issue of women's health, particularly in more developed countries.
Locke notes that in the 1990s the great interest in menopause can likely be
attributed to "the sheer number of women, baby boomers, soon to become
old, and hence a burden to society."[16]

Increased longevity conjures up images of better diet and exercise, reduced
smoking, greater financial security, and access to sophisticated medical interventions to fight cancer and heart disease and other ailments that chiefly
afflict people in their later years in rich countries. All of these are signs of
an increase in wealth. But as noted, these are not necessarily the forces driving the increase in women's longevity. For most women, increased longevity
is the result of simple medical interventions at birth (which applies to men
too) and at the point of giving birth. In industrialized countries, these can
be complex and expensive interventions. But the interventions that have the
biggest impact are inexpensive. Ensuring healthy infants (reducing infant
mortality) involves the health of the mother and access to prenatal care and
nutrition. In the case of maternal mortality, the critical factors are women's
access to nutrition during pregnancy and access to medical assistance and
possibly emergency care during childbirth. Ensuring healthy childbirth need
not take a lot of money or fancy hospitals, but it does take the will to provide
education to women and to trust community-based people to deliver basic
care. Such critical interventions, which should be available to all, are not in
themselves signs of the end of poverty. The fact that women are living longer
does not mean they are leaving poverty.

The perceptions of older women as "unproductive" and "dependent" are
ingrained in government policies that fail to compensate women for their
labor and focus on the elderly solely receiving goods through social security

and welfare programs.[17] Faced with the prospect of discrimination and lack of financial support in their later years, many women must attempt to find paid employment throughout their lives. Retirement for the vast majority of people in the world is a luxury. According to the United Nations Development Programme (UNDP), only a fifth of people over sixty worldwide have income security, and this group is likely to be predominantly male.[18] Since men are more likely to work in the formal economy and to serve in pensioned jobs like the military, and since they die sooner, they have greater financial security as they age than do women. The work that women perform, including care of children and other relatives, as well as labor in the informal sector, is under-compensated or not compensated at all. As noted earlier, women earn only 10% of the world's income but contribute about 60% of the work. In the developing world, only 53% of females are in the formal paid workforce, versus 84% of males. This discrepancy is a result of lack of education, sex discrimination in the work place, and women's household duties.[19] According to demographers Ronald Lee and John Haaga, failure to fairly compensate women's labor applies even in the case of systems such as Social Security in the United States.[20]

For many women in poorer countries, retirement or the end of labor is out of the question. A study in Botswana, for example, revealed that women over sixty continued to spend 16% of their time on work outside the home and one quarter of their time on household work, in addition to time spent providing care for themselves and others.[21] The UN International Institute on Ageing has reported that 41% of all women over the age of fifteen are involved in the formal economy while another 10% to 20% work in the informal economy and remain part of the informal economy well into their older years.[22]

Even if women are involved in the formal economy, it is difficult to receive benefits. Writing on pension standards laid out by the World Bank, Suzanne and James Paul observed that when Latin American governments reduced pensions to comply with World Bank standards, women seeking jobs in the paid work force found themselves doubly disadvantaged by being women and elderly. Unable to find jobs, many had no choice but to depend upon the support of families, forced into positions of dependence and vulnerability.[23] In Ghana, the government's policy of offering free healthcare is available to

WOMEN'S COURAGE: AIBONITO, PUERTO RICO. Envejecer Juntas (Growing Old Together) was founded in Aibonito, Puerto Rico, in 2004, by a group of older feminist lawyers, sociologists, and activists who, not having an established retirement plan, recognized that services available to women over fifty, particularly those living alone (divorced women, widows, and women single by choice), were severely lacking in their region. The group comments that "The issue of aging is not discussed, and we avoid addressing it until we are already old women. To be an old woman is a shame and it is necessary to hide it in every way. However, it constitutes a natural occurrence from which we cannot escape." The group adds that "The capacity of women at forty-five is still accepted in many arenas, but beyond sixty-five we are considered beings without feelings, without needs, the only [women over sixty-five] who are accepted are grandmothers; we are seen as incapable, asexualized, our abilities are negated and the sexuality of an elderly woman is a source of repugnance and mocking."

Envejecer Juntas programs involve petitioning for meetings with local legislators and senators to enact legal measures to benefit older women, and developing resources from local agencies to be able to intervene in cases of mistreatment of elderly women by their families, husbands, friends, and children. The group's priority is to advocate for public policies that will improve the lives of women of la tercera edad ("the third age"), "especially against violence and mistreatment of older women and laws that include more health and social benefits."

only those over the age of seventy, though official life expectancy is listed at fifty-five, and retirement age is set at sixty, making it nearly impossible for older women to receive benefits.[24]

Older Women as Caregivers

The perception that older women are useless or unproductive means that their contributions often go unrecognized. However, contributions from older women are critically important to the functioning and maintenance of society. In most societies in the world, older women are with us at our most significant transitions: the moment of birth and the moment of death. Care giving and nurturing are seen as the stereotypical female roles. When we consider the lives of older women, we see how significant and important these roles can be, even as they continue to be undervalued by society in general.

Although the transitions of birth and death are beginning to be medicalized and institutionalized in many societies, it is still true that for the vast majority of people in the world, the first and the last person that we see in our lives is a woman. Tish Sommers, the founder of the Older Women's League, connects the birth and death experiences by noting that at the time of dying, a person is likely to be tended by a woman: "the nurse's aide (significantly one of the least paid and least valued workers in our society). . . . These are, in a sense, the midwives of death."[25]

Women's care-giving activities are of course not limited to the moments of life and death. As they have for generations, women also tend the young, the sick, and the very old. The UN International Institute on Ageing observes that "Women at midlife and older years play a key role in both economic development and family stability in the Latin American and Caribbean region, far beyond that which would be anticipated by their numbers. This is true to such an extent that, if their productive resources and care-giving roles were suddenly withdrawn and abandoned, the effects on the region's economy and social structure would be devastating."[26] In fact, elderly women as caregivers for the young, the ill, and the even older provide more health care than the health care system. The elderly receive 80% of their care informally, from family, friends, and neighbors, the majority of whom are female caregivers.[27] Most of us would agree that such care from family and friends can be a very good thing. But for the caregiver—often uncompensated and unrelieved—such work can be both debilitating and impoverishing.

THE SPECIAL CASE OF HIV/AIDS

In the face of HIV/AIDS in particular, many women are becoming essential parts of social service systems as they become the sole caretakers of their grandchildren and of the sick and dying. The important role of grandmothers as caregivers extends around the world, but it is particularly vital in Africa, where AIDS is destroying a generation of younger adults. Elders, especially older women, are pressed into service, caring for young adults dying of AIDS and for their surviving grandchildren.[28] Over 60% of orphaned children currently live in grandparent-headed households in Namibia, South Africa, and Zimbabwe, and over 50% do in Botswana, Malawi, and Tanzania.[29]

Because government and international intervention is uneven at best, the victims of AIDS have little access to help, and their caretakers have little or no financial or social support. This burden adds a great weight of responsibility, particularly as the majority of the women are widowed and already attempting to survive on very little. In one study of elders caring for people with AIDS or AIDS orphans in Zimbabwe, 89% of the caretakers had no monthly or yearly income whatsoever.[30] The Reproductive Health Outlook highlights many of the ways that HIV/AIDS affects older women. As they state: "A few studies in Africa and Asia have catalogued many negative effects on individual elderly caregivers. These include:

- physical exhaustion from around-the-clock nursing in addition to household chores and child care.

- loneliness and social isolation, either because they cannot leave the sickbed or because they are shunned by friends and neighbors.

- poverty and financial hardships due to lack of time to tend fields or do paid work, the loss of their children's income, and the need to pay for treatment as well as food and clothing for their children and grandchildren.

- emotional distress, grief, and depression."[31]

Caring for a person dying of AIDS or becoming the primary caretaker for young children represents a huge burden for the elderly who have already spent their lives caring for others without any financial compensation. In addition to financial difficulty, these people face physical illness and psychological distress as a result of their difficult roles.[32] Older women are stepping in where governments fail to care for the sick, shouldering the burden of caretaking at great personal cost. Furthermore, because caregiving is traditionally a female role, growing reliance on such home-based care is reinforcing gender inequalities.[33]

These elderly caregivers currently receive little support from the health care system, but international organizations are beginning to focus attention on their needs. These include supplies and training so that older women can do a better job of nursing sick family members and so that they can protect themselves from infection by using standard precautions. They also need counseling to cope with the emotional stress and stigma of their situation, some kind of income support to keep them out of poverty, and affordable health care for their own medical problems.[34] Home- and community-based care programs, such as the "Grandma Cares" project in Thailand, may be an effective and affordable way to meet their needs.[35] Another approach has been proposed in Swaziland: paying women U.S.$30 per month to look after orphans, in an effort to both recognize the value of women's work and also to provide essential economic support.[36]

Health Consequences of a Lifetime of Work

The economic, social, and political inequalities that women face throughout their lifetime are magnified in old age, and many older women in poorer countries live in chronic ill health, according to the World Health Organization (WHO). For example, poverty at older ages often reflects poor economic status earlier in life and is a determinant of health at all stages of life. Countries that have data on poverty by age and sex (mostly the developed countries) show that older women are more likely to be poor than older men.[37]

The WHO reports that poverty is also linked to inadequate access to food and nutrition, and the health of older women often reflects the cumulative impact of poor diets.[38] Years of child bearing, heavy physical labor, and sacrificing her own nutrition to that of her family leaves the older woman with chronic anemia and general malnutrition.[39]

The gendered division of domestic tasks further contributes to older women's poor health. Women often procure and carry water, exposing themselves to malaria and the waterborne diseases of hookworm and schistosomiasis. Additionally, the water may be polluted with agricultural pesticides. Long-term exposure to pesticides has been linked to development of certain cancers and nervous-system impairment.[40] In most societies, women are in charge of cooking. Women in many developing countries spend between three and seven hours each day near an indoor stove, preparing food.[41] Of all deaths attributable to indoor air pollution, 59% are primarily due to chronic obstructive pulmonary disease and lung cancer, with the vast majority of these being of women.[42]

These factors, almost all derived from WHO sources, emphasize that although women may lead longer lives than men, a longer life does not translate into a healthier life. WHO studies in forty-five countries conclude that women can generally expect to spend more years of their lives with some

WOMEN'S COURAGE: JERUSALEM, PALESTINE. The Patient's Friends Society–Jerusalem, founded in 1980, focuses on older women's health and offers the only organized support services for breast cancer patients and survivors in the area, as well as a telephone help line and outreach and community health education. During 2004, the Society organized and implemented 116 health education lectures on osteoporosis, breast cancer/disease, midlife women's health, and STD/HIV. The Sunrise Group, the Society's main project, was established in 2000. It is currently made up of sixty-eight Palestinian breast cancer survivors from various locations who meet monthly for social support and to share ideas and information. In March of 2003, two members of the Sunrise Group attended the Reach to Recovery International Conference in Portugal and were the only breast cancer survivors from the Arab world attending. The Society is currently expanding its osteoporosis project to create a reference data set to understand the prevalence of osteoporosis among Palestinian women, and to provide health education lectures and outreach screening tests.

functional limitations than men.[43] Men are more likely to die—from diseases such as heart failure, stroke, or cancer—whereas women live longer but suffer declining health because of such diseases as arthritis, osteoporosis, and diabetes—as well as cancer, stroke, and heart disease. Although with modern medical care the balance may shift, it is still true that, on a global scale, "men die from their diseases, women live with them."[44]

Social Exclusion and Loss

Discrimination often affects women past reproductive age particularly severely, directly because of ageism compounded with sexism, and indirectly because of the lifelong denial of opportunities that women experience. Older women face isolation, abandonment, social exclusion, and deprivation of choices, status, finances, and property. Whether with a partner or alone, women have less access than do men to assets like land and savings, and, if widowed, they may face cultural barriers that limit their activity and independence[45] or strip them of their homes. In parts of Kenya and Zimbabwe, for example, when a woman is widowed, she and her possessions become the property of her husband's family, usually a brother. Although this practice is slowly changing, to challenge it means further isolation for the widow.[46]

WOMEN'S COURAGE: ENUGU, NIGERIA. The Widows Development Organization (WIDO), which has a membership of about fifty women, was established in 1996 by four women in Eastern Nigeria who wanted to: sensitize the general public to the plight of widows in Nigeria and bring about social change in traditional customs affecting them; create awareness about the rights of widows; provide counseling and support for widows; and develop collaborative ties with other organizations with similar objectives.

In Nigeria, many customary practices do not recognize a women's right to inherit her husband's property, and many widows are rendered destitute when their in-laws take virtually all of the deceased husband's property. Widows are routinely subjected to unhealthy rites and unfavorable conditions as a result of discriminatory traditional customs and economic deprivation. WIDO, among many accomplishments, has documented these and other practices and human rights violations against widows in Nigeria, and has presented this information to several public bodies.

WIDO was the lead group behind a bill in the Enugu State Assembly, signed into law in 2002, designed to protect the rights of widows, and the group continues to advocate for similar legislation in other parts of Nigeria. WIDO conducts public information campaigns through radio, television, and print media to raise awareness of the value of this legislation and to encourage more women to seek protection and redress under its provisions.

Women are likely to face old age without a husband because of the combination of shorter male lifetimes and the practice of older husbands taking younger wives. In Indonesia, 58% of older women are widowed. Among older men, only 11% are.[47] In sub-Saharan Africa, 90% of older men are married, compared with only 25% to 50% of older women. Men not only find younger spouses more easily than do women, but they also have a greater incentive to marry because of gender roles. Men who remarry gain in a woman her traditional role of companion and nurse for their old age.[48] Thus to be married in later years confers real advantage and at least a modicum of security.

In contrast, widows, who have spent time and energy caring for their dying spouses, are often stigmatized. In India, women may be blamed for their husbands' deaths, evicted from their property, and viewed as "socially dead." This is not a past practice now eliminated in a thriving India but

WOMEN'S COURAGE: NAIROBI, KENYA. The Kenya Widows and Orphans Support Programme was founded in 2000 specifically to help widows directly affected by HIV/AIDS. Five of the eight founders of the group were widows themselves; they understood the need to empower women and ensure their social and economic status after the deaths of their husbands. The Programme provides education on the prevention of mother-to-child transmission of HIV/AIDS through safe breast-feeding. In addition, it offers home-care services to widows who are ill and cannot afford hospitalization.

Traditionally in Kenya, widows may be denied inheritances and may be expelled from the family land. The Support Programme counters these practices by lobbying for women's rights on local and national levels. Also, to increase economic independence, on the local level, the Programme trains women to manage their own businesses and fosters the education of orphaned girls by offering scholarships. Through these measures, the Support Programme decreases women's dependency on men for money and provides women with greater capacity to negotiate safer sex practices.

one that continues today, as Susannah Froman and Patrick May reported in 2006.[49] In many parts of Africa, a woman cannot inherit land, and upon the death of her husband, a woman's land is passed on to her son or to her husband's family.[50]

Accusations of witchcraft are often directed at older women. In Mozambique, accusations lead to attacks on older women and sometimes to killings. In Tanzania, an estimated 500 women are murdered every year as a result of witchcraft accusations. Older women receive the majority of witchcraft allegations because they embody certain characteristics (grey hair, wrinkled skin, red eyes, living alone) associated with witches. This issue became so serious that it was made the theme for International Women's Day in Tanzania in 1999.[51]

In some African countries, structural discrimination against women is intensified by the reality of the HIV/AIDS pandemic. In parts of Kenya, for example, women who lose their husbands have little or no control over their husbands' belongings and property. Even the woman herself may be handed over to her husband's relatives with the rest of his possessions.[52] I think of Lily, a woman I met in 2004 in western Kenya whose husband died of AIDS. It was assumed that she would be inherited by her husband's brother (who was HIV positive), along with her late husband's other "possessions." She refused, an almost unheard of response, and was isolated and alone until women at a local community group, the Rural Education and Economic Enhancement Programme (REEP), reached out to her to offer support and community.[53] Lily now has her own hut, in which she is caring for seven AIDS orphans.

On the other hand, desperation and poverty caused by HIV/AIDS and the presence of many orphans and widows leads some families to neglect traditional obligations, leaving widows alone without traditional support systems. After their husbands die, many older women have no option but to beg for support for themselves and for grandchildren left in their care.[54]

Not only can cultural attitudes of widow's rights and appropriate roles lead to social exclusion, but growing urbanization also leaves older women increasingly isolated, as we saw in Doña Eulogia's story. Rural women in poorer countries are often left behind by younger family members migrating to cities in search of jobs. These women continue to perform the labor of subsistence farming for themselves and children. Women cultivate 80% of the food but own only 1% of the land in sub-Saharan Africa.[55] In Ghana, 65% of food farmers are middle-aged and elderly women, many enduring lifelong poverty.[56] As Doña Eulogia explained at the beginning of this chapter, "The work is the hardest thing, but how can I stop? We would have nothing to live on." Rural life for elderly women is harsh, since it results in their being isolated, cut off from health and other services, and unable to access opportunities for training or paid employment.

Older women living in cities confront a different set of challenges, but like their rural counterparts, they face exclusion and isolation. Both Kenya and Brazil report the practice of abandoning older family members in health care facilities. Families drop off elders and never return to pick them up. In Kenya, 15-30% of elderly patients are abandoned in hospitals.[57] Treatment is little better inside medical facilities. The head of a hospital in Kenya explains, "Older people are a big headache and a waste of scarce resources, the biggest favor you could do . . . is to get them out of my hospital."[58] Though apparently less extreme, the needs and autonomy of older women in India are frequently denied by their family members. Elderly women fear being a burden on family members, explaining that they do not want to inconvenience family

WOMEN'S COURAGE: KAUNAS, LITHUANIA. The Elderly Women's Activities Center (EWAC) was formed in 1994 to "enhance the quality of life of elderly women in Lithuania." It has been difficult for elderly women in particular to adapt to the political, social, and economic transitions happening in Lithuania. Many have lost financial security; they are not familiar with lobbying for their social rights and protections; and their concerns are often overshadowed by more vocal sectors of society. EWAC provides elderly women with training opportunities to encourage creativity and help them participate more fully in society. EWAC sees bridging generations as a way to improve the lives of both elderly and younger women.

EWAC notes that, "the situation of elderly women can only be significantly improved by the active integration of them into society, developing voluntary help for old and young to help to improve the self-esteem of elderly women and to strengthen the relationships between generations." The Kaunas Senior Citizen Council, a group that EWAC helped create, runs a self-defense course that includes discussion sessions about preventing violence against women in the home and workplace. From this project emerged an EWAC program to train members and volunteers to talk with students and community groups about the experiences and situation of elderly women in Lithuania. EWAC hopes to build a network of skilled volunteers who will run workshops for other groups and serve as models to improve services for the elderly throughout the country.

members to escort them or pay for their medical needs. However, even when a woman decides that she requires medical treatment, it is often at "the sole discretion of the children to decide whether she needs medical assistance or not."[59] An older woman in Kenya asserts similar sentiments: "You can be living with your family but are still isolated and not taken care of."[60]

Feelings of social exclusion, disintegration of rural communities, poor nutrition, physical exertion, poor living conditions, lack of employment opportunities, and grieving for the loss of loved ones strain women's mental health. It is not surprising, therefore, that older women experience much higher rates of mental illness and depression.[61] Unfortunately, there is a dearth of information on the mental health of older women in developing countries. What has been written focuses on the experience of growing older but can be used to analyze mental health. For example, an older woman in Kyrgyzstan eloquently voices the role of emotional health in aging: "I thought washing the crockery was the main thing for older people, but it seems that feelings are more important. . . . When we become old we are all the same; we are all alone. When you look back, take off your hat; when you look forward, be ready to work hard."[62]

Characteristics of Older Women in Poorer Countries

Older women in poorer countries are particularly hard to discuss because so little has been written about them. Although there have been studies of menopause and aging among women in richer countries, even the UN International Research and Training Institute for the Advancement of Women (INSTRAW) agrees that little is known about older women in poorer countries because so few formal studies have been published.[63] Organizations addressing the needs of older women in poorer countries are nearly as scarce as scholarship on the topic. Nevertheless, there are many ways to learn, and it is often through anecdotes, experience, reports from women's groups, and stories that the characteristics of older women in poorer countries can be revealed. It is known that older women in poorer countries share many of the following characteristics:

- Most are poor.
- Most suffer ill health.
- Most lack access to health care, food, and paid employment.
- Most are illiterate.
- Most are alone, unless they are caregivers for others.
- Many suffer violence.
- Most live in rural areas.
- Most are invisible, their lives not having been studied or written about.
- Most are assumed to have no value in society.
- Many are important as care givers of the young, the sick, and the older old.
- Many are the custodians of cultural traditions.[64]

Earlier in this chapter, it was noted that virtually all problems of older women seem to be an outgrowth of problems in earlier life, many of which have been described throughout this book. Young women who are literate and able to earn money will fare better in later years than their less educated and poorer counterparts—because they hold onto those assets and the strength that comes with them. There are no doubt disadvantages for them compared to wealthy older males, but these are not as dire as for poor women. Thus, to create a population of secure, powerful elderly women, it is vital to empower and provide opportunities to girls and young women. In doing so, it sets the stage for their later years to turn out differently. Lifting young women out of poverty, educating them, and giving them access to services and opportunities are prerequisites to solving the problems of destitute older women.

Hopeful Signs

Desperation and practical necessity are beginning to change the lives of some older women. In many countries, the vital roles of older women as caretakers and nurturers are beginning to be appreciated, particularly among populations devastated by HIV/AIDS. Although there is little evidence that these important caretakers are being sought out and paid, there is beginning to be some recognition, particularly by non-governmental organizations that are encouraging older people to come together to share their concerns.

In the last twenty years, there has been a rapid growth of women's groups around the world—some of them described throughout this book—and this is a hopeful sign for all women. The work of groups focusing on the well-being of women who are already older is desperately needed, and more and more older women are coming together around the world to offer connection and support to each other. Older peoples' clubs, like those formed in Thai Nguyen, Thailand,[65] and Chisinau, Moldova, offer older caregivers a place where they can discuss their problems and receive support from peers.[66] Some older peoples' clubs organize and mobilize for political action in their communities and abroad.

With the support of HelpAge International, older people from thirty-two countries had a voice in the development of the Madrid International Plan of Action on Aging, described below.[67] In 2002, the Madrid International Plan

WOMEN'S COURAGE: BUENOS AIRES, ARGENTINA. Desde Nosotras (From Us) works to counteract the invisibility experienced by lesbians over forty, while also providing services for all women. In October of 2003, the organization opened La Casa del Encuentro (The Meeting House), which is "a space for lesbian feminists, open to all women." La Casa's programs include cultural programs; consciousness-raising through workshops and educational opportunities, particularly for older lesbians; and activities and publications addressing issues of oppression and discrimination.

The group notes that "In Argentina, no place exists where we can develop our potential and create solidarity against the discrimination and oppression we face. In countries like ours, the cultures of consumption and development are based on youth and beauty, and lesbians entering the second half of their lives are completely excluded." Among its activities, La Casa has run discussion groups for lesbians over forty, classes on basic technology and Internet skills, performing arts workshops, and an "Introduction to Feminism" workshop.

of Action on Aging formally recognized the contributions of older caregivers, committing member states to "introduce policies to provide . . . support, health care, and loans to older caregivers to assist them in meeting the needs of children and grandchildren in accordance with the Millennium Declaration."[68]

The Madrid International Plan of Action on Aging champions "the potential of the aging population as the basis for future development,"[69] and strongly urges recognition of the productivity, authority, and knowledge of older people. Community-based projects designed with input from older women can effectively incorporate their knowledge, skills, and experience. For example, the attitudes of older women are crucial to the continuation or cessation of female genital mutilation in traditional societies. As this generation of better-educated women ages, we can expect that alternative rituals related to practices like female genital mutilation, already being introduced in some countries, will become more common. In emergency situations, older women contribute not only as caregivers, but also as guardians of community knowledge about past crises and coping strategies.[70] Older women are often the only birth attendants available in refugee situations, a contribution

WOMEN'S COURAGE: N'DJAMENA, CHAD. Founded as an informal women's saving group in 1999, Groupement Arc in Ciel's mission is to give all women—from teenage mothers to older widows—the tools and knowledge to support themselves financially and to protect their health. The group holds monthly meetings to train women in income-generating activities; the meetings are also an opportunity for members to learn about health and legal issues. Additional activities include literacy classes and counseling workshops, as well as training programs for women to become community educators.

that has been acknowledged by international health organizations that now provide these midwives with tools and training.[71] The vital roles of elderly women have been affirmed in recent academic studies that highlight the special importance of maternal grandmothers in supporting and positively influencing grandchildren.

The assumption that older people, particularly older women, are unproductive has led to the exclusion of the elderly from many discourses on development. Yet evidence indicates that older women play a pivotal role in the health and survival of their families and communities. As the population of older women grows, they should be viewed as contributors to, not just beneficiaries of, development. To do anything less violates elderly women's rights to independence, health, self-fulfillment, dignity, and participation.[72]

In 2002, 159 government representatives adopted the Madrid International Plan of Action on Aging. In doing so, they committed their governments to include aging in all social and economic development policies, including poverty reduction.[73] Defending the rights of older people worldwide, the Madrid Plan declares, "We commit ourselves to eliminate all forms of discrimination. We also recognize that persons, as they age, should enjoy a life of fulfillment, health, security and active participation in the economic, social, cultural and political life of their societies. We are determined to enhance the recognition of the dignity of older persons and to eliminate all forms of neglect, abuse, and violence."[74]

Though the ideals expressed in the Madrid Plan are far from being realized in most regions of the world, older women and women's groups are beginning to grow in number and strength, and are working for the rights of women worldwide.

If the first woman God ever made
was strong enough to turn the world
upside down, all alone
together women ought to be able to turn it
rightside up again.

—Sojourner Truth, U.S., 19th Century[1]

Someone, I tell you,
will remember us.

—Sappho, Greece, 6th Century B.C.

Turning The World Rightside Up

In her thought-provoking book *The Creation of Patriarchy*, Gerda Lerner takes up the question of women's subordination, and she also discusses why there has been such a long delay (more than 3500 years) in women's "coming to consciousness" of their own subordinate position in society. "What could explain it?" she asks. What could explain women's "historical complicity in upholding the patriarchal system that subordinated them and in transmitting that system, generation after generation, to their children of both sexes?" [2] One has to read her book to find her answers to such questions. A quick and possibly accurate answer might be that women have been too busy working, caregiving, producing, and reproducing to take on the struggles for our own equality. Suffice it to say, however, that the long delay is over. Women's "coming to consciousness" is part of most women's experiences now, and it has been for many women for the past century.

Because of and despite the deprivation and pain that women have experienced, they are coming together to change their situations. The examples in this book are only a few of the thousands of women's groups that have emerged to address the kinds of human rights and health issues that have been described in these pages. Amrita Basu, Professor of Political Science and Women's and Gender Studies at Amherst College, confirms that the evidence is clear that a global women's movement exists, comprised of "a range of struggles by women against gender inequality."[3] The activist and author Peggy Antrobus describes the movement as "recognizable in its understanding of how 'common difference' links us all in a political struggle for recognition and redistributive justice. Its difference from other social movements lies not only in the absence of homogeneity . . . but in the value it places on diversity, its commitment to solidarity with women everywhere, its feminist politics, and its methods of organizing."[4]

The Global Women's Movement

All over the world, women are addressing complicated and difficult issues that affect their own lives and the fabric of their communities and therefore their health. They are empowering themselves to speak out about issues that in the past were invisible or unspeakable—issues such as genital mutilation, reproductive rights, violence against women, trafficking in women, and women's right to accessible and safe health care. New women's groups addressing such issues are emerging at a very rapid rate all over the world.

Being the founding president of the Global Fund for Women has given me a unique vantage point from which to watch the development of the international women's movement.[5] The power of the movement is demonstrated in the thousands of proposals submitted to the Global Fund describing the work of women in every country in the world. The movement of women empowered to improve their lives and their societies is booming.

The current work of activists for women's equality and improved health care rests on a foundation of work that goes back to at least the mid-nineteenth century, during the "first wave" of the international women's movement. Gita Sen, professor of international health at Harvard University, describes the three waves of the global women's movement. According to Sen, the first wave had three "strands": these were the emergence of social reform movements focusing on "cultural practices affecting civil laws, marriage and family life," mobilizing both men and women. The second comprised the debate within "the social democratic and communist organizations of the late nineteenth and early twentieth centuries . . . [which] was the most explicit about the connections between . . . private property, the control over material assets, and women-men relationships within families and society. A third . . . was the liberal strand that combined the struggle for the vote with the struggle to legalize contraception." Sen continues: "The second wave [of the global women's movement] was in the mid-twentieth century, which was dominated by struggles against colonial domination, in which women were present in large numbers. . . . Many women also went through the experience of being in the thick of anti-colonial struggles and then being marginalized in the postcolonial era. . . . The third wave, that we understand as the modern women's movements, had its roots in the social and political ferment of the 1960s. . . . The anti-imperialist and anti-Vietnam War movements, civil rights struggles, challenges to social and sexual mores and behaviour, and above all the rising up of young people, brewed a potent mixture from which emerged many of the social movements of the succeeding decades worldwide. What was specific to the women's movement among these was its call for recognition of the personal as political."[6]

These waves have come together in our time to constitute a global women's movement, which is described by Peggy Antrobus—a founding member of both the Caribbean Association for Feminist Research and Action and of DAWN, a network of women promoting development alternatives—in her book, *The Global Women's Movement*.[7] In country after country, women's groups and individual women have begun to play much greater roles in their own development and in that of their societies.

From Development to Human Rights to Paradigm Change

In recent years, there has been a change in the nature of the women's movement, illustrated in the programs of women's groups at grassroots, national, and international levels. In the 1960s, 1970s, and 1980s, people concerned with poverty were implementing "women in development" programs, creating income-generating programs and projects designed to increase women's participation in existing economic and social systems. Access to loans, to education, and to health care were high in the minds of development professionals. More and more young women began to go to medical school and law school, soon becoming 50% or more of the professional school classes, at least in the United States.

But lack of real progress with regard to women's rights rankled, and many continued to be frustrated. As the years went by, the nature of the requests from women's groups around the world to the Global Fund for Women, for example, changed, moving much more toward a concern with violence against women, women's legal rights, and the elimination of human rights abuses; shifting, in other words, from purely development issues to human rights issues.

It had been known for some time that the development approach to addressing such problems as widespread poor health, poverty, and inequality in education were often ineffective. In 1987, "It had become clear that new ways of approaching problems, new players (especially women), and different kinds of institutions were badly needed."[8] But, as discussions in this book have suggested, the situation remains dire, especially for women in poorer countries, where three-fourths of the world's people live.

Moving toward a human rights and now a systemic approach, more and more women's groups have emerged to work on policy change, political participation, and advocacy. They are using modern technology and media in strategic ways. They are exhibiting major concern with the effects of globalization on women and the ramifications of the rise of fundamentalism. They are linking social change to spiritual growth. They are even speaking of "love" as a force for social change. In other words, women in groups around the world are seeing very clearly that just having more participation in the dominant economic and social systems is not going to transform the lives of women or men. Instead, organizational paradigms and systems themselves need to change.

Back in 1985, at the end of the UN Decade for Women, feminist activists like Gita Sen were seeing what is obvious now. They realized the compelling need to "question in a more fundamental way the underlying processes of development into which we have been attempting to integrate women." Sen states: "In many of the discussions and actions generated throughout the Decade [1975-85], it has been implicit that women's main problem in the Third World has been insufficient participation in an otherwise benevolent process of growth and development. Increasing women's participation and improving their shares in resources, land, employment, and income relative to men were seen as both necessary and sufficient to effect dramatic changes in their economic and social position. Our experiences now lead us to challenge this belief."[9] Sen wrote this in 1985, when women and other marginalized people were only beginning to see that systemic change was becoming more and more necessary.

Others, such as Edward Whitmont, a Jungian psychologist, were also seeing the inevitability and need for paradigm change, and his words provided background and rationale for the very creation of the Global Fund for Women.[10] In 1982, he described our time as a "low point of cultural development that has led us into the deadlock of scientific materialism, technological destructiveness, religious nihilism, and spiritual impoverishment."[11] In such a time, he argued, it is both necessary and inevitable that certain values, commonly perceived as "feminine," receive much greater prominence. In the dynamic growth of the women's, indigenous, and environmental movements, for the most part based on the principle of diversity and dedicated to different ways of organizing, such feminist values as nurturing the earth, respecting the cycles of the earth, and expressing a love and concern for the generations that follow are being given reality.

In practical terms, how are the kinds of changes that Sen and Whitmont wrote about going to happen? Few real-world examples of transformative change have been evident, though those few may be found in the global women's movement. Currently, there appears to be increasing credence given to different ways of effecting successful international development and addressing issues of poverty and widespread poor health—exhibited in the writings of Georgina Ashworth and her colleagues, William Easterly, Hans Enzensberger, Anne Firth Murray, Amartya Sen, Gita Sen, and Marilyn Waring, for example.[12]

Moving away from and increasingly being critical of the programs and approaches of traditional donors, mulitlateral agencies, and governments that set agendas from afar, such writers are focusing more on the need for community-based solutions to development and human rights issues. They are basing their ideas on the reality of successful development, which takes place when the voices of people at very local levels are heard and local people themselves are empowered to make change "on the ground." Here and there, in country after country, there are success stories, some of which have been presented in these pages. But the compelling need to support many individual groups at grassroots and village levels and support them with generosity, respect, trust, mutual empowerment, and true partnership has not yet "taken off" in the wider development and donor communities.

Health officials at donor agencies and elsewhere bemoan the reality that they did not attain the goal of "health for all by the year 2000," a goal set by the powers that were in Alma Ata, USSR, back in September 1978. Clearly, strategies set by leaders in the field did not translate well. Now we have the Millennium Goals,[13] which are valuable but are already being adjusted as the current powers that be realize that they will not be met within the previously envisioned time frame.

In attempting to meet such goals—or perhaps just getting on with the business of helping people better their own health—there are lessons to be learned from the many women's and civil society groups that are proliferating around the world. People who operate from the centers of power around the world cannot solve the global problems of poverty, climate change, and ill health alone. They need to join forces with and learn from people at every level, and very particularly at individual grassroots and community levels.

The Nature of Feminist Activism

The growth of the international movement for women has been quiet but steady in its commitment to principles as the basis for action. The movement is characterized by passionate commitment, collaboration, diversity, and, where it is most successful, mutual respect and valuing of individual people. The spread of modern technology and the internet has helped the international women's movement immensely, as women's groups are able to collaborate at all levels of planning, sharing, educating, and taking action.

Such collaboration is not new, however; it is a continuation of decades of activism. Marilyn Waring reveals an example of "issues-based advocacy networks" from the early twentieth century in her article entitled "Civil Society, Community Participation, and Empowerment in the Era of Globalization." She states: "Such networks might well work with more speed in the 21st century, but I have stood in the library archives of Ishikawa Fusae (feminist, journalist, union activist, and independent senator) in Tokyo, Japan, and examined letters and magazines she was receiving from suffrage leaders in New Zealand about the first women elected as mayors and councilors in local government elections there, and also her correspondence with Jeanette Rankin, the first woman elected to the United States Congress in 1917. I saw archived correspondence from women throughout the Pacific congratulating Ishikawa Fusae on establishing the first union for women in Japan. They wrote by hand or antique typewriter, and traveled to international feminist gatherings by ship, yet their language and issues have resonance in our era of notebook computers and business class air travel. . . . For generations now, we women would have described our methods as transparent, community-based, empowering, and political. We are doing what women have always had to do."[14] She continues, "But let's not for one moment relax our vigilance, or our sense of risk and our sense of humour. We'll need them all for this round."[15]

This talk of organizations and programs that are "transparent, community-based, collaborative, diverse, respectful, and valuing of individual people"—in a word, *feminist*—is finding some basis in reality as more and more thoughtful public health experts argue for community-based approaches to health issues that include people at the grassroots levels and that give reality to the truth that people nearest to the problems know best what is needed to solve them.

We need to work in all parts of the system and create new systems. It is imperative to realize new ways of leading, to encourage women's creativity in addressing issues of violence, for example, not just at the family level but at all levels of society. Thus, the "new" approaches that can be seen among many women's groups that have developed since the Fourth United Nations Conference on Women, held in Beijing, China, in 1995, recognize the need for major change. Women's groups are increasingly using modern technology in the formation of worldwide networks at the same time as they are challenging leadership structures and focusing on policy and politics. Some examples are presented in this chapter. Other groups are not neglecting the steady work at the grassroots: basic support, access to nutritious food, access to clean water. Yes, women can collaborate and operate at community levels while at the same time caring about, supporting, and respecting each other, as women move into leadership, political, and policy positions.

While women have been working at community levels, creating organizations and pasting together budgets with bits of money raised from here and there, some major events were happening at the level of the United Nations. In 1975, 1985, and the 1990s, culminating in the Fourth United Nations Conference on Women, held in China in 1995, milestone conferences were held. Out of these came "platforms of action" and other documents and conventions, some of which have been useful to advocates around the world. To me, the major benefits of these huge official gatherings, especially those held in 1985 in Kenya and 1995 in China, were found in the concomitant non-governmental organization (NGO) meetings held alongside the official UN meetings. These huge gatherings of women from the NGO community were exhilarating and inspiring for the vast majority of women who were able to attend.

Out of those meetings came a determination by women to take matters into their own hands, create organizations, and begin to address compelling issues directly rather than to depend on governments and huge multi- and bilateral agencies located in distant capitals to solve these problems. Women's groups themselves defined the issues that would bring about systems change, and they began to create organizations that demonstrate:

- commitment to operating in terms of sincerely held principles.

- respect for indigenous and women's ways of knowing.

- new kinds of leadership, advocacy, and political empowerment.

- sophisticated use of media and communication.

- networking, especially with other marginalized people (indigenous, disabled, rural).

- bridge-building among diverse religious and ethnic communities.

Hope for major change flourishes in the proliferation of courageous women's groups in every country in the world, groups exemplified by the eight described in the paragraphs that follow.

WOMEN'S COURAGE: CHIMBOTE, PERU. In 1984, La Casa de la Mujer Chimbote (Women's House Chimbote) was formed to promote women's rights through the introduction of women into political positions. The women were concerned with the low number of females in local government: women filled only 5% of the positions. As a result, members of the organization sought to educate women to effect policy action in Peru, raise awareness and encourage women's participation in government, educate women about their political rights, and provide gender equality training to both men and women. Members of the group have worked in elementary school settings to instruct teachers and students about the importance of gender equity in society. La Casa de la Mujer hopes to enable women in the region to exercise power and autonomy in public and private life.

WOMEN'S COURAGE: MONTEVIDEO, URUGUAY. Mujer Ahora (Woman Now) was founded in 1989 as a response to ultraconservative forces that had limited the rights of women in Uruguay. At that time, there was little female participation in government. Furthermore, the government was highly permeable to conservative religious forces, making it difficult for some progressive bills to pass. Mujer Ahora has launched local campaigns to bring attention to women's issues such as domestic violence and access to abortion. Through its efforts, Mujer Ahora hopes to end gender-based violence and secure Uruguayan women's rights to sexual and reproductive health.

WOMEN'S COURAGE: PHNOM PENH, CAMBODIA. After the Fourth World Conference on Women in 1995, a group of concerned women established Strey Khmer in Cambodia, a group that mobilizes Cambodian women to participate in the country's male-dominated political system. The group firmly believes that for women's voices and needs to be heard and respected, there must be female representation in the government. Strey Khmer provides workshops in language training and leadership skills, and informational classes on gender-based violence and women's health, and it works collaboratively with male supporters of women's rights. It produces a monthly publication about gender equity issues, reaching about 3000 women. With its great efforts to raise the female voice in society, the group hopes to meet its 30% quota for female seats in the government in the near future.

WOMEN'S COURAGE: BANGKOK, THAILAND. The Alternative Asean Network of Burma (Altsean) operates out of Bangkok, Thailand, to promote Burmese women's participation in a possible democratic process in their home country. The group also concerns itself with raising awareness about society's attitude toward women in Burma. Founded in 1996, Altsean has organized workshops to promote women's involvement in the political process. The programs include teaching women how to create networks and mobilize support for their movement. Very importantly, Altsean also addresses many female trainees' concerns about working in an environment with men; the group therefore provides skills-training to boost women's confidence socially. Altsean has published the *Women's Voice Anthology*, to report on the situation of women in Burma. In hopes of raising local support for the women's movement, Altsean has augmented its readership by translating recent editions of the anthology into various Burmese dialects.

WOMEN'S COURAGE: KADJEBI, VOLTA REGION, GHANA. The Kadjebi Disabled Women's Association, founded in 1998, provides rights education and vocational training in order to increase disabled women's employment opportunities and financial independence. The Association recognizes that Ghana's poor economy and high unemployment rates pose special challenges for disabled women. Women with disabilities in these regions face two layers of discrimination: one for being female and the other for being disabled. As a result, the group advocates for equal employment opportunities for people with disabilities. Recently, the group began to train women with disabilities in vocations of their choice, to help them gain economic independence. Because of the high prevalence of HIV/AIDS in Ghana, the Association also includes disease prevention education in its services to further improve the lives of disabled women in the region.

WOMEN'S COURAGE: COLORADO, U.S.A. The Global Culture of Women Project is a group of women dedicated to "empowering women to use our wisdom and voice." They have joined together to create a world of balance and
interdependence wherein all life is considered sacred. "We believe empowering women to act from our most ancient wisdom will form the starting point
for this much needed transformation. Through the world-wide collaboration of extraordinary everyday women, the Global Culture of Women Project
develops opportunities for women to explore and celebrate the power, voice,
and beauty of the unique and unified expressions of our female identity as if
human survival depended upon our doing so." The Global Culture of Women
has a website where women can connect by email with their stories. The site
will soon include audio archives of women's stories, told in their own voices. It
will also make available: stories of women in Middle East and Northern Africa;
the Story Gatherers Handbook (how to become a witness to women's beautiful stories); and a documentary film on the project. Women around the globe
are invited to participate.

WOMEN'S COURAGE: KATHMANDU, NEPAL. Tewa is a women's foundation
that provides funds to small women's groups in rural parts of Nepal. Drawing
together a very diverse group of Nepali women from different castes and ethnicities, the founders of Tewa (which means "support") created an organization that not only makes grants to women's organizations in rural Nepal, but
also invites individual people in that country to become involved and support
the effort. Tewa fundraises successfully in a country where asking local people
directly for money to support efforts to strengthen women was completely
new. Since its beginnings in 1996, Tewa has operated with shared leadership
and thrived, having acquired land and built five buildings to create a women's
center and a permanent place for Tewa in Kathmandu. Consistently fostering
the values expressed in its processes and structures in a conflict-ridden Nepal,
Tewa is successfully integrating development, environment, and culture through
its land and building development project. At the same time, the women are
ensuring Tewa's sustainability and continuing contributions in a difficult economic climate.

WOMEN'S COURAGE: NEW YORK, U.S.A. FIMI, or the Foro Internacional de Mujeres Indígenas (International Indigenous Women's Forum) is hosted by Madre, an international women's rights association. The recent history of the formation of FIMI follows: One of the first times that indigenous women from many countries were able to meet was at the 1995 UN women's meeting in Beijing, China. At the end of the conference, indigenous women issued their own declaration, firmly asserting their identity and their struggles. In 2000, the International Indigenous Women's Forum (FIMI) was founded as a network of Indigenous women leaders from Asia, Africa, and the Americas. FIMI's mission is to bring together indigenous women activists, leaders, and human rights promoters to coordinate agendas, build unity, develop leadership and advocacy skills, increase indigenous women's role in international decision-making processes, and advance women's human rights. One of the dreams of the women of FIMI has been to create an Indigenous Women's Fund—an economic and philanthropic arm to provide resources for indigenous women from the seven geo-cultural regions defined by the UN Permanent Forum on Indigenous Issues. This dream came true in March 2007, with the creation of the IWF, whose mandate is "to support the capacity of the indigenous women's movement and Indigenous women's leadership, and to strengthen the institutions that advance indigenous women's rights." The IWF is dedicated to providing indigenous women with resources in a way that will increase their sense of dignity and self-esteem and that respects the visions, priorities, and perspectives that are compatible with the self-determination of their peoples.

The noble ideals as well as the pains and joys of human life are often captured in poetry and song. From Sappho to modern times and in all countries, women have sung and written their hopes and dreams and their struggles. Women around the world are uniting consciously to "turn the world right-side up" for the benefit of all.

Endnotes

Unless otherwise noted, electronic resources were accessed between January 2006 and August 2007.

PROLOGUE: DARKNESS AND LIGHT

1. Linthwaite, 1987, p. 158.
2. Some say that there are no "poor" countries, only "poor" people. Others argue that "poor" people in reality are "resource-poor" or "economically disadvantaged" people who in fact may lead rich lives of community, family, and positive traditions. For lack of better terms, we have used "poor," "poorer," and "developing" as adjectives to describe the people and places that are the focus of this book, understanding that the terms do not fully describe the strong and resilient people at the center of change.
3. Banister, 2003.
4. Sen, Amartya, 2001.
5. UNICEF, 2005. Gender Achievements and Prospects in Education.
6. Rahman and Toubia, 2000, p. 6.
7. UNICEF, 2002.
8. Population Reference Bureau (PRB), 2002b.
9. Population Information Program and the Center for Health and Gender Equity (CHANGE), 1999, p. 3.
10. Some forty major conflicts are going on in the world today. In armed conflicts since 1945, 90% of casualties have been civilians. See http://www.world revolution.org/projects/globalissuesoverview/overview2/BriefPeace.html. Accessed June 12, 2006.
11. Stories of women and girls throughout the text of the book are based on real people; in some cases their names have been changed to protect their privacy.
12. Population Reference Bureau, 2002a.
13. Preamble to the Constitution of the World Health Organization as adopted by the International Health Conference, New York, June 19–22, 1946; signed on July 22, 1946, by the representatives of 61 States (Official Records of the World Health Organization, no. 2, p. 100) and entered into force on April 7, 1948. The definition of "health" has not been amended since 1948.
14. Avotri and Walters, 2001.
15. Information about the vast majority of the groups described throughout this book came from the grantee files of the Global Fund for Women.

16. The UN report "The World's Women, 2005: Trends and Statistics" is the first document to comprehensively analyze which countries collect official statistics by sex and which do not. The report makes clear that better information is needed in order to develop effective solutions to persistent problems.

17. Sen, Gita et al., 2002.

18. Ibid, p. 2.

19. Ibid, p. 5.

20. It is interesting to note that the word "taboo" or "tabu," which was originally used in Polynesia, means "set apart" or "consecrated to a special purpose, restricted to the use of a god, a king, priests, or chiefs, while forbidden to general use; prohibited to a particular class (especially to women)," according to the Oxford English Dictionary.

21. For the full text of the Universal Declaration of Human Rights, see http://www.un.org/Overview/rights.html.

CHAPTER I WOMEN'S HEALTH, POVERTY AND RIGHTS

1. Hirshfield, 1994, p. 63.

2. Eleanor Roosevelt, at the presentation of "In Your Hands: A Guide for Community Action for the 10th Anniversary of the Universal Declaration of Human Rights, March 27, 1958, at the United Nations, New York. See http://www.udhr.org/history/Biographies/bioer.html for further quotes by Eleanor Roosevelt on human rights.

3. "World population reached 6.4 billion in 2004 and it continues to grow by some 80 million each year." Population Reference Bureau, World Population Highlights, 2004.

4. World Bank, 2000, p. 3.

5. Ibid.

6. United Nations Womenwatch, 2000.

7. United Nations Human Development Programme (UNDP) Report, 1997b.

8. United Nations Womenwatch, 2000.

9. United Nations, 1995, paragraphs 48 and 50.

10. Population Reference Bureau, 2003a.

11. Ibid.

12. Adler et al., 1999, p. 181-82.

13. For example, in high-mortality African villages, deaths among infants and young children occur ten times more frequently than among the elderly because of the large proportion of children and a high incidence of infectious diseases. In low-mortality settings, such as Europe and North America, infant and child deaths have become rare relative to adult deaths. An infant mortality rate of 50 deaths per 1,000 births in a sub-Saharan African village could signal an improvement in infant and possibly maternal health, while the same rate would mean a significant decline in health in a richer country. Population Reference Bureau 2003a, p. 10.

14. United Nations Development Programme 1997b, p. 2.

15. United Nations, 2000.

16. Population Reference Bureau, 2003, p. 10.

17. Kim, Jim Y. et al., 2000, p. 4.

18. Ibid.

19. Mann et al. 1999, p. 1. Jonathan Mann was the Founding Director of the Francois Xavier Bagnoud Center for Health and Human Rights at Harvard University and the first director of the Global Programme on AIDS at the World Health Organization; his untimely death in 1998 cut short a distinguished career in the field of health and human rights.

20. For the full text of the Universal Declaration of Human Rights, see http://www.un.org/overview/rights.html

21. Human Rights Watch: http://www.hrw.org/women. Accessed June, 12, 2006.

22. Ibid.

23. Text available at http://www.un.org/womenwatch/daw/cedaw/text/econvention.htm

24. Text available at http://www.unhchr.ch/html/menu3/b/k2crc.htm

25. Mann et al., 1999, p. 1.

26. Population Reference Bureau, 2003a.

27. It should be noted that claiming biological/mental inferiority has been the final refuge of all discrimination against all peoples.

28. This devaluation of one sex, female, is particularly ironic given that sex determination resides with the male. Two chromosomes—the X and the Y chromosome—determine the sex of the child; females have 2 X chromosomes; males have 1 X and 1 Y chromosome. Each parent contributes one half of each chromosome pair to the child; the mother always contributes an X chromosome to the child. The father may contribute an X or a Y, therefore it is the father that determines the sex of the child.

29. Lerner, 1986, p. 5.

30. Kim, Jim Y. et al., 2000, p. xiv.

CHAPTER 2 FROM THE BEGINNING: A DEADLY PREFERENCE

1. Emecheta, 1983.

2. Bumiller, 1990, p. 102.

3. The Population Reference Bureau (PRB), 2003a, p.4, updated for 2005: see http://www.prb.org.

4. Miller, 1981.

5. Leonhardt, David. "It's a Girl! (Will the Economy Suffer?)" *New York Times*, October 26, 2003.

6. "The ratio of women's to men's median annual earnings [in the U.S.] was 77.0 in 2005 . . . for full-time, full-year workers, statistically the same as in 2004 (76.6) and virtually unchanged from 2001 (76.3)." Institute for Women's Policy Research, Fact Sheet (IWPR #C350), April 2007.

7. Sen, Amartya, 2001, p. 3. Every year, about 137,350,692 people are born around the world, about 50% of whom are female.

8. Ibid.

9. Banister, 2003.

10. Bumiller, 1990, p. 102.

11. Charles Feng, class paper, Stanford University, Fall 2003.

12. Carmichael, Mary. "No Girls, Please," *Newsweek*, January 26, 2004, based on reports from the Chinese Fifth National Census.

13. Miller, Barbara D., 1981.

14. Haldar and Battacharyya, 1969.

15. Gordon, John E. et al., 1965, p. 906-07.

16. United Nations Development Programme, 1995.

17. World Bank, 2000, p. 34-35.

18. Sen, Amartya, 2001, p. 4.

19. UNICEF, 1997.

20. Sen, Amartya, 2001.

21. Bumiller, 1990, p. 115.

22. Ibid, p. 102.

23. Arora, 1996, p. 420-24.

24. Ganatra et al., 2001, p. 109-24.

25. The Institute of Population Research at Beijing University is a World Health Organization collaborating center in reproductive health and population science. Chu Junhong, 2001.

26. Carmichael, Mary. "No Girls, Please," *Newsweek*, January 26, 2004.

27. Statistics from the State Statistics Administration of the Government of China, reported by China News Service, May 9, 2002.

28. China News Service (CNS), May 9, 2002.

29. *New York Times*, July 23, 2004.

30. Carmichael, Mary. "No Girls, Please," *Newsweek*, January 26, 2004.

31. Joyce et al., 2001.

CHAPTER 3 CHILDHOOD: THE HOPE OF EDUCATION
AND THE PERSISTENCE OF DISCRIMINATION

1. Global Fund for Children, 2003.

2. Asian Center for Women's Human Rights, p. 247.

3. Linthwaite, 1990, p. 135.

4. UNICEF, State of the World's Children, 2005. See www.unicef.org/sowc05.

5. United Nations Womenwatch, 2000.

6. Visaria, 2002.

7. Griffiths et al., 2002.

8. United Nations, 1948.

9. Visaria, 2002, p. 89.

10. Population Reference Bureau, 2002a.

11. UNICEF, 2007, p. 133.

12. For information about absolute enrollment levels, refer to UNESCO Institute for Statistics, 2004 figures.

13. UNESCO website. See: http://portal.unesco.org/education/en/ev.php-URL_ID=41576&URL_DO=DO_TOPIC&URL_SECTION=201.html.

14. World Bank, 2000, p. 18.

15. Population Reference Bureau, 2002a.

16. World Bank, 1992, p. 1.

17. Ibid.

18. Ibid.

19. Ibid.

20. Dervarics, Charles, "Tiny Successes," Population Reference Bureau, 2004.

21. "African Girls' Route to School is Still Littered With Obstacles," *New York Times*, December 14, 2003.

22. "Literacy: A Key to Women's Empowerment." *United Nations, Beijing Declaration and Platform for Action*. Fourth World Conference on Women, 1995, p. 5-6.

23. "Links" Oxfam Newsletter, October 2003, p. 7.

24. Personal observations, October 2003 and March 2004.

25. UNESCO website. See: http://portal.unesco.org/education/en/ev.php-URL_ID=41576&URL_DO=DO_TOPIC&URL_SECTION=201.html.

26. The Forum for African Women Educationalists (FAWE), 1995, p. 5.

27. Editorial, "Links" Oxfam Newsletter, October 2003, p. 2.

28. United Nations Childrens' Fund (UNICEF), 2003a.

29. Joint United Nations Programme on HIV/AIDS (UNAIDS), 2004d.

30. Editorial, "Links" Oxfam Newsletter, October 2003, p. 2.

31. ActionAid International, 2004.

32. Population Reference Bureau, 2001, p. 1.

33. Ibid.

34. Ibid.

35. There is debate about the effects of male circumcision; some see it as an abrogation of boys' human rights; some argue that it affects sexual function; others seek to show that circumcised men are less likely to contract sexually transmitted infections, and recent studies in South Africa have confirmed this positive health effect, particularly with regard to HIV/AIDS. Extensive comments and discussion can be found on various sites on the world wide web.

36. For a discussion of FGM/FC, its prevalence in various countries, and legal status, see WHO fact sheet on female genital mutilation, 2006 at: http://www.who.int/mediacentre/factsheets/fs241/en.

37. For information on the practice and its legal status, see AmnestyInternational: http://web.amnesty.org/library/Index/ENGACT770071997?open&of=ENG.2AF and/or Rahman, 2000.

38. Elimu Yetu Coalition, 2005, p. 108.

39. World Health Organization, 2000, p. 2.

40. Rahman and Toubia, 2000, p. 5–6.

41. World Health Organization, 2000.

42. Njiru, 2003.

43. World Health Organization, 2000.

44. Ibid.

45. WHO website. See http://www.who.int/mediacentre/news/releases/2006/pr30/en/index.html.

46. Rahman et al., 2000, p. 10.

47. Equality Now. See http://www.equalitynow.org/english/navigation/hub_ en.html.

48. Taina Bien Aime, executive director of Equality Now, at a symposium on Muslim women's equality and rights, April 9, 2005, Toronto, Canada.

49. Inter Press Service News Industry, June 2004.

50. Ibid.

51. Population Reference Bureau, 2001, pp. 17-19.

52. Hosken, Fran, 1993.

53. UNICEF 2005. See http://www.unicef.org/protection/index_exploitation. html

54. Altink, 1995, p. 7.

55. Amnesty International. See http://www.amnesty.org.uk/sextraffic.

56. International Labour Organization website. Fact Sheet: Poverty in Africa.

57. UNICEF 2005: See http://www.unicef.org/protection/index_childlabour .html.

58. Ibid.

59. United Nations, 1990, Convention on the Rights of the Child. Text available at http://www.unhchr.ch/html/menu3/b/k2crc.htm. Note: The United States of America has not ratified this convention, making it one of only three countries not to do so. The others are Somalia and East Timor.

60. Ibid.

CHAPTER 4 ADOLESCENCE: CHANGE AND VULNERABILITY

1. Cosman, 1988, p. 49.

2. Quoted by Peter Piott, Executive Director, UNAIDS, in his keynote address at the first World Congress against the Commercial Sexual Exploitation of Children, held in Stockholm, 1996.

3. With women's groups from the Philippines and Singapore, the Global Fund for Women supported this 1992 meeting in an attempt to strengthen women's regional efforts.

4. For the most part we use World Health Organization (WHO) data.

5. International Center for Research on Women, 2001a.

6. Stone and Church, 1973, p. 418.

7. Apter, 1991.

8. International Labour Organization. See http://article.wn.com/view/2006/10/31 /Youth_unemployment_soars_worldwide_ILO.

9. International Center for Research on Women, 2001a.

10. Ibid.

11. "Low-birthweight babies . . . face a greatly increased risk of dying during their early months and years. Those who survive have impaired immune function and face increased risk of disease, including that of diabetes and heart disease later in life. They are also likely to remain malnourished and to have lower IQ and cognitive disabilities, leading to school failure and learning difficulties. Weight at birth is a good indicator not only of the mother's health and nutritional status but also of the newborn's

chances for survival, growth, long-term health and psychosocial development."
United Nations Children's Fund. See http://www.unicef.org/specialsession/about
/sgreport pdf/15_LowBirthweight_D7341Insert_English.pdf

12. Joint United Nations Programme on HIV/AIDS, 2004d.

13. On a global scale, complications from unsafe abortions result in 13–17% of
all maternal deaths. In 1996, the Pan American Health Organization revealed that
unsafe abortion is the primary cause of maternal death in Argentina, Chile, Guatemala, Panama, Paraguay and Peru. Reported by Flora Tristan, Peruvian Women's
Center, September 2004.

14. Save the Children, *State of the World's Mothers*, 2004.

15. International Center for Research on Women, 2001.

16. Alan Guttmacher Institute, 1998.

17. Ibid.

18. United Nations Children's Fund, 2002.

19. Ibid.

20. International Center for Research on Women, 2003.

21. Ibid.

22. Ibid.

23. Ibid.

24. Save the Children, an international non-governmental organization, issues
a yearly report on "early motherhood risk," relying on three indicators: early marriage (percentage of females aged fifteen to nineteen ever married); early motherhood (number of births per 1,000 females aged fifteen to nineteen); and risk to babies
(infant mortality rate for children born to mothers under age twenty). In 2004, fifty
countries were listed with high-risk scores where early motherhood is most common
and where the consequences are the most devastating. In these countries, girls' education levels were low. In Afghanistan, Bangladesh, Chad, Guinea, Mozambique, and
Uganda, for example, about half of all girls aged fifteen to nineteen are married. In
Mali, Niger, and Uganda, about 20% of women aged fifteen to nineteen give birth
each year; and in Afghanistan, Liberia, Mali, Mozambique, Niger, and Tanzania,
one out of six children born to teen mothers dies within the first year of life. "Given
that these figures are not universally collected, and exclude the youngest mothers
under age fifteen, the death toll is likely much higher." Save the Children, *State of
the World's Mothers*, 2004.

25. International Center for Research on Women, 2003.

26. Ibid.

27. United Nations Children's Fund, 2001.

28. Ibid.

29. Population Reference Bureau, 2000a.

30. Lewis, 2004.

31. Population Reference Bureau, 2000a.

32. *Pandemic: Facing Aids*, video, 2002. Rory Kennedy, producer.

33. Joint United Nations Programme on HIV/AIDS, 2002a.

34. Joint United Nations Programme on HIV/AIDS, 2004d.

35. Ibid.

36. UNICEF, 2002.

37. Joint United Nations Programme on HIV/AIDS, 2003b.

38. Kaiser Foundation, Global HIV/AIDS Epidemic Fact Sheet, 2004, p. 1.

39. United Nations Children's Fund, Joint UN Program on HIV/AIDS, 2004.

40. Ibid.

41. Ibid.

42. Global Health Council, Global AIDS Link, 2003-04.

43. Joint United Nations Programme on HIV/AIDS, 2001.

44. Stephen Lewis, head of UNAIDS office, interviewed on the BBC, July 2004.

45. Altman, Lawrence K., "HIV Risk Greater for Young African Brides." *New York Times*, February 29, 2004.

46. XV International AIDS Conference, Bangkok, Thailand, July 13, 2004.

47. United Nations Children's Fund/Center for Disease Control, 2004.

48. Joint United Nations Programme on HIV/AIDS, 2004b.

49. Joint United Nations Programme on HIV/AIDS, 2001.

50. Ibid.

51. International Center for Research on Women, 2002.

52. As cited by Melody and Ooms, Medécins Sans Frontières Coordinators, 21 October 2002.

53. Joint United Nations Programme on HIV/AIDS, 2001.

54. Joint United Nations Programme on HIV/AIDS, 2002.

55. Moreno, 1997.

56. Joint United Nations Programme on HIV/AIDS, 2004d.

57. United Nations Children's Fund/Center for Disease Control, 2004.

58. Ibid.

59. Ibid.

60. Chase, Marilyn, "Saying No to 'Sugar Daddies.'" *The Wall Street Journal*, February 25, 2004.

61. Joint United Nations Programme on HIV/AIDS, 2004a.

62. International Center for Research on Women, 2001a, p. 2.

63. Joint United Nations Programme on HIV/AIDS, 2004a.

64. Epstein, Helen, "The Fidelity Fix." *New York Times Magazine*, June 19, 2004.

65. Population Reference Bureau, 2000a.

66. United Nations Children's Fund. See http://www.unicef.org/protection/index_exploirtation.html. Accessed December 2004.

67. Joint United Nations Programme on HIV/AIDS, 2004d.

68. United Nations document: SG/SM/8436.

CHAPTER 5 THE MATERNITY DEATH ROAD:
REPRODUCTIVE AND SEXUAL HEALTH

1. Cosman, 1988, p. 289.

2. World Neighbors interview at Hewlett Foundation, 1986.

3. Population Reference Bureau, 2002b.

4. Fathalla, 1997, p. 249.

5. Population Reference Bureau, 2002a.

6. Cited in Fathalla, 1997, p. 249.

7. Ibid, p. 255-57.

8. Population Reference Bureau, 2000c.

9. Fathalla, p. 251.

10. Pradhan et al., 2002.

11. Ravindran, Sundari, 1990, p. 13.

12. Ibid.

13. Population Reference Bureau, 2002b, p. 3.

14. Merali, Isfahan, 2000, p. 610.

15. De Bruyn, Maria, 1999.

16. Merali, Isfahan, 2000, p. 610.

17. De Bruyn, Maria, 1999, p. 4.

18. Kristof, Nicholas, "Alone and Ashamed." *New York Times*, May 16, 2003f.

19. Fathalla, Mahmoud, 1997, p. 245.

20. The "crude birth rate" of a population is the number of childbirths per 1,000 persons per year. The fertility rate is defined as the average number of babies born to women during their reproductive years. Population Reference Bureau, 1998.

21. World Development Indicators (WDI) online database. See http://devdata .worldbank.org/dataonline/ .

22. Center for Reproductive Rights, See http://www.reproductiverights.org /ww_asia_1child.html

23. Bulatao, 1998, p. xii.

24. Ibid.

25. Merali, 2000, p. 610.

26. United Nations Population Fund. See http://www.unfpa.org/mothers /contraceptive.htm. Accessed June 19, 2006.

27. Population Reference Bureau, 2002c.

28. United Nations Population Fund: See http://www.unfpa.org/mothers /contraceptive.htm. Accessed June 19, 2006.

29. Simpson, 2003.

30. Cited in Ibid.

31. Cited in Ibid.

32. United Nations Population Fund. See http://www.unfpa.org/mothers /contraceptive.htm

33. Population Reference Bureau (PRB), 2002c.

34. Ibid.

35. Ibid.

36. Center for Disease Control (CDC)/National Center for Health Statistics, 1998.

37. Joint United Nations Programme on HIV/AIDS (UNAIDS), 1997.

38. Population Council and International Family Health, 2000.

39. For a discussion of contraceptive methods, see Trussell J. "Contraceptive efficacy" in Hatcher R.A., Trussell J, Stewart F, Cates W, Stewart GK, Kowal D, Guest F, *Contraceptive Technology: Seventeenth Revised Edition.* New York, NY: Irvington Publishers, 1998.

40. World Health Organization, 2003a.

41. Alan Guttmacher Institute, 1999.

42. Hord, Charlotte, 1999.

43. World Health Organization, 2003a, p. 7.

44. Population Reference Bureau, 2002b, p. 2.

45. World Health Organization, 1999, p. 1.

46. Ibid, pp. 24-25.

47. Alan Guttmacher Institute, 1999.

48. World Health Organization, 2003a, p. 13.

49. For a list of contraceptive methods and failure rates, see http://www .sexuality.org/1/sex/contfail.html.

50. Paternostro, 1999.

51. World Health Organization, 2003b.

52. World Health Organization, 1999, p. 24.

53. For information on abortion rates, legal status, etcetera, see the Alan Guttmacher Institute website, http://www.agi-usa.org.

54. Alan Guttmacher Institute, 1999, pp. 28-29.

55. Population Action International, 2001, p. 8.

56. The Center for Reproductive Law and Policy (CRLP), a non-profit organization dedicated to promoting women's equality worldwide. See http://www.crlp.org /about.html.

57. Kristof, Nicholas, "Killing Them Softly." *New York Times*, September 20, 2003h.

58. "The War Against Women," *New York Times*, Editorial Desk, January 12, 2003g.

59. Sexually Transmitted Infection (STI) is now the more commonly used term for what used to be known as Venereal Disease (VD) or Sexually Transmitted Disease (STD). An STI is an infection that is passed from one person to another through sexual activity, although the person may not have any signs or symptoms of the infection. STD refers to a situation in which the person displays signs or symptoms of the infection.

60. Population Action International, 2001.

61. Shelton, James, 2001.

62. Population Reference Bureau, 2003c.

63. Population Action International, 2001, p. 8.

64. Ibid.

65. World Health Organization, 1994.

66. United Nations, 1995.

67. For the text of the Beijing Declaration, see http://www.un.org/womenwatch /daw/beijing/platform/declar.htm.

68. Miller et al. (1999) discuss lesbian existence in the framework of health and human rights, making visible a subset of women typically ignored even within the women's movement.

69. See http://www.lesbianhealthinfo.org.

70. Fathalla, Mahmoud, 1997, p. 245.

CHAPTER 6 VIOLENCE AGAINST WOMEN: ABUSE OR TERRORISM?

1. Barnstone and Barnstone, 1990, p. 71.
2. World Health Organization, 2005.
3. Population Information Program and the Center for Health and Gender Equity, 1999, p. 3. The report of the Population Information Program and the Center for Health and Gender Equity on "Ending Violence Against Women" is a comprehensive review of intimate partner violence globally, including health and societal effects. These statistics come from a series of studies done in various countries and regions during the 1990s among populations ranging in age from about fifteen through adulthood.
4. Population Information Program and the Center for Health and Gender Equity, 1999, p. 5.
5. United Nations Children's Fund, 1997, reported that a quarter to half of women around the world have suffered violence from an intimate partner.
6. Population Reference Bureau, 2000b, p. 2.
7. Communication with R. Allen, Spring 2004.
8. Family Violence Prevention Fund, 1998b.
9. Ibid, p. 5.
10. Population Information Program and the Center for Health and Gender Equity, 1999, p. 5.
11. Carrillo, 1990, p. 22.
12. Ibid.
13. Population Information Program and the Center for Health and Gender Equity, 1999, p. 4.
14. Ibid, p. 5.
15. Population Information Program and the Center for Health and Gender Equity, 1999, p. 1.
16. Majumdar, 2003. See http://www.womensenews.org/article.cfm/dyn/aid/1591.
17. World Health Organization, 2005.
18. U.S. Department of Justice, 2000.
19. Bureau of Justice Statistics, 1997, p. 5.
20. Heise, 1994, p. 18.
21. Reference for whole paragraph: Hesperian Foundation Facts about Domestic Violence and Abuse, 1997.
22. See: http://www.ivillage.co.uk/ivillageuk/dom/features/articles/0,,181901_182762,00.html. For a discussion of this issue in the U.S., see U.S. General Accounting Office, May 2002, "Violence against Women: Data on Pregnant Victims and Effectiveness of Preventive Strategies."
23. Interagency Gender Working Group and Population Reference Bureau, 2002, p. 8.
24. Ibid, p. 6.
25. Personal communication with R. Allen, Spring 2004.
26. Raine, 1998.
27. Ibid.

28. The Commonwealth Fund, "First Comprehensive National Health Survey of American Women Finds Them at Significant Risk" (News Release). New York: The Commonwealth Fund, July 14, 1993.

29. Caralis and Musialowski, 1997; McCauley et al., 1998; Friedman et al., 1992; Rodriguez et al., 1996.

30. Population Information Program and the Center for Health and Gender Equity, 1999.

31. The Centers for Disease Control have calculated that in the United States alone, the expense resulting from domestic violence amounts to about $5.8 billion per year. Department of Health and Human services and Centers for Disease Control and Prevention, National Center for Injury Prevention and Control, 2003.

32. World Health Organization, 2004b.

33. Jaffe and Sudermann, 1995.

34. United Nations High Commission for Human Rights, 2000. Quoted from a speech given by Mary Robinson, the United Nations High Commissioner for Human Rights for The United Nations Special Rapporteur on Violence Against Women before the United Nations Human Rights Commission on April 10, 2000.

35. United Nations High Commission for Human Rights, 2000.

36. "Honor Killings." *New York Times* Editorial, November 12, 2000.

37. Mydans, Seth, "A Friendship Sundered by Muslim Code of Honor." *New York Times*, February 1, 2003.

38. Katz, 2003.

39. "Europe Tackles Honour Killings." British Broadcasting Company (BBC) News, June 22, 2004.

40. United Nations Children's Fund, 2000a.

41. United Nations Development Fund for Women, 2003.

42. Ibid.

43. Bose, Brinda, personal conversation, Bellagio, Italy, October 2004.

44. Adcock, 2003, p. 16.

45. United Nations, 1993.

46. The World Health Organization (WHO) campaign for violence prevention (see http://www.who.int/violence_injury_prevention/violence/global_campaign /en/index.html) and the WHO multi-country study on women's health and domestic violence (see http://www.who.int/gender/violence/en) are recent examples of important initiatives.

47. United Nations, 1948.

CHAPTER 7 WOMEN CAUGHT IN CONFLICT AND REFUGEE SITUATIONS

1. http://condor.depaul.edu/~rrotenbe/aeer/aeer13_1/Darvas.html.

2. Margaret Mead's "Warfare Is Only an Invention" first appeared in the journal *Asia* in August 1940. See http://faculty.millikin.edu/~moconner.hum.faculty .mu/in151/mead.html

3. Survivors Fund, 2003.

4. The induction of women into war as soldiers and more recently as key members of government administrations responsible for war, such as Secretary of State

Condoleezza Rice, has so far done little to change the reality of war as a primarily male activity which is devastating to women.

5. Save the Children, 2002.
6. Cited by Human Rights Watch, 2001a.
7. Save the Children, 2002.
8. Walker, Anne S., 2002.
9. Ibid.
10. The Center for Defense Information, 2003.
11. Walker, Anne S., 2002.
12. Ibid.
13. Nikolic-Ristanovic, 2000, p. 195.
14. See http://www.peacewomen.org/un/sc/1325.html for details of the resolution.
15. Secretary General's Statement to the Security Council on Women, Peace and Security, October 28, 2002.
16. United Nations Development Fund for Women, 2002c.
17. Rabia Women's Hospital remained open.
18. United Nations Children's Fund/Center for Disease Control, 2002.
19. Yuval-Davis, 1997.
20. Ibid.
21. Nikolic-Ristanovic 2000, p. 197.
22. Lindsey, Charlotte, 2001, p. 77, author of the International Committee of the Red Cross study.
23. United Nations Development Fund for Women, 2002, p. 38.
24. Ibid.
25. Lindsey, 2001, p. 51.
26. Ibid, p. 112.
27. Women's Human Rights Net. See http://www.whrnet.org/docs/issue-refugees.html
28. McKinley, James C., "Legacy of Rwanda Violence: The Thousands Born of Rape." *New York Times*, September 23, 1996.
29. Lentin, Ronit, 1997, p. 10.
30. Human Rights Watch, 2000.
31. Nikolic-Ristanovic, 2000.
32. Halsell, 1993.
33. Lacey, Marc, "Amnesty Says Sudan Militias Use Rape as a Weapon." *The New York Times*, July 19, 2004.
34. Nikolic-Ristanovic, 2000, p. 204.
35. Ibid, p. 205.
36. Knonstantinovic-Villic, 2000, p. 132.
37. Martin, 1991.
38. Farha, 1998.
39. Personal Communication at Global Fund for Women.
40. Bennett, Olivia et al., 1995, p. 36.
41. Human Rights Watch, 2001b.

42. Ibid.

43. Human Rights Watch, 2003.

44. United Nations Development Fund for Women. See   http://www
.womenwarpeace.org/issues/landmines/landmines.htm

45. Bilukha et al., 2003.

46. United Nations Development Fund for Women, 2002c.

47. International Labour Organization, 1998.

48. Bennet et al., 1995, pp. 177–78.

49. UN Integrated Regional Information Network, 2002.

50. Crawley, 1999.

51. Mrvic-Petrovic, 2000.

52. Howarth et al., 1997.

53. Women's Human Rights Net. See http://www.whrnet.org/docs/issue-refugees
.html, July 2003.

54. Ibid.

55. Centers for Disease Control and Prevention/National Center for Health
Statistics, 2004.

56. World Health Organization, 1995.

57. World Health Organization, 2004.

58. Personal interviews, Lu, Irene. "The Needs of Afghan Women in Post-
Conflict Reconstruction and Development." Unpublished Undergraduate Honors
Thesis, Stanford University, 2004.

59. Cited in Cohen, 1998.

60. Boelaert et al., 1999, p. 166.

61. Ibid.

62. Ibid, p. 168.

63. Ellis, 2001, p. 74.

64. Ibid, p. 70.

65. Goodyear, 2002.

66. Ibid.

67. United Nations Development Fund for Women (UNIFEM), 2002a, p. 37.

68. Mrvi-petrovic, 2000, p. 165.

69. United Nations Development Fund for Women (UNIFEM), 2002a, p. 23.

70. Martin, 1991, p. 21.

71. Both Amnesty International and Human Rights Watch report on violence
against women in refugee camps.

72. Meintjes, Sheila, Anu Pillay, and Meredeth Turshen, 2001.

73. World Health Organization , 2002c.

74. Amnesty International, 2004a.

75. "Fort Bragg Killing Raises Alarm about Stress." CNN, July 27, 2002.

76. Richard, 1999.

77. Amnesty International, 2004b.

78. Amnesty International, 2004a.

79. Amnesty International, 2004b.

80. United Nations Development Fund for Women, 2002a, p. 40.

81. Ibid, p. 42.

82. Bennett et al., 1995, pp. 37–38.

83. Lindsey, 2001, p. 54.

84. This figure is approximately 10% of women estimated to have been raped in the war. Survivors Fund, 2003.

85. Human Rights Watch, 1996.

86. Ibid.

87. Population and Development Program at Hampshire College, 2003.

88. Bennett, Olivia et al., 1995, pp. 174–75.

CHAPTER 8 LABORING IN A GLOBALIZED WORLD

1. Lorde, Audre, from a commencement address at Oberlin College, May 29, 1989, in Alexander et al., p. 533.

2. Linthwaite, 1990, p. 135.

3. Meadows, 1989, p. 16.

4. Sleightholme and Sinha, 1996, p. 20, citing "Two Halves Make a Whole": Balancing Gender Relations in Development. The Canadian Council for International Cooperation, 1991, p. 3.

5. United Nations Development Programme, 1995, p. 88.

6. Sen and Grown, 1987.

7. UN Womenwatch, June 2000, Commission on the Status of Women. See ww.un.org/womenwatch/daw/followup/session/presskit/fs1.htm.

8. United Nations Development Programme, 1995, p. 97.

9. Waring, 1988b.

10. Women's Action for New Directions, 1994.

11. See "concept of informal sector," www.worldbank.org. According to the World Bank Group, "the informal sector consists of: 1) Coping strategies (survival activities): casual jobs, temporary jobs, unpaid jobs, subsistence agriculture, multiple job holding; 2) Unofficial earning strategies (illegality in business): 2.1) Unofficial business activities: tax evasion, avoidance of labor regulation and other government or institutional regulations, no registration of the company; and 2.2) Underground activities: crime, corruption—activities not registered by statistical offices."

12. Radcliffe Public Policy Center and Women in Informal Employment Globalizing and Organizing, 2000.

13. Elson, 1992.

14. For a discussion of women's property rights, poverty, and health, see Strickland, International Center for Research on Women, 2004.

15. Food and Agriculture Organization of the United Nations, 2006.

16. Freedman, 2002, p. 131.

17. Association for Women's Rights in Development, 2002, p. 4.

18. Wichterich, 2000.

19. Ibid.

20. Center for Strategic and International Studies, 2005.

21. See *Businessweek*, June 18, 2007, cover story: "The Real Cost of Offshoring."

22. See William Greider, "The Establishment Rethinks Globalization," *The Nation*, April 30 2007.

23. Department. of Sociology, Emory University. See http://www.sociology.emory.edu.

24. Sutherland and Sewell, 1998.

25. Rosenberg, 2002.

26. Rockefeller Foundation, 2001, p. 13.

27. Raghavan, 1996.

28. Ibid.

29. Ibid.

30. Rockefeller Foundation, 2001, p. 13.

31. Women's Rights and Economic Change, 2003. See http://www.awid.org/wrec.

32. Center for Strategic and International Studies, 2005.

33. Seguino, 1995, p. 1.

34. Ibid.

35. African Women's Economic Policy Network, 1996, p. 3.

36. Ibid.

37. Ibid, p. 9.

38. Ibid.

39. Women's Action for New Directions, 1994.

40. Wichterich, 2000.

41. Ibid.

42. Sassen, 2002. (At the same time, though, as discussed in Chapter 6, domestic violence may rise as women's wages reach or even excess those of their partners.)

43. Ehrenreich and Hochschild, 2002, p. 6.

44. Ibid.

45. Ibid, p. 40.

46. Ibid, p. 41.

47. Ibid, p. 42.

48. Arizpe, 1997, p. 238.

49. Ibid, p. 230.

50. Heyzer, 1981, p. 70.

51. Ibid, p. 72.

52. Htun, 1998, p. 11.

53. The North American Free Trade Agreement (NAFTA), a trade agreement between Mexico, the United States, and Canada, stipulates that restrictions on the free-flow of goods and services would be gradually removed over a period lasting between ten and fifteen years.

54. Brenner et al., 2000, p. 299.

55. Personal story from women's group working in the border region.

56. In the film *Global Assembly Line*, about maquiladora work in Mexico.

57. Nathan, 1999, p. 140.

58. Brenner et al., 2000.

59. Eskenazi et al., 1993, p. 674.

60. Brenner et al., 2000, p. 276.

61. Hynes and Raymond, 2002 p. 197.

62. U.S. Dept. of State, 2006; and UNESCO, "Trafficking Project."

63. Trafficking includes "all acts involved in the recruitment, abduction, transport, harboring, transfer, sale, or receipt of persons; within national or across international borders; through force, coercion, fraud, or deception; to place persons in situations of slavery or slavery-like conditions, forced labor or services, such as forced prostitution or sexual services, domestic servitude, bonded sweatshop labor, or other debt bondage." Richard, 1999, p. v.

64. United Nations Office of Drugs and Crime, "Trafficking in Persons: Global Patterns" April 2006, p. 7. The United Nations Convention Against Transnational Organized Crime, entered into force on September 29, 2003. The Protocol to Prevent, Suppress, and Punish Trafficking in Persons, Especially Women and Children entered into force on December 25 2003. The Protocol Against the Smuggling of Migrants by Land, Sea, and Air, entered into force on January 28 2004.

65. Ibid, p. 52.

66. The Protocol Against the Smuggling of Migrants by Land, Sea, and Air, p. 41.

67. United Nations Office of Drugs and Crime, 2006, p. 51.

68. Although the UN 2000 Protocol on Trafficking does recognize the distinction between voluntary prostitution and forced prostitution, it fails to define the phrase "exploitation of prostitution of others or other forms of sexual exploitation." This lack of definition reveals the divide between groups working on trafficking and human rights and their perceptions of prostitution. Some groups, notably the Coalition Against Trafficking in Women (CATW), argue that trafficking should include all forms of recruitment and transportation for prostitution, regardless of consent, and offers that "Prostitution is not sex work; it is violence against women. It exists because significant numbers of men are given social, moral and legal permission to buy women on demand. It exists because pimps and traffickers prey on women's poverty and inequality. It exists because it is a last-ditch survival strategy, not a choice, for millions of the world's women." (Raymond, 2005.) In contrast, groups in the Human Rights Caucus, like the Global Alliance Against Trafficking in Women and the Network of Sex Workers Project, support the distinction between voluntary and involuntary prostitution. These groups defend the right to self-determination, the right to work, and the right to self expression, believing that women can make informed choices about engaging in consensual commercial sex. CATW and its international partners question the wider socioeconomic and cultural context within which such "choices" are being made, and caution that legalizing "voluntary" prostitution reifies larger systems of male dominance and oppression against women. However, both CATW and groups in the Human Rights Caucus see the Protocol's inability to clearly define "exploitation of prostitution of others or other forms of sexual exploitation" as highly problematic for national governments that are deciding how to address prostitution in their domestic laws.

69. Article 4: No one shall be held in slavery or servitude; slavery and the slave trade shall be prohibited in all their forms.

Article 5: No one shall be subjected to torture or to cruel, inhuman or degrading treatment or punishment.

Article 13: 1. Everyone has the right to freedom of movement and residence within the borders of each State. 2. Everyone has the right to leave any country, including his own, and to return to his country.

The Universal Declaration of Human Rights may be accessed at http://www .hrweb.org/legal/udhr.html

70. Phinney, 2001.

71. Brown, 2000, p. 66.

72. Altink, 1995.

73. Derks (Southeast Asia); May (Mexico).

74. Altink, 1995, p. 4.

75. Sleightholme and Sinha, 1996, p. 73.

76. Raymond et al., 2002.

77. Sleightholme and Sinha, 1996, p. 73.

78. Poudel and Carryer, 2000.

79. Raymond et al., p. 71.

80. Raymond, 2001; Vulliamy, 2005.

81. Hyland, 2001, p. 43.

82. Altman, 2001, pp. 1ff.

83. McMahon, 1999.

84. Swedish Deputy Prime Minister Margareta Winberg, cited in Lochhead, 2003.

85. Hyland, 2001, p. 37.

86. These profits are hard to monitor, so estimates vary widely. See SAGE, Information Center; UNESCO "Trafficking Project."

87. Hyland, 2001, p. 38.

88. Organized crime syndicates found to be involved in trafficking were either structured hierarchically, with clearly defined roles, or as "core groups," where a small number of individuals are surrounded by a network of "associates." United Nations Office of Drugs and Crime, 2006, p. 69.

89. Landesman, 2004, p. 36.

90. Ibid, p. 37.

91. Poudel and Carryer, 2000.

92. Altink, 1995.

93. UN Development Fund for Women (UNIFEM), 2002d.

94. Worldlink TV, "No Experience Necessary." See http://www.internews.org /prs/worldlink/corps_2002_11_26.htm.

95. An article on the topic quotes a founder of one of these agencies thus: "It all started with women's lib," said Sam Smith . . . who founded I Love Latins in Houston. "Guys are sick and tired of the North American *me, me, me* attitude." Porter, Eduardo, "Law on Overseas Brides is Keeping Couples Apart." *New York Times,* July 19, 2007.

96. Richard, 1999, p. 27.

97. Ibid.

98. Ibid, p. 28.

99. Gorman, Anna, "Behind Closed Doors: A Life of Abuse, Fear." *Los Angeles Times,* August 12, 2005.

100. The Coalition to Abolish Slavery & Trafficking. See: http://www.castla .org.

101. Landesman, 2004, p. 32

102. Derks, Amnesty International; and Kathleen Kim, Professor, School of Law, Stanford University, in a lecture on November 13, 2006.

103. Richard, 1999.

104. The Coalition to Abolish Slavery & Trafficking, 2001.

105. Richard, 1999, p. vi.

106. Sleightholme and Sinha, 1996.

107. Lee, 1991, p. 85.

108. Ibid, p. 87.

109. Ibid, p. 97.

110. East-West Center, 2002.

111. *New York Times*, January 3,2005.

112. Hyland, 2001, p. 32.

113. Ibid, p. 67.

114. McMahon, 1999.

115. Ibid.

CHAPTER 9 AGING IN A MAN'S WORLD

1. *New York Times*, June 27, 2007. See:http://www.nytimes.com/2007/06/27/arts/ 27malaika.html?ex=1340596800&en=876672adca28cb8b&ei=5088&partner=rssnyt &emc=rss

2. Linthwaite, 1990, p. 182.

3. HelpAge International, 2006a.

4. Population Reference Bureau, 2005.

5. Population Reference Bureau, 2003a.

6. World Health Organization, 2000b.

7. World Health Organization, 1998.

8. Population Reference Bureau, 1999.

9. Ibid.

10. HelpAge International, 2000.

11. The UN International Institute on Ageing, 1991b.

12. Clara Pratt, quoted in the United Nations International Research and Train-ing Institute for the Advancement of Women, 1999, p. v.

13. Ibid.

14. Population Reference Bureau, 2003a.

15. Locke, Margaret, 1994, p. xx.

16. Ibid, p. xviii.

17. The UN International Institute on Ageing, 1991b.

18. Cited in Women's Health Collection, 1999b.

19. The Population Resource Center, 2001.

20. Lee and Haaga, 2002.

21. Zeilinger, 1999.

22. The UN International Institute on Ageing, 1991d.

23. Paul and Paul, 1995.

24. HelpAge International, 2000.

25. Sommers, 1994.

26. The UN International Institute on Ageing, 1991d.

27. The UN International Institute on Ageing, 1991c.

28. World Health Organization, 2002b.

29. HelpAge International, 2006b

30. World Health Organization, 2002b, p. 10.

31. Reproductive Health Outlook, 2006, citing Lindsey et al., 2003; Saengtienchai and Knodel, 2001; Williams and Tumwekwase, 2001; WHO, 2002. See http://www .rho.org/html/older_keyissues.htm#hivaids.

32. Reproductive Health Outlook, 2006, citing World Health Organization, 2002. See http://www.rho.org/html/older_keyissues.htm#hivaids.

33. Reproductive Health Outlook, 2006, citing Health and Development Networks, 2004.

34. Reproductive Health Outlook, 2006, citing HelpAge, 2003; International HIV/AIDS Alliance, 2004; UNAIDS, 2002; WHO, 2002.

35. Reproductive Health Outlook, 2006, citing HelpAge International, 2002.

36. Reproductive Health Outlook, 2006.

37. World Health Organization, 2000b.

38. Ibid.

39. Ibid.

40. World Health Organization, 2006.

41. World Health Organization, 2005a.

42. Ibid.

43. World Health Organization, 2000b.

44. That women live longer than men is explained in part by the balance of two forces, according to Thomas Perls, a geriatrician at Harvard Medical school: "One is the evolutionary drive to pass on her genes, the other is the need to stay healthy enough to rear as many children as possible. . . . Menopause . . . protects older women from the risks of bearing children late in life, and lets them live long enough to take care of their children and grandchildren." It appears that life spans are correlated with the length of time the offspring remain dependent on adults; in humans this is a longer period than for most other animals. Another perspective on women's longevity is behavioral: between the ages of fifteen and twenty four, men are four to five times more likely to die than females, and most of the fatalities are due to reckless behavior or violence. A lot of these differences in behavior can be attributed to hormones. Male testosterone seems to promote aggressive behavior and increases levels of low-density lipoprotein, raising a male's risk of heart disease. In contrast, estrogen in women lowers levels of low-density lipoprotein and raises high-density lipoprotein, or good cholesterol, which lowers risk of heart disease. At other ages, the difference in mortality narrows until later in life, in the fifties and sixties, when more men than women die, mostly because of heart disease. "Why Women Live Longer than Men," by Thomas T. Perls and Ruth C. Fretts. *Scientific American Presents: Women's Health: A Lifelong Guide*, 1998. Other insights about women living longer than men include the belief that the reason for this inequality is that males

engage in more risky behavior than females do. But new research published in *Science*, September 2002, reports on a study by Sarah L. Moore and Kenneth Wilson of the University of Stirling that may suggest that males are more likely than females to succumb to parasites: "With their generally larger size, males may just make more attractive targets." Ian P.F. Owens of Imperial College London notes that "In the United States, United Kingdom and Japan, men are approximately twice as vulnerable as women to parasite-induced death. . . . In countries with a higher overall incidence of deaths due to parasites, such as Kazakhstan and Azerbaijan, men are four times as vulnerable as women are. Still others (for example, Ronald Lee, a demographer at the University of California, Berkeley) posit that nurturing children into old age may result in people living longer.

45. The World Bank, 2001.

46. Personal observations in East Africa, 2004.

47. Population Reference Bureau, 1999.

48. United Nations International Research and Training Institute for the Advancement of Women, 1999, p. 6.

49. Frohman, Susanna and Patrick May, "Journey into the 'City of Widows.'" *San Jose Mercury News*, April 2, 2006.

50. HelpAge International, 2002a.

51. HelpAge International, 2000.

52. Lacey, Marc, "Rights Group Calls for End to Inheriting African Wives." *New York Times*, March 5, 2003.

53. I visited community groups in Western Kenya in October 2003; a trip report was provided to the Firelight Foundation, Santa Cruz, a sponsoring organization.

54. "Africa's Homeless Widows." *New York Times*, June 16, 2004.

55. Ibid.

56. The UN International Institute on Ageing, 1991a.

57. WHO/INPEA, 2002.

58. Ibid, p. 20.

59. Ibid, p. 18.

60. HelpAge International, 2002a.

61. Carreño, 2001.

62. Participant in roundtable discussion, "Establishing inter-sector cooperation to improve the situation of vulnerable older people in Kyrgyzstan." Held November 16, 2004. Quoted in *Kyrgyzstan Newsletter* February 2005, Issue 3.

63. The United Nations International Research and Training Institute for the Advancement of Women, 1999.

64. Ibid.

65. HelpAge International/ International HIV/AIDS Alliance, 2003.

66. "Reintegration of Older People into Moldovan Society: Good Practice Manual." Pontos: Chisinau, 2004. Manual accessed at http://www.helpage.org /Resources/Manuals#1118082365-0-10

67. Ageways, 2002.

68. Madrid International Plan of Action on Aging, 2002; United Nations Report on the Second World Assembly on Aging April 8–12, 2002, A/CONF. 197/9, Paragraph 81. As cited in HelpAge International/International HIV/AIDS Alliance, 2003.

69. Madrid International Plan of Action on Aging, 2002; United Nations Report on the Second World Assembly on Aging April 8–12, 2002, A/CONF. 197/9, Paragraph 16. As cited in Ageways, 2002.

70. HelpAge International, 2002a.

71. HelpAge International, 2002b.

72. HelpAge International, 2000.

73. Ageways, 2002.

74. Ibid.

CHAPTER 10   TURNING THE WORLD RIGHTSIDE UP

1. Linthwaite, 1990, p. 129.

2. Lerner, 1986, p. 5.

3. Basu, 1995.

4. Antrobus, 2004, p. 25.

5. For information about the purpose and creation of the Global Fund for Women, see Murray, 2005.

6. Sen, Gita, "The Politics of the International Women's Movement," in Srilatha Batliwala and David Brown, eds. Kumarian Press, *Claiming Global Power: Transnational Civil Society and Global Governance*, as quoted in Antrobus, 2004.

7. Antrobus, 2004.

8. Murray, Anne Firth, "President's Statement," annual report of the Global Fund for Women, 1989.

9. Sen, with Grown, 1985, p. 11.

10. Murray, 2006.

11. Whitmont, 1982.

12. See bibliography.

13. See www.un.org/millenniumgoals.

14. Waring, 2004, p. 1-2.

15. Ibid, p. 8.

Bibliography

Unless otherwise noted, electronic resources were accessed between January 2006 and August 2007.

ActionAid International
2004 *Stop Violence Against Girls in School*. Johannesburg, South Africa: ActionAid International.

Adler, Nancy, Thomas Boyce, Margaret A. Chesney, Sheldon Cohen, Susan Folkman, Robert L. Kahn, and S. Leonard Syme
1999 "Socioeconomic Status and Health: The Challenge of the Gradient," in *Health and Human Rights: A Reader*. Mann, Jonathan M., Sofia Gruskin, Michael A. Grodin, and George J. Annas (eds). New York, NY: Routledge, pp. 182–88.

African Women's Economic Policy Network
1996 "Women Standing Up to Adjustment in Africa." Uganda: AWEPON.

Ageways
2002 "Special Issue on the Second World Assembly on Ageing." *Ageways*, Issue 60, July.

Alan Guttmacher Institute
1998 "Young Women in a Changing World" in *Into a New World: Young Women's Sexual and Reproductive Lives*. New York: The Alan Guttmacher Institute.
1999 *Sharing Responsibility: Women, Society, and Abortion Worldwide*. New York, NY: The Alan Guttmacher Institute. http://www.agi-usa.org/pubs/sharing.pdf.

Alexander, M. Jacqui, Lisa Albrecht, Sharon Day, and Mab Segrest, eds.
2003 *Sing, Whisper, Shout, Pray!*. Fort Bragg, California: Edgework Books.

Altink, Sietske
1995 *Stolen Lives: Trading Women into Sex and Slavery*. New York, NY: Harrington Park Press.

Altman, Dennis
2001 *Global Sex*. Chicago: University of Chicago Press.

Altman, Lawrence K.
2004 "HIV Risk Greater for Young African Brides." *The New York Times*, February 29.

Amnesty International
"Trafficking of Persons: Fact Sheet: Stop Violence Against Women."
1999 "The Rationale of Honor Killings: Commodification of Women and the Honor Code." September.
2004a "Violence against Women." New York.
2004b "'So does it mean that we have the rights?' Protecting the human rights of women and girls trafficked for forced prostitution in Kosovo." New York.

Angier, Natalie
2002 "Weighing the Grandma Factor." *The New York Times*, November 5.

Antrobus, Peggy
2004 *The Global Women's Movement: Origins, Issues, and Strategies*. London: Zed Books.

Apter, Terri
1991 *Altered Loves: Mothers and Daughters During Adolescence*. New York, NY: Fawcett Books.

Arizpe, Lourdes
1997 "Women in the Informal-Labor Sector: The Case of Mexico City." *The Women, Gender and Development Reader*. Nalini Visvanathan, Lynn Duggan, Laurie Nisonoff, and Nan Wiegersma (eds). London: Zed Books.

Arora, Dolly
1996 "The Victimizing Discourse of Sex-Determination Technologies and Policy." *Economic and Political Weekly* Vol. 31, No. 7.

Arthur, Joyce
1997 "Psychological After-Effects of Abortion: The Real Story." *The Humanist Magazine*. New York, March/April, Vol. 57, No. 2.

Ashworth, Georgina
1995 *A Diplomacy of the Oppressed: New Directions in International Feminism*. London: Zed Books.

Asian Center for Women's Human Rights
1998 *Common Grounds: Violence against Women in War and Armed Conflict Situations*, Indai Lourdes Sajor, ed.

Association for Women's Rights in Development
2002 "The International Covenant on Economic, Social and Cultural Rights Primer." *Women's Rights and Economic Change No. 3*. Toronto: Association for Women's Rights in Development, August.

Avotri, Joyce Yaa, and Vivienne Walters
2001 "We Women Worry a Lot About Our Husbands: Ghanaian women talking about their health and their relationships with men." *Journal of Gender Studies* Vol. 10, No 2.

Badran, Margot, and Miriam Cooke
1990 "Zainaba." *Opening the Gates: A Century of Arab Feminist Writing.*
Bloomington: Indiana University Press.

Banister, Judith
2003 "Shortage of Girls in China Today: Causes, Consequences, International
Comparisons, and Solutions." Powerpoint Presentation. Beijing: Javelin
Investments. From Pop.Ref.Bureau Graphics Bank.

Barnstone, Aliki, and Willis Barnstone
1980 *A Book of Women Poets.* New York, NY: Schocken.

Barry, Jane
2005 *Rising Up in Response: Women's Rights Activism in Conflict.* Urgent Action
Fund for Women's Human Rights.

Basu, Amrita, ed.
1995 *The Challenge of Local Feminisms: Women's Movements in Global Perspective.*
Colorado: Westview Press.

Bennett, Olivia, Jo Bexley, and Kitty Warnock, eds.
1995 *Arms to Fight, Arms to Protect: Women Speak Out About Conflict.* London: Panos.

Berer, Marge, and Sunanda Ray
1993 *Women and HIV/AIDS: An International Resource Book.* London: Pandora.

Bilukha, Oleg O., Muireann Brennan, and Bradley A. Woodruff
2003 "Injuries Associated with Landmines and Unexploded Ordinance—
Afghanistan 1997–2002." *Journal of the American Medical Association*, October 8.

**Boelaert, Marleen, Fabienne Vautier, Time Dusauchoit, Wim Van Damme,
and Monique VanDormael**
1999 "The Relevance of Gendered Approaches to Refugee Health: A Case Study
in Hagadera, Kenya." *Engendering Forced Migration: Theory and Practice.* New
York: Berghahn Books, pp. 165–76.

Brenner, Joel, Jennifer Ross, Janie Simmons, and Sarah Zaidi
2000 "Neoliberal Trade and Investment and the Health of Maquiladora Workers
on the US–Mexico Border." In *Dying for Growth*, Jim Yong Kim, Joyce V.
Millen, Alec Irwin, and John Gershman (eds). Monroe, ME: Common
Courage Press, pp. 261–90.

British Broadcasting Company (BBC)
2004a "Europe Tackles Honour Killings." BBC News, June 22.
2004b "Interview with Stephen Lewis, Head of UNAIDS Office." BBC News, July.

Brown, Louise
2000 *Sex Slaves: The Trafficking of Women in Asia*. London: Virago Press.

Bulatao, Rodolfo
1998 *The Value of Family Planning Programs in Developing Countries*. Washington DC: RAND.

Bumiller, Elisabeth
1990 "No More Little Girls." In *May You Be the Mother of a Hundred Sons: A Journey Among the Women of India*. New York: Fawcett Columbine.

Bureau of Justice Statistics
1997 *Violence-Related Injuries Treated in Hospital Emergency Departments (NCJ-156921)*, August.

Butler, Robert, Myrna Lewis, and Trey Sunderland
1998 *Aging and Mental Health*. Boston: Allyn and Bacon.

Cammack, Diana
1999 "Gender Relief and Politics During the Afghan War." In *Engendering Forced Migration: Theory and Practice*. New York: Berghahn Books, pp. 94–121.

Canadian Council for International Cooperation
1991 "'Two Halves Make a Whole': Balancing Gender Relations in Development." Ottawa: Canadian Council for International Cooperation.

Caralis, P., and R. Musialowski
1997 "Women's Experiences with Domestic Violence and Their Attitudes and Expectations Regarding Medical Care of Abuse Victims." *South Medical Journal*, Vol. 90: 1075–80.

Carmichael, Mary
2004 "No Girls, Please." *Newsweek*, January 26.

Carreño, Dolly
2001 "On Growing Older: Some Observations on Important Issues." *Women and Mental Health: Reflections of Inequality*, Women's Health Collection 6. Adriana Gómez and Deborah Meacham (eds). Santiago, Chile: Latin American and Caribbean Women's Health Network.

Carrillo, Roxanna
1990 "Violence Against Women: An Obstacle to Development" *Human Development Report*.

Center for Research on Women
2000 Kahn, Janet, and Susan Bailey. "Shaping A Better World: Global Issues, Gender Issues."

Center for Disease Control/National Center for Health Statistics
1995 "Vital Health Statistics." National Center for Health Statistics. Series 20 and 23.
1998 "Surgical Sterilization in the United States: Prevalence and Characteristics, 1965–95." Center for Disease Control and National Center for Health Statistics.
2004 "Global Perspective: Refugee Reproductive Health." www.cdc.gov/nccdphp/dhr/logistics/global_rrh.htm.

Center for Defense Information (CDI)
2003 "The World At War—January 1, 2003." In *Defense Monitor* Vol. XXXII, No. 1, January/February.

Center for Strategic and International Studies (CSIS)
2005 "What is Globalization?" www.globalization101.org/p.1

Center for Reproductive Rights
2004 "Female Circumcision/Female Genital Mutilation (FC/FGM): Legal Prohibitions Worldwide." February. http://www.crlp.org/pub_fac_fgmicpd.html.

Center for Women's Global Leadership
1994 "Testimonies of the Global Tribunal on Violations of Women's Human Rights." New Jersey: Plowshares Press.

Chu Junghong
2001 "Prenatal Sex Determination and Sex-Selective Abortion in Rural Central China." *Population and Development Review*, Vol. 27, No. 2, June.

CNN
2002 "Fort Bragg Killing Raises Alarm about Stress." CNN, July 27.
2004 *Nightline.* CNN, May 4.

Chase, Marilyn
2004 "Saying No to 'Sugar Daddies.'" *The Wall Street Journal*, February 25.

The Coalition to Abolish Slavery and Trafficking
2001 "Educational Briefing." Presentation.

Coburn, Broughton
1991 *Nepali Aama: Portrait of a Nepalese Hill Woman.* Singapore: Tien Wah Press.

Cohen, Susan A.
1998 "The Reproductive Health Needs of Refugees: Emerging Consensus Attracts Predictable Controversy." In *The Guttmacher Report on Public Policy 1998*, Vol. 1, No. 5: 10–20.

The Commonwealth Fund
1993 *First Comprehensive National Health Survey of American Women Finds Them at Significant Risk* (News Release). New York: The Commonwealth Fund, July 14.

Cook, Rebecca J., ed.
1994 *Human Rights of Women: National and International Perspectives*. Philadelphia: University of Pennsylvania

Cosman, Carol, Joan Keefe, and Kathleen Weaver, eds.
1988 *The Penguin Book of Women Poets*. London: Penguin.

Crawley, Heaven
1999 "Women and Refugee Status in the UK." In *Engendering Forced Migration: Theory and Practice*, Doreen Indra (ed). New York: Berghahn Books.

Crose, Royda
1997 *Why Women Live Longer than Men . . . and What Men Can Learn From Them*. San Francisco: Jossey-Bass.

Dalsimer, Marlyn, and Laurie Nisonoff
1997 "Abuses against Women and Girls under the One-Child Family Plan of the People's Republic of China." *The Women, Gender and Development Reader*. London: Zed Books.

De Bruyn, Maria
1999 "Intersecting Health Risks: Adolescent Unwanted Pregnancy, Abortion, and AIDS." *Initiatives in Reproductive Health Policy* Vol. 3, No. 1, North Carolina: Ipas.

De Lima, Maria Santiago
1997 "Reproductive Risks of Rural Workers." *Women's Health Collection 2*, Deborah Meacham (ed). Santiago, Chile: Latin American and Caribbean Women's Health Network.

Department of Health and Human Services and Centers for Disease Control and Prevention, National Center for Injury Prevention and Control
2003 "Costs of Intimate Partner Violence Against Women in the United States."

Derks, Annuska
2000 "Combating Trafficking in South-East Asia: A Review of Policy and Programme Responses." Geneva, Switzerland: International Organization for Migration, Migration Research Series. February.

Dervarics, Charles
2003 "African Girls' Route to School is Still Littered With Obstacles." *The New York Times*, December 14.

Doress-Worters, Paula B., and Diana Laskin Siegal
1994 *The New Ourselves, Growing Older: Women Aging with Knowledge and Power.* The Boston Women's Health Book Collective. New York: Simon & Schuster.

Drezner, Daniel
2004 "Globalization Without Riots." *The New York Times*, April 18.

Dugger, Celia
2000 "Kerosene, Weapon of Choice for Attacks on Wives in India." *The New York Times*, December 26.

East-West Center
2002 "Human Trafficking, Challenge of Globalization in Asia–Pacific–US." *East-West Center Observer*, Fall 2002.

Easterly, William
2006 *The White Man's Burden.* New York, NY: Penguin Press.

Ehrenreich, Barbara, and Arlie Russell Hochschild, eds.
2002 *Global Woman: Nannies, Maids, and Sex Workers in the New Economy.* New York: Metropolitan Books.

Elimu Yetu Coalition
2005 "The challenge of educating girls in Kenya" in *Beyond Access: Transforming Policy and Practice for Gender Equality in Education.* Sheila Aikman and Elaine Unterhalter (eds). London: Oxfam Great Britain.

Ellis, Deborah
2001 *Women of the Afghan War.* Westport, Connecticut: Praeger Publishers.

Elson, Diane
1992 "Male Bias in Structural Adjustment." *Women and Adjustment Policies in the Third World.* Haleh Afshar, Carolyne Dennis (eds). New York: St Martin's Press.

Emecheta, Buchi
1983 *Second Class Citizen.* New York, NY: George Braziller.

Ensler, Eve
2000 *The Vagina Monologues.* New York, NY: Random House Inc.

Enzensberger, Hans Magnus
1993 *Civil Wars: from L.A. to Bosnia.* New York, NY: New Press.

Epstein, Helen
2004 "The Fidelity Fix." *The New York Times Magazine*, June 19, pp. 54–59.

Eskenazi, B., S. Guendelman, and E. P. Elkin
1993 "A Preliminary Study of Reproductive Outcomes of Female Maquiladora Workers in Tijuana, Mexico." *American Journal of Industrial Medicine* Vol. 24: pp. 667–76.

Family Violence Prevention Fund
1994 "Health Care Response to Domestic Violence Fact Sheet." *End Abuse*. San Francisco: Family Violence Prevention Fund.
1998a Levi, Robin. "Cambodia: Rattling the Killing Fields." Ending Domestic Violence: Report from the Global Frontlines, Leni Marin, Helen Zia, and Esta Soler (eds). San Francisco: Family Violence Prevention Fund.
1998b Ganley, A. "Domestic Violence: Strategies for Screening, Assessment, Intervention, and Documentation." Trainer's Manual for Health Care Providers. San Francisco: Family Violence Prevention Fund.

Farha, Leilani
1998 "The case of forced evictions." In *The Women and War Reader*. New York: New York University Press, pp. 77–109.

Farmer, Paul
1996 "Women, Poverty, and AIDS." *Women, Poverty, and AIDS: Sex, Drugs, and Structural Violence*. Monroe, ME: Common Courage Press.

Fathalla, Mahmoud
1997 *Obstetrics and Gynecology to Women's Health*. New York, NY: Parthenon Publishing Group.
2007 *Issues in Women's Health: International and Egyptian Perspectives*. Assiut, Egypt: Assiut University Press.

Filkins, Dexter
2003 "'Honor Killings Defy Turkish Efforts to End Them." *The New York Times*.

Food and Agriculture Organization of the United Nations
2003 "Women and Food Security." August.
2006 "Women and Food Security." June.

The Forum for African Women Educationalists (FAWE)
1995 *Girls and African Education: Research and Action to Keep Girls in School*. Nairobe, Kenya: FAWE International House.

Freedman, Estelle
2002 *No Turning Back: The History of Feminism and the Future of Women*. New York: Ballantine Books.

French, Howard W.
2005 "A Village Grows Rich Off Its Main Export: Its Daughters." *The New York Times*, January 3.

Friedman L., J. Samet, M. Roberts, M. Hudlin, and P. Hans
1992 "Inquiry About Victimization Experiences: A Survey of Patient Preferences and Physician Practices." *Archives of Internal Medicine* Vol. 152: pp. 1186–90.

Frohman, Susanna, and Patrick May
2006 "Journey into the 'City of Widows.'" *San Jose Mercury News*, April 2.

Ganatra, Bela, Siddhe Hirve, and V.N. Rao
2001 "Sex-Selective Abortion: A Community-Based Study in Western India." *Asia-Pacific Population Journal* Vol. 16, No. 2.

Global Fund for Children
2003 *Annual Report 2002–03.* http://www.globalfundforchildren.org/about_us/ GFC_AR0203.pdf.

Goodyear, Lorlei
2002 "Reproductive Health and Rights: Reaching the Hardly Reached Article 5: Reaching Refugees and Internally Displaced Persons." Seattle: PATH. http:// www.path.org/files/RHR-Article-5.pdf.

Gordon, John E., Sohan Singh, and John B. Wyon
1965 "Causes of Death at Different Ages by Sex and by Season in a Rural Population of Punjab 1957–1959." *Indian Journal of Medical Research*, September.

Gorman, Anna
2005 "Behind Closed Doors: A Life of Abuse, Fear." *Los Angeles Times*, August 12.

Griffiths, P., Z. Mathews, and A. Hinde
2002 "Gender, family, and the nutritional status of children in three culturally contrasting states of India." *Social Science & Medicine* Vol. 55, pp. 775–90.

Haddad, Lawrence, Christine Peña, Chizuru Nishida, Agnes R. Quisumbing, and Alison Slack
1996 "Food Security and Nutrition Implications of Intrahousehold Bias: A Review of Literature." Washington, DC: Food Consumption and Nutrition Division, International Food Policy Research Institute, September.

Haldar, A.K., and N. Battacharyya
1969 "Fertility and Sex Sequence of Children of Indian Couples." *Sankhya*, Series B 31:144.

Halsell, Grace
1993 "Women's Bodies a Battlefield in War for 'Greater Serbia.'" In *Washington Report on Middle East Affairs*, April/May 1993, Vol. XI, No. 9.

The Harvard University Gazette
1998 Cromie, William J., "Why Women Live Longer Than Men." *The Harvard Universty Gazette*, October 1.

HelpAge International
2000a "The Mark of a Noble Society: Human Rights and Older People," Briefing Paper, HelpAge International, November.
2000b "Witchcraft—a violent threat." Ageing and Development News No. 6. HelpAge International, July.
2002a "Gender and Ageing Briefs." HelpAge International, April.
2002b "UNHCR Older Refugees: a resource for the refugee community. " Health and Community Development Division, n.d. cited in Gender and Ageing Briefs, HelpAge International.
2004 "Reintegration of Older People into Moldovan Society: Good Practice Manual." Pontos: Chisinau. Manual accessed June 12, 2006 at http://www.helpage.org/Resources/Manuals#1118082365-0-10.
2006a "Case Study: Doña Eulogia." http://www.helpage.org/Worldwide/@24026
2006b "Older women lead response to HIV/AIDS." http://helpage.org/News/Latestnews/@27680.

HelpAge International and International HIV/AIDS Alliance
2003 "Forgotten Families: Older people as carers of orphans and vulnerable children." HelpAge International/International HIV/AIDS Alliance.

Heise, Lori L., Jacqueline Pitanguy, and Adrienne Germain
1994 *Violence Against Women: The Hidden Health Burden*. World Bank Discussion Papers, 255. Washington DC: World Bank.

The Hesperian Foundation
1997 "Facts about Domestic Violence and Abuse." August Burns, Ronnie Lovich, Jane Maxwell, et al., *Where Women Have No Doctor: A Health Guide for Women*. Berkeley, CA: The Hesperian Foundation.

Heyzer, Noeleen
1981 "Toward a Framework of Analysis." In *Women at Work*. 1985, Cambridge: Overseas Development Network, pp. 70–74.

Hirshfield, Jane, ed.
1994 *Women in Praise of the Sacred*. New York, NY: Harper Collins.

Hord, Charlotte
1999 "ICPD Paragraph 8.25: A Global Review of Progress." North Carolina: Ipas.

Hosken, Fran
1993 *The Hosken Report: Genital and Sexual Mutilation of Females, Fourth Revised Edition*. Massachusetts: Women's International Network Press.

Howarth, John P., Timothy D. Healing, and Nicholas Banatvala
1997 "Health care in disaster and refugee settings." In *Lancet* Vol. 349, No. 9068s.

Htun, Mala
1998 *Women's Rights and Opportunities in Latin America: Problems and Prospects.*
Washington, DC: Women's Leadership Conference of the Americas.

Human Rights Watch
1996 "Shattered Lives: Sexual Violence During the Rwandan Genocide and its
Aftermath." New York: Human Rights Watch.
2000 "Federal Republic of Yugoslavia: Rape as a Weapon of 'Ethnic Cleansing.'"
New York: Human Rights Watch.
2001a "'Fueling Afghanistan's War.'" New York: Human Rights Watch.
2001b "Sexual Violence Within the Sierra Leone Conflict." New York: Human
Rights Watch.
2003 Landmine Moniter Report. August, Human Rights Watch. http://www.icbl.
org/lm/2003.

Hyland, Kelly
2001 "Protecting Human Victims of Trafficking: An American Framework."
Berkeley Women's Law Journal, pp. 29–71.

Hynes, Patricia H., and Janice Raymond
2002 "Put in Harm's Way: The Neglected Health Consequences of Sex
Trafficking in the United States." In *Policing the National Body: Sex, Race, and
Criminalization*. Jael Silliman and Anannya Bhattacharjee (eds). Cambridge:
South End Press.

Illich, Ivan
1982 *Gender*. New York, NY: Random House, Inc.

Inter Press Service News Industry
2004 Mulama, Joyce. "A Disturbing Trend in Female Genital Mutilation." *Inter
Press Service News Agency*, June 9. http://www.ipsnews.net/africa/interna.
asp?idnews=24098.

**Interagency Gender Working Group (IGWG) and Population Reference
Bureau (PRB)**
2002 "Gender-Based Violence and Reproductive Health & HIV/AIDS."
Washington DC: IGWG and PRB, October.

International Centre for Research on Women (ICRW)
2001a "The Critical Role of Youth in Global Development." *ICRW Issue Brief*,
December.
2001b Caraël, Michael, and King K. Holmes, "Dynamics of HIV Epidemics
in Sub-Saharan Africa: Introduction." *AIDS Information Bulletin*, Vol. 15,
Supplement 4.

2002 "What Every Planner Needs to Know: How AIDS Affects Young Women and Girls and What Programs Can Do." *ICRW Information Bulletin*, February.
2003 "Child Marriage." *ICRW Policy Advisory*.
2004 Strickland, "To Have and to Hold," June.

International Institute on Ageing

1991a Apt, Nana Araba, "Elderly Women's Economic Participation: Problems and Prospects in Africa." *Bold: Quarterly Journal of the International Institute on Aging (United Nations–Malta)* Vol. 2, November 1.
1991b "The Role of Statistics in Changing the Image of Elderly Women as Productive Partners." *Bold: Quarterly Journal of the International Institute on Aging (United Nations–Malta)* Vol. 2, November 1.
1991c Havens, Betty. "Interface of the Formal System and Informal Care." Quarterly Journal of the International Institute on Aging (United Nations–Malta) Vol. 2, November 1.
1991d Hoskins, Irene. "Older women's Issues 1985–1991: Invisibility, Vulnerability and Empowerment." Bold: Quarterly Journal of the International Institute on Aging (United Nations–Malta) Vol. 2, November 1.

International Labour Organization

1998 "Gender Guidelines for Employment and Skills Training in Conflict-Affected Countries." Geneva: ILO.

International Women's Health Coalition (IWHC)

1989 *Special Challenges in Third World Women's Health*. Presentations at the 117th Annual Meeting of the American Public Health Association. Chicago, Illinois. October.
1991 *Reproductive Tract Infections in Women in the Third World: National and International Policy Implications*. Report of a Meeting at the Bellagio Study and Conference Center. Lake Como, Italy. April 29 – May 3.

Izett, Susan, and Nahid Toubia

1999 *Learning About Social Change*. New York: Rainbo.

Jaffe, P., and M. Sudermann

1995 "Child Witness of Women Abuse: Research and Community Responses," in Stith, S., and M. Straus (eds). Understanding Partner Violence: Prevalence, Causes, Consequences, and Solutions. Families in Focus Services, Vol. II. Minneapolis, MN: National Council on Family Relations.

Jang, Deeana, Debbie Lee, and Rachel Morello-Frosch

1997 "Domestic Violence in the Immigrant and Refugee Community: Responding to the Needs of Immigrant Women." *RESPONSE* Issue 77, Vol. 13, No 4.

Joint United Nations Programme on HIV/AIDS (UNAIDS)
1997 "The Female Condom and AIDS." April. www.unaids.org/publications/ documents/care/index.html#female.
2001 Feinstein, Noah, and Becky Prentice "Gender and AIDS Almanac."
2002 "Mother-to-Child Transmission of HIV." *Factsheet*, January 2.
2003a "HIV/AIDS and Youth: At a Glance." December. http://wbln0018. worldbank.org/HDNet/hddocs.nsf/0/62beb610bb2fc69085256df800582d70? OpenDocument.
2003b "AIDS Epidemic Update." December.
2004a "Violence against Women and AIDS." *Factsheet*, February 2.
2004b "Microbicides, Women, and AIDS." *Factsheet*, February 2.
2004c "World AIDS Campaign 2004: Women, Girls, HIV and AIDS, A Strategic Overview and Background Note." January 28.
2004d "HIV/AIDS and Young People: Hope for Tomorrow." April.

Joyce, Colin, and Keiko Iguchi
2001 "Japanese Parents Hope: Daughters Will Take Care of Us." Japan: *PANOS*, January 1.

Kaiser Foundation
2004 Global HIV/AIDS Epidemic Fact Sheet. http://www.kff.org/hivaids/3030.cfm.

Katz, Nikki
2003 "What You Need to Know About Honor Killings." *Women's Issues*, November 4. http://womensissues.about.com/cs/honorkillings/a/honorkillings.htm.

Kerr, Joanna
1993 *Ours by Right: Women's Rights as Human Rights*. London: Zed Books.

Klapper, Bradley S.
2005 "U.N. Says 90 Million Girls Not Getting Education." *AP/Seattle Post Intelligencer*, November 25.

Kim, Jim Y., Joyce V. Millen, Alec Irwin, et al.
2000 *Dying For Growth: Global Inequality and the Health of the Poor*. Monroe, ME: Common Courage Press.

Knonstantinovi-Villi, Slobodanka
2000 "Psychological Violence and Fear in War and Their Consequences for the Psychological Health of Women." In *Women, Violence and War: Wartime Victimization of Refugees in the Balkans*, Vesna Nikolic-Ristanovic (ed). Budapest: Central European University Press.

Kristof, Nicholas
2003a "Alone and Ashamed." *The New York Times*, May 16.
2003b "Killing Them Softly." *The New York Times*, September 20.

Kyrgyzstan Newsletter
2005 "Establishing inter-sector cooperation to improve the situation of vulnerable older people in Kyrgyzstan." Roundtable Discussion, November 16, 2004, as cited in February, Issue 3.

Lacey, Marc
2003 "Rights Group Calls for End to Inheriting African Wives." *The New York Times*, March 5.
2004 "Amnesty Says Sudan Militias Use Rape as a Weapon." *The New York Times*, July 19.

Landesman, Peter
2004 "The Girl Next Door." *The New York Times Magazine*, January 25, pp. 30–75.

Lee, Ronald, and John Haaga
2002 "Government Spending in an Older America." Reports on America 3.1. Washington DC: Population Reference Bureau, May.

Lee, Wendy
1991 "Prostitution and Tourism in South-East Asia." In *Working Women: International Perspectives on Labour and Gender Ideology*. Nanneke Redclift and M. Thea Sinclair (eds). New York, NY: Routledge Press, pp. 79–103.

Lentin, Ronit (ed.)
1997 *Gender and Catastrophe*. London: Zed Books.

Leonhardt, David
2003 "It's A Girl! (Will the Economy Suffer?)" *The New York Times*, October 26.

Lerner, Gerda
1986 *The Creation of Patriarchy*. New York, NY: Oxford University Press.

Levinson, David
1989 "Family Violence in Cross-Cultural Perspective," *Frontiers of Anthropology*, Volume 1. California: Sage Publishers.

Lewis, Stephen
2004 Microbicides Conference Keynote Speech. London, March 30.
2005 *Race Against Time*. Toronto: House of Anansi Press.

Lindsey, Charlotte
2001 *Women Facing War: ICRC study on the impact of armed conflict on women*. Geneva: International Committee for the Red Cross (ICRC).

Linthwaite, Illona
1987 *Ain't I a Woman!* New York: Peter Bedrick Books.

Lock, Margaret
1994 *Encounters With Aging: Mythologies of Menopause in Japan and North America.* Berkeley: University of California Press.

Lockhead, Carolyn
2003 "Sex Trade uses Bay Area to Bring in Women, Kids." *San Francisco Chronicle*, February 26, 2003.

Lu, Irene
2004 "The Needs of Afghan Women in Post-Conflict Reconstruction and Development." Unpublished Undergraduate Honors Thesis, Stanford University.

Majumdar, Swapna
2003 "In India, Domestic Violence Rises with Education." http://www.womensenews.org/article.cfm/dyn/aid/1591.

Mann, Jonathan M., Sofia Gruskin, Michael A. Grodin, George J. Annas, eds.
1999 *Health and Human Rights: A Reader.* New York: Routledge.

Martin, Susan Forbes
1991 *Refugee Women.* New Jersey: Zed Books.

Matlou, Patrick
1999 "Upsetting the Cart: Forced Migration and Gender Issues, the African Experience." *Engendering Forced Migration: Theory and Practice.* New York: Berghahn Books, pp. 128–43.

May, Meredith
2006 "Sex Trafficking: San Francisco is a Major Center." *San Francisco Chronicle*, October 6.

McCauley J., R. Yurk, M. Jenckes, and D. Ford
1998 "Inside 'Pandora's Box': Abused Women's Experiences Wghgggyyyith Clinicians and Health Services." *Archives of Internal Medicine* Vol. 13: 549–55.

McCourt, Frank
1996 *Angela's Ashes.* New York, NY: Scribner.

McKinley, James C.
1996 "Legacy of Rwanda Violence: The Thousands Born of Rape." *The New York Times*, September 23.

McMahon, Kathryn
1999 "Introduction to the Trafficking of Women: A Report from Los Angeles." Paper presented at Berkshire Conf. on History of Women, June 3-6.

Mead, Margaret
1940 "Warfare Is Only an Invention—Not a Biological Necessity." *Asia*, August.
http://faculty.millikin.edu/~moconner.hum.faculty.mu/in151/mead.html.

Meadows, Donella
1989 "Thoughts While Cleaning the Living Room." *Caring For Families* Vol. 21,
Spring, p. 16.

Meintjes, Sheila, Anu Pillay, and Meredeth Turshen
2001 *The Aftermath: Women in Post-Conflict Transformation*. London: Zed Books.

Melody, David, and Gorik Ooms
2002 Medécins Sans Frontières Coordinators, Maputo, October 21. Accessed June
20, 2006. http://www.msf.org/msfinternational/invoke.cfm?component=article
&objectid=1C3A8933-16B6-4CA6-B551EAE6AF5E562B&method=full_html.

Merali, Isfahan
2000 "Advancing women's reproductive and sexual health rights: using the
International Human Rights system." *Development in Practice* Vol. 10, No. 5,
November.

Mertus, Julie A.
2000 *War's Offensive on Women: The Humanitarian Challenge in Bosnia, Kosovo, and
Afghanistan*. Bloomfield: Kumarian Press.

Miller, Barbara D.
1981 *The Endangered Sex*. Ithaca, NY: Cornell University Press.

Miller, Alice, Ann, Janette Rosga, and Meg Satterthwaite
1999 "Health, Human Rights, and Lesbian Existence." *Health and Human Rights*.
New York, NY: Routledge.

Moreno, Garcia
1997 "Women Are Not Just Transmitters." *The Women, Gender and Development
Reader*. London: Zed Books.

Moulton, Jeanne
1997 *Formal and Non-formal Education and Empowered Behavior: A Review of the
Research Literature*. Support for Analysis and Research in Africa (SARA)
Project, April.

Mrvic-Petrovic, Nataša, and Ivana Stevanovic
2000 "Life in refuge—changes in socioeconomic and familial status." In *Women,
Violence and War: Wartime Victimization of Refugees in the Balkans*. Budapest:
Central European University Press.

Murray, Anne Firth
1989 *President's Statement.* The Global Fund for Women: The First Two Years, 1987–89. Annual Report, October.
2006 *Paradigm Found: Leading and Managing for Positive Change.* Novato, California: New World Library.

Mydans, Seth
2003 "A Friendship Sundered by Muslim Code of Honor." *The New York Times,* February 1.

Nath, Madhu Bala
2001 *From Tragedy Towards Hope.* London: Commonwealth Secretariat.

Nathan, Debbie
1997 "Death Comes to the Maquilas: A Border Story." In *Perspectives: Women's Studies.* Renae Bredin, (ed). Bellevue, IA: CourseWise Publishing, pp. 139–43.

The National Council for Research On Women
2000 *The World's Women: A Demographic and Statistical Overview.* New York, NY: The National Council for Research on Women.

The National Institute of Mental Health (NIMH)
1982 *Television and Behavior: Ten Years of Scientific Progress and Implications for the Eighties.* Pearl, David, L. Bouthilet, and J. Lazar (eds). Rockville, Maryland: National Institute of Mental Health.

The New York Law Journal
2003 Adcock, Thomas. "Guatemalan Asylum Case Helps Push Envelope in Abuse Matters." *New York Law Journal* Vol. 229, p. 16, May 23.

The New York Times
1996 September 23.
2000 "Honor Killings." *The New York Times* editorial, November 12.
2003 "The War Against Women." *The New York Times,* Editorial Desk, January 12.
2004 "Africa's Homeless Widows." *The New York Times,* June 16.
2004 A Population Crisis in the Most Populous Nation." *The New York Times,* May 30.

Njiru, Haron
2003 "The Poverty of Female Genital Mutilation (FGM)." Presentation. Austin, Texas: Fourth Trapped by Poverty/Trapped by Abuse Conference, October.

Nikolic-Ristanovic, Vesna
2000 *Women, Violence and War: Wartime Victimization of Refugees in the Balkans.* Budapest: Central European University Press.

Older Women's League
1993 "Violence Against Older Women." *The OWL Observer 13.4.* Washington
    DC: Older Women's League, Summer.

Oxfam
2003 "Links." Editorial, *Oxfam Newsletter,* October.

Paternostro, Silvana
1999 *In the Land of God and Man: A Latin Woman's Journey.* New York, NY: Plume
    Books.

Paul, Suzanne, and James Paul.
1995 "The World Bank, Pensions, and Income (In)Security in the Global South."
    International Journal of Health Services 25.4. New York: Baywood Publishing Co.

Perls, Thomas T., and Ruth C. Fretts
1998 "Why Women Live Longer than Men." *Scientific American Presents: Women's
    Health: A Lifelong Guide.* Scientific American.

Petchesky, Rosalind P.
1997 "Spiraling Discourses of Reproductive and Sexual Rights: A Post-Beijing
    Assessment of International Feminist Politics." *Women Transforming Politics:
    An Alternative Reader.* New York: New York University Press.
2003 *Global Prescriptions: Gendering Health and Human Rights.* London: Zed Books.

Pillay, Anu
2001 "Violence Against Women in the Aftermath." In *The Aftermath: Women in
    Post-Conflict Transformation.* Meintjes, Sheila, A. Pillay, and M. Turshen, (eds).
    London: Zed Books.

Pitanguy, Jacqueline, ed.
2007 *Violence Against Women in the International Context,* CEPIA, Rio de Janeiro,
    June

Phinney, Alison
2001 *Review of Trafficking of Women and Children, for the Inter-American
    Commission of Women,* Organization of American States, October.

Population Action International
1998 Conly, Shanti R. *Educating Girls: Gender Gaps and Gains.* Washington, DC:
    Population Action International.
2001 "A World of Difference: Sexual and Reproductive Health and Risks. The
    PAI Report Card 2001." Washington DC: Population Action International.

Population Council and International Family Health
2000 "The Case for Microbicides: A Global Priority." New York, NY: Population
    Council and International Family Health.

Population and Development Program at Hampshire College
2003 "Ten Reasons Why Militarism is Bad for Reproductive Freedom." *Different Takes* No. 20, Winter.

Population Information Program and Center for Health and Gender Equity (CHANGE)
1999 "Ending Violence Against Women." Population Reports, Vol. XXVII, No. 4, December.

Population Reference Bureau
1998 Haupt, Arthur, and Thomas Kane. *Population Reference Bureau's International Population Handbook*, 4th Edition. Washington DC: Population Reference Bureau.
1999 "The Coming Age of Older Women." *Population Today*, Vol. 27, No. 2, February.
2000a "The World's Youth 2000 Data Sheet." Washington, DC: Population Reference Bureau.
2000b "Conveying Concerns: Women Report on Gender-Based Violence." Washington, DC: Population Reference Bureau, April.
2000c "Making Pregnancy and Childbirth Safer." Washington, DC: Population Reference Bureau, May.
2001 "Abandoning Female Genital Cutting: Prevalence, Attitudes, and Efforts to End the Practice." Washington, DC: Population Reference Bureau, August.
2002a "2002 Women of Our World." Washington, DC: The Population Reference Bureau.
2002b Ashford, Lori, "Hidden Suffering: Disabilities From Pregnancy and Childbirth in Less Developed Countries." Washington, DC: The Population Reference Bureau, November.
2002c "Family Planning Worldwide 2002 Data Sheet." Washington, DC: Population Reference Bureau.
2003a "World Population Data Sheet of the Population Reference Bureau: Demographic Data and Estimates for the Countries and Regions of the World." Washington, DC: Population Reference Bureau.
2003b "Sex Ratio Imbalance in India: Too Few Girls." Powerpoint Presentation, Population Reference Bureau.
2003c Roudi-Fahimi, Farzaneh. "Female Education in the Middle East and North Africa." Washington, DC: Population Reference Bureau, October.
2005 "Global Aging: The Challenge of Success." *Population Bulletin*, Washington, DC: Population Reference Bureau, March.

Population Reports
1995 "Female Genital Mutilation: A Reproductive Health Concern." Supplement to *Population Meeting the Needs of Young Adults*, Series J, No. 41, Vol. XXIII, No. 3, October.

The Population Resource Center
2001 Executive Summary: *The Status of Women Around the World*. Princeton, New Jersey: The Population Resource Center.

Poudel, Praima, and Jenny Carryer
2000 "Girl-Trafficking, HIV/AIDS, and the Position of Women in Nepal."
Gender and Development, Vol. 8, No. 2.

Pradhan, Elizabeth Kimbrough, Keith P. West, Jr., Joanne Katz, Parul Christian, Subarna K. Khatry, Steven C. LeClerq; Sanu Maiya Dali; Sharada Ram Shrestha.
2002 "Risk of death following pregnancy in rural Nepal." *Bulletin of the World Health Organization*. November, Vol. 80, No.11: pp. 887-91. Available online at http://www.scielosp.org/scielo.php?script=sci_arttext&pid=S0042-96862002001100009&lng=en&nrm=iso.

Premi, Mahendra K.
2001 "The Missing Girl Child." *Economic and Political Weekly*, Vol. XXXVI, No. 21, May 26.

Radcliffe Public Policy Center (Harvard) & Women in Informal Employment Globalizing and Organizing (WIEGO)
2000 "Rethinking the informal economy: a dialogue between academics and activists." *International Perspectives on Work and the Economy* Vol. 1, Issue 2.

Raghavan, Chakravarthi
1996 "TNCs Control Two Thirds of the World Economy." *Third World Resurgence* 65/66.

Rahman, Anika, and Nahid Toubia
2000 *Female Genital Mutilation: A Guide to Laws and Policies Worldwide*. New York, NY: Center for Reproductive Law and Policy.

Raine, Nancy Venable
1998 *After Silence: Rape and My Journey Back*. New York, NY: Three Rivers Press.

Ramdas, Kavita N.
2004 "Ending Trafficking" Talk Given in Chicago, March 8.

Ramirez, F.O.
1997 "Progress, Justice and Gender Equality: World Models and Cross-National Trends." *Bring Back the Iron Cage*. Stanford, CA: Stanford University.

Ravindran, Sundari
1990 "The Untold Story: How the Health Care System Contributes to Maternal Mortality." *Maternal Mortality & Morbidity: A Call to Women for Action*. Special Issue, May 28.

Raymond, Janice
2005 "Sex Trafficking is Not 'Sex Work.'" *Conscience* Vol. XXVI, No. 1. Accessed June 12, 2006. http://action.web.ca/home/catw/readingroom.shtml?x=74355.

Raymond, Janice, and Donna Hughes

2001 "Sex Trafficking of Women in the U.S." Coalition Against Trafficking in
    Women, March.

**Raymond, Janice, Jean D'Cunha, Siti Dzuhayatin, H. Patricia Hynes,
Zoraida Rodriguea, and Aida Santos**

2002 "A Comparative Study of Women Trafficked in the Migration Process:
    Patterns, Profiles, and Health Consequences of Sexual Exploitation in Five
    Countries (Indonesia, the Philippines, Thailand, Venezuela, and the United
    States.)" http://action.web.ca/home/catw/readingroom.shtml?x=17062.

Reproductive Health Outlook (RHO)

2006 "Impact of HIV/AIDS on Older Women." *Key Issues: Older Women.* PATH.
    http://www.rho.org/html/older_keyissues.htm.

Richard, Amy O'Neil

1999 *International Trafficking in Women to the United States: A Contemporary
    Manifestation of Slavery and Organized Crime.* November. www.cia.gov/csi/
    monograph/women/trafficking.pdf.

Rockefeller Foundation

2001 "Challenging Inequities in Health: From Ethics to Action." *Summary.*
    New York: The Rockefeller Foundation and the Swedish International
    Development Cooperation Agency.

Rodriguez, M., S.S. Quiroga, and H. Bauer

1996 "Breaking the Silence: Battered Women's Perspective on Medical Care."
    Archives of Family Medicine, Vol. 5: 153–58.

Roosevelt, Eleanor

1958 *In Your Hands: A Guide for Community Action for the 10th Anniversary of the
    Universal Declaration of Human Rights.* Presentation at the United Nations,
    New York, March 27.

Rosenberg, Tina

2002 "The Free-Trade Fix." *The New York Times Magazine*, August 18, pp. 28–74.

Sachs, Jeffrey

1999 "Helping the World's Poorest." August 14. http://www.cid.harvard.edu/
    cidsocialpolicy/sf9108.html.
2000 "Sachs on Globalization: A New Map of the World." *The Economist*, June 24.

SAGE (Standing Against Global Exploitation)

"Information Center: Key Statistics." http://www.sagesf.org/html/info_statistics.htm.

Sánchez, Celia Sarduy
2001 "Who Cares for the Caregivers? The Vicious Cycle of Illness." *Women and Mental Health: Reflections of Inequality*. Women's Health Collection 6. Adriana Gómez and Deborah Meacham (eds). Santiago, Chile: Latin American and Caribbean Women's Health Network.

Sancho, Nelia
1997 "The 'Comfort Women' System During World War II: Asian Women as Targets of Mass Rape and Sexual Slavery by Japan." In *Gender and Catastrophe*. London: Zed Books, pp. 50–63.

Sassen, Saskia
2002 "Global Cities and Survival Circuits." In *Global Woman: Nannies, Maids, and Sex Workers in the New Economy*. Barbara Ehrenreich and Arlie Russell Hochschild, (eds). New York, NY: Henry Holt.

Save the Children
2002 "The State of the World's Mothers 2002."
2004 "The State of the World's Mothers 2004."

Seguino, Stephanie
1995 "Structural Adjustment." *Trialogue* Vol. 1, No. 1.

Sen, Amartya
1999 *Development as Freedom*. New York, NY: Random House.
2001 "Many Faces of Gender Inequality." *Frontline, India's National Magazine*, Vol. 18, Isssue 22, October/November.

Sen, Gita, and Caren Grown
1985 *Development, Crisis, and Alternative Visions: Third World Women's Perspectives*. New York: Monthly Review Press.

Sen, Gita, Asha George, and Priosko Ostlin, eds.
2002 *Engendering International Health: The Challenge of Equity*. Boston: MIT Press.

Sen, Gita
1997 "Subordination and Sexual Control: A Comparative View of the Control of Women." *The Women, Gender and Development Reader*. London: Zed Books.
2005 "The Politics of the International Women's Movement." In *Claiming Global Power: Transnational Civil Society and Global Governance*. Batliwala, Srilatha, and David Brown (eds). Bloomfield, Connecticut: Kumarian Press.

Shelton, James
2001 "Women's Reproductive Health: the Public Health Perspective." *Reproductive Health, Gender and Human Rights: A Dialogue*. Washington, DC: Program for Appropriate Technology in Health (PATH).

Shiva, Vandana
1997 "GATT, Agriculture, and Third World Women." In *Perspectives: Women's Studies*. Renae Bredin (ed). Bellevue, IA: CourseWise Publishing, pp. 144–51.

Simpson, Trudy
2003 "Jamaica Teen Pregnancy Controversy Heats Up, Cooler Heads Prevail" *Panos Features*, December 17. Accessed June 12, 2006. http://www.panos.org .uk/newsfeatures/featureprintable.asp?id=1175

Sleightholme, Carolyn, and Indrani Sinha
1996 *Guilty Without Trial: Women in the Sex Trade in Calcutta*. Calcutta: STREE.

Sommers, Tish
1994 " Death—A Feminist View." *The New Ourselves, Growing Older*. The Boston Women's Health Book Collective. New York, NY: Simon & Schuster.

Sorensen, Birgitte
2001 "Women and Post-Conflict Reconstruction: Issues and Sources." War-Torn Societies Project Occasional Paper 3. Retrieved May 16, 2002, from the War-Torn Societies Project. http://www.unrisd.org/wsp/op3/toc.htm.

Stone, Joseph L., and Joseph Church
1973 *Childhood and Adolescence*. New York, NY: Random House.

Summers, Lawrence H.
1992 "Investing in All the People: Educating Women in Developing Countries." *EDI Seminar Paper* No. 45. Washington, DC: The World Bank.

Survivors Fund (SURF)
2003h "Remember Rwanda: 10 Years On." http://www.survivors-fund.org.uk/ remember/widows/w_13.htm.

Sutherland, Peter and John Sewell
1998 "Gather the Nations to Promote Globalization." *The New York Times*, February 8.

Swiss, Shana, Peggy J. Jennings, Gladys V. Aryee, Grace H. Brown, Ruth M. Jappah-Samukai, Mary S. Kamara, Rosana D. H. Schaack, and Rojatu S. Turay-Kanneh
1998 "Violence Against Women During the Liberian Civil Conflict." *The Journal of the American Medical Association* Vol. 279, No. 8, February 25.

Ullman, Liv
1977 *Changing*. New York, NY: Random House, Inc.

The United Nations
1948 *Universal Declaration of Human Rights*. Geneva: United Nations. http://www
.unhchr.ch/udhr/lang/eng.htm.
1990 *Convention on the Rights of the Child*. Geneva: United Nations. http://www
.unhchr.ch/html/menu3/b/k2crc.htm.
1993 *Declaration on the Elimination of Violence against Women*. Geneva: United
Nations Secretariat Centre for Human Rights. http://www.hri.ca/uninfo
/treaties/ViolWom.shtml.
1995 "Literacy: A Key to Women's Empowerment." *United Nations, Beijing
Declaration and Platform for Action*. Fourth World Conference on Women,
September. http://www.un.org/womenwatch/daw/beijing/platform.
2000 "The World's Women 2000: Trends and Statistics." Geneva: United Nations.
2002 "Secretary General's Statement to the Security Council on Women, Peace
and Security, October 28, 2002." United Nations Document SG/SM/8461
SC/7551WOM/1366. Geneva: United Nations.
2005 "The World's Women 2005: Trends and Statistics." Geneva: United Nations.

The United Nations Children's Fund (UNICEF)
1997 The Progress of Nations. New York, NY: UNICEF.
2000a "UNICEF Opens Global Drive to Halt Killings of Women." *The New York
Times Company*, March 9. http://www.peace.ca/unicef.htm.
2000b "UNICEF Executive Director Targets Violence Against Women." New
York, NY: UNICEF, March 7. http://www.unicef.org/newsline/00pr17.htm.
2001 "Early Marriage: Child Spouses." *Inocenti Digest*, No. 7, March. http://www.
unicef-icdc.org/publications/pdf/digest7e.pdf.
2002 "Young People and HIV/AIDS." New York, NY: UNICEF, February.
http://www.unicef.org/publications/test.pdf.
2003a "Africa's Orphan Crisis: Worst is Yet to Come." Press Release, November
26. New York, NY: UNICEF. http://www.unicef.org/media/media_16287.
html.
2003b *The State of the World's Children 2004: Girls, Education, and Development*.
New York, NY: UNICEF.
2007 *The State of the World's Children 2007: The Double Dividend of Gender Equality*,
New York, NY: UNICEF.

**The United Nations Children's Fund (UNICEF)/Center for Disease
Control (CDC)**
2002 "Afghanistan is Among Worst Places on Globe to be Pregnant." Joint Press
Release, November 6. http://www.unicef.org/media/media_19233.html.

**The United Nations Children's Fund (UNICEF), Joint United Nations
Programme on HIV/AIDS (UNAIDS) and the U.S. Agency for
International Development**
1997 *Annual Report: The Progress of Nations*.
2004 *Children on the Brink 2004*. XV International AIDS Conference. Bangkok,
Thailand, July 13.
2005 "The State of the World's Children 2005—Childhood Under Threat."
http://www.unicef.org/sowc05/english/index.html.

The United Nations Development Fund for Women (UNIFEM)

2000 "Trafficking in Women and Children." *UNIFEM Gender Fact Sheet*, New York: UNIFEM. http://www.unifem.org/global_spanner/e_se_asia.html.

2002a Rehn, Elizabeth and Ellen Johnson Sirleaf. *Women, War, Peace: The independent experts' assessment on the impact of armed conflict on women and women's role in peace-building*. New York: UNIFEM.

2002b "Progress of the World's Women, 2002: Gender Equity and Millennium Development Goals." UNIFEM Biennial Report. http://www.unifem.org/index.php?f_page_pid=10m.

2002c "Women, War, Peace and Landmines Issue Brief." http://www.womenwarpeace.org/issues/landmines/landmines.htm.

2002d "Combating Trafficking in Women and Children: A Gender and Human Rights Framework." November. http://www.hawaii.edu/global/projects_activities/Trrafficking/Noeleen.pdf

2003 "Not A Minute More." New York, NY: UNIFEM, November 25. http://www.observatorioviolencia.org/Upload%5CDOC20_Informe%20UNIFEM%20Violencia%202003%20Not%20a%20minute%20more1.pdf.

2006 "Reducing Risk by Offering Contraceptive Services." Accessed June 19, 2006. http://www.unfpa.org/mothers/contraceptive.htm.

The United Nations Development Programme (UNDP)

1995 "Still an Unequal World: Human Development Report 1995." United Nations Development Programme. New York, NY: Oxford University Press.

1997a *Status and Economic Development of Women in Kazakhstan: Project of the Government of Kazakhstan Phase 1*. Department for External Aid Co-ordination.

1997b *Human Development Report 1997: Human Development to Eradicate Poverty*. New York, NY: United Nations Development Programme.

The United Nations Educational, Scientific, and Cultural Organization (UNESCO)

2002 *Financing Education*. UNESCO Institute for Statistics.

2005 *Trafficking Project: Statistics Data Base*, Bangkok. http://www2.unescobkk.org.

The United Nations General Assembly

1993 *Declaration on the Elimination of Violence against Women*. Proceedings of the 85th Plenary Meeting, Geneva, December 20.

The United Nations High Commission for Human Rights

2000 Robinson, Mary. *Speech: The United Nations High Commissioner for Human Rights for The United Nations Special Rapporteur on Violence Against Women Before the United Nations Human Rights Commission*. April 10.

The United Nations Integrated Regional Information Network (IRIN)

2002 "SUDAN: NGO expresses concern for neglected 'lost girls.'" http://www.irinnews.org/report.asp?ReportID=20879&SelectRegion=East_Africa&SelectCountry=SUDAN%E2%80%9D.

The United Nations and International Research and Training Institute for the Advancement of Women (INSTRAW)
1999 *Ageing in a Gendered World: Women's Issues and Identities*. Santo Domingo: Dominican Republic.

The United Nations Office of Drugs and Crime
2006 "Trafficking in Persons: Global Patterns" April. http://unodc.org/pdf/crime/a_res_55/res5525e.pdf.
The United Nations Womenwatch
2000 *Women 2000: Gender Equality, Development, and Peace for the Twenty-First Century*. New York, NY: UN Department of Public Information, May. http://www.un.org/womenwatch/daw/followup/session/presskit/fs1.htm.

U.S. Department of Justice
2000 Rennison, C.M., and S. Welchans, *Intimate Partner Violence*. Special Report NCJ 178247. Washington, DC: U.S. Department of Justice.

U.S. Department of Labor, and Bureau of International Labor Affairs.
1995 *Forced Labor: The Prostitution of Children*. U.S. Department of Labor, and Bureau of International Labor Affairs. Papers from a symposium co-sponsored by the U.S. Department of Labor, Bureau of International Labor Affairs, the Women's Bureau, and the U.S. Department of State, Bureau of Democracy, Human Rights and Labor, held on September 29, 1995 at the U.S. Department of Labor in Washington, DC.

U.S. Department of State
2006 "Trafficking in Persons Report," Washington, DC. http://www.state.gov/g/tip/rls/tiprpt/2006.

U.S. General Accounting Office (GAO)
2002, "Violence against Women: Data on Pregnant Victims and Effectiveness of Preventive Strategies Are Limited."

Visaria, Leela
2002 "Education and Health in South Asia: What Do We Know?" *Asia Pacific Population Journal*, December.

Vulliamy, Ed
"Streets of Despair." *Amnesty International Magazine*. Washington, DC, Winter 2005.

Walker, Anne S.
2002 "Fact Sheet on Women and Armed Conflict." Prepared by the UN NGO Working Group on Women, Peace and Security, circulated at the UN on October 23, 2002. In *GlobalNet #212*. New York: International Women's Tribune Center.

Waring, Marilyn
1988a *Counting for Nothing: What Men Value and What Women Are Worth.*
    Wellington, New Zealand: Allen & Unwin.
1988b *If Women Counted.* San Francisco: Harper.
2004 "Civil Society, Community Participation, and Empowerment in the Era
    of Globalization." In *Spotlight* No.1, May. Association for Women's Rights in
    Development. http://www.awid.org/go.php?cid=32.

Weaver, Mary Anne
2000 "Gandhi's Daughters: India's poorest women embark on an epic social
    experiment." *The New Yorker,* January 10.

Whitmont, Edward C.
1982 *Return of the Goddess.* New York: Crossroad Publishing.

Wichterich, Christa
2000 *The Globalized Woman: Reports from a Future of Inequality.* Patrick Camiller
    (trans). London: Zed Books.

Women's Action for New Directions (WAND)
1994 "The Valuing of Women's Unwaged Work." *WAND Occasional Paper.*

Women's Health Collection
1999a Gómez, Adriana, and Deborah Meacham (eds). "Conversations With
    Lesbians Growing Older." *Go Gray! Reflections and Experiences of Women
    Growing Older.* Women's Health Collection 4. Santiago, Chile: Latin
    American and Caribbean Women's Health Network.
1999b Gómez, Adriana and Deborah Meacham (eds). "Introduction." *Go
    Gray! Reflections and Experiences of Women Growing Older.* Women's Health
    Collection 4. Santiago, Chile: Latin American and Caribbean Women's
    Health.

Women's Rights and Economic Change
2003 "Ten Principles for Challenging Neoliberal Globalization." *AWID* 6.

World Bank
1992 Summers, Lawrence H. "Investing in All the People: Educating Women in
    Developing Countries." *EDI Seminar Paper* No 45. Washington, DC: World
    Bank.
2000 *World Development Report: Attacking Poverty.* New York: Oxford University Press.
2001 "The World Bank Activities and Position on Aging." Washington, DC:
    World Bank. http://www.un.org/esa/socdev/ageing/worldbank200106.htm.

World Health Organization (WHO)
1994 "International Plan of Action on Population and Development."
1995 "Women's health: improve our health, improve the world." WHO position
    paper for Fourth World Conference on Women, September 4–15; Beijing, China.

1998 "Population Ageing—a Public Health Challenge." WHO Fact Sheet No. 135, updated Septmber. http://www.who.int/inf-fs/en/fact135.html.

1999 *Abortion in the Developing World.* New Delhi: Vistaar Publications.

2000a "Female Genital Cutting." WHO Fact Sheet No. 241.

2000b "Women, Ageing, and Health." WHO Fact Sheet No. 252.

2002a "Adolescent Health and Development: A WHO Regional Framework 2001.

2002b "Impact of AIDS on Older People in Africa: Zimbabwe Case Study." http://www.who.int/hpr/ageing/zimaidsreport.pdf.

2002c *Missing Voices: views of older persons on elder abuse.*

2002d "World Report on Violence and Health." http://www.who.int/violence_injury_prevention/violence/world_report/wrvheng/en.

2003a *Safe Abortion: Technical and Policy Guidance for Health Systems*

2003b *Misoprostol: Review of Application by Expert Committee Member,* February 26. http://www.who.int/medicines/organization/par/edl/expcom13/misoprostol_review.doc.

2004a Child and Adolescent Health Development Focus. WHO, Manila, Philippines.

2004b "Making Pregnancy Safer." WHO Fact Sheet 276. http://www.who.int/mediacentre/factsheets/fs276/en.

2004c Economic Dimensions of Interpersonal Violence. http://www.who.int/violence_injury_prevention/publications/violence/economic_dimensions/en/

2005a "Indoor Air Pollution and Health." WHO Fact Sheet No. 292, June.

2005b *WHO Multi-Country Study on Women's Health and Domestic Violence Against Women: Initial results on prevalence, health outcomes and women's responses.* http://www.who.int/gender/violence/who_multicountry_study/en/index.html.

2006 "Agrochemicals: linking health and environmental management" WHO Policy Brief, Health and Environment Linkages Initiative. Accessed June 10, 2006. http://www.who.int/heli/risks/toxics/chemicals/en.

2007 Most recent figures can be obtained from: www.who.int/en.

Yuval-Davis, Nira.

1997 *Gender and Nation.* London: Sage Publications.

Zeilinger, Irene.

1999 "Family Support Systems and Older Women in Sub-Saharan Africa." In *Ageing in a Gendered World: Women's Issues and Identities.* Dominican Republic: INSTRAW.

Zurayk, Huda

2002 "The Meaning of Reproductive Health for Developing Countries: The Case of the Middle East." *Women's Global Network for Reproductive Rights, Newsletter* 75.

Some Useful Resources

Journals on International Health
American Journal of Public Health: http://www.ajph.org
Economic Development and Cultural Change: http://www.journals.uchicago.edu
/EDCC/home.html
Global Public Health: http://www.tandf.co.uk/journals/titles/17441692.asp
Health Policy and Planning: http://heapol.oxfordjournals.org
Human Organization: http://www.sfaa.net/ho
International Family Planning Perspectives: http://www.guttmacher.org/archive/
IFPP.jsp
International Journal of Health Services: http://www.baywood.com/journals
/previewjournals.asp?id=0020-7314
The Lancet: http://www.thelancet.com
The New England Journal of Medicine: http://content.nejm.org
Medical Anthropology Quarterly: http://www.medanthro.net/maq/index.html
Medical Anthropology: http://www.tandf.co.uk/journals/titles/01459740.html
Perspectives on Sexual and Reproductive Health: http://www.guttmacher.org
/archive/PSRH.jsp
Social Science and Medicine: http://www.elsevier.com/wps/find/
journaldescription.cws_home/315/description#description

International Governmental Organizations
BILATERAL OR BINATIONAL ORGANIZATIONS:
Canadian International Development Assistance (CIDA): http://www.acdi-cida
.gc.ca/index.htm
Canadian International Development Research Centre (IDRC): http://www.idrc
.ca/index_en.html
Danish International Development Assistance (DANIDA): http://www
.um.dk/en/menu/DevelopmentPolicy/DanishDevelopmentPolicy/
DanishDevelopmentPolicy
German Corporation for International Development Cooperation (GTZ): http://
www.gtz.de/en/index.htm
Japan International Cooperation Agency (JICA): http://www.jica.go.jp/english
Swedish International Development Assistance (SIDA): http://www.sida.se

United Kingdom Department for International Development (DFID): http://
www.dfid.gov.uk

United States Agency for International Development (USAID): http://www.usaid.gov

MULTILATERAL OR MULTINATIONAL ORGANIZATIONS OR
INTERGOVERNMENTAL ORGANIZATIONS:

United Nations: http://www.un.org

United Nations Organizations

Food and Agricultural Organization (FAO): http://www.fao.org

UNAIDS: http://www.unaids.org/en

United Nations Children's Fund (UNICEF): http://www.unicef.org

United Nations Development Programme (UNDP): http://www.undp.org

United Nations Division for the Advancement of Women: http://www.un.org
/womenwatch/daw

United Nations Educational, Scientific, and Cultural Org. (UNESCO): http://
www.unesco.org

United Nations Women's Fund (UNIFEM): http://www.unifem.org

World Health Organization (WHO): http://www.who.int

Regional branches of the WHO:

Regional Office for Africa (AFRO): http://www.afro.who.int

Regional Office for Eastern Mediterranean (EMRO): http://www.emro.who.int

Regional Office for Europe (EURO): http://www.euro.who.int

Pan American Health Organization (PAHO): http://www.paho.org

Regional Office for South-East Asia (SEARO): http://www.searo.who.int

Regional Office for the Western Pacific (WPRO): http://www.wpro.who.int

MULTINATIONAL BANKS:

The World Bank: http://www.worldbank.org

Asian Development Bank: http://www.adb.org

Inter-American Development Bank: http://www.iadb.org

African Development Bank: http://www.afdb.org

Non-Governmental Organizations (NGOs)

*(There are thousands of NGOs—organizations that are sometimes described as
"voluntary agencies" or "civil society organizations." This list is an illustrative sample
rather than a comprehensive survey.)*

American College of Nurse-Midwives, Silver Spring, MD

*ACNM supports the development of the profession of midwifery in the U.S. through
providing research, promoting continuing education, establishing clinical practice
standards, and facilitating legislative activities.*

http://www.acnm.org

Birthing Project USA, Sacramento, CA

*Birthing Project is an international organization and resource center for improving
birth outcomes for women of color.*

http://www.birthingprojectusa.com

CARE, Washington, DC
CARE fights global poverty through community-based efforts to increase poor women's capacity for self-help.
http://www.care.org

Center for Global Development, Washington, DC
CGD is a research and policy institute that works to reduce global poverty and inequality by encouraging policy change in the developed world.
http://www.cgdev.org

Center for Health and Gender Equity (CHANGE), Takoma Park, MD
CHANGE is a U.S.-based NGO focused on the effects of U.S. international policies on the health and rights of women, girls, and other vulnerable populations in Africa, Asia, and Latin America.
http://www.genderhealth.org

Center for Reproductive Rights, New York, NY
The Center for Reproductive Rights is a nonprofit legal advocacy organization dedicated to promoting and defending women's reproductive rights worldwide.
http://www.reproductiverights.org

Centre for African Family Studies (CAFS), Nairobi, Kenya
CAFS is an African institution dedicated to strengthening the capacities of organizations and individuals working in the field of reproductive health, population, and development.
http://www.cafs.org

Centre for Development and Population Activities (CEDPA), Washington, DC
CEDPA is a non-profit organization that improves the lives of women and girls in developing countries by increasing educational opportunities, ensuring access to health information and services, and strengthening leadership capacity.
http://www.cedpa.org

Centre for Health Education, Training, and Nutrition Awareness (CHETNA), Gujarat, India
CHETNA is a support organization based in Gujarat, India, that focuses on raising awareness and building capacity concerning issues of children, adolescents, and women.
http://www.chetnaindia.org

CONRAD, Arlington, VA
CONRAD facilitates the rapid development of safe, acceptable, affordable products and methods that provide contraception and/or prevent the sexual transmission of infections such as HIV.
http://www.conrad.org

CORE Group, Washington, DC
The CORE Group is a coalition of NGOs working across the developing world to aid mothers, fathers, and community leaders in improving the health of their children.
http://www.coregroup.org

DKT International, Washington, DC
DKT International employs social marketing with a focus on family planning and AIDS prevention.
http://www.dktinternational.org

Engender Health, New York, NY
   *Engender Health is an international organization that works to make reproductive
   health services safe, available, and sustainable for women and men worldwide.*
   http://www.engenderhealth.org
Family Care International, New York, NY
   *FCI works to ensure that women and adolescents have access to services and information
   to improve their health, experience safe pregnancy and childbirth, and avoid unwanted
   pregnancy and HIV infection.*
   http://www.familycareintl.org
Family Health International, Research Triangle Park, North Carolina
   *FHI manages research and field activities in more than 70 countries to meet the public
   health needs of vulnerable people.*
   http://www.fhi.org
Family Violence Prevention Fund, San Francisco, CA
   *The Family Violence Prevention Fund works to prevent violence against women and
   children around the world through developing legislation and promoting community
   leadership.*
   http://www.endabuse.org
Female Cancer Program Foundation, Amsterdam, the Netherlands
   *The Female Cancer Program Foundation supports research, screening, and treatment
   of cervical cancer with a focus on high incidence areas.*
   http://www.femalecancerprogram.org
FEMNET (African Women's Development and Communication Network),
   Nairobi, Kenya
   FEMNET is a communications network of African women
   http://www.femnet.or.ke
Fistula Foundation, Santa Clara, CA
   *The Fistula Foundation is dedicated to the treatment and prevention of obstetric fistulae
   through support of the Hamlin Fistula Hospitals in Ethiopia.*
   http://www.fistulafoundation.org
Global Alliance for Women's Health, New York, NY
   *GAWH works with coalitions of organizations around the world to promote and implement
   women's health care service improvements at local, national, and international levels.*
   http://www.gawh.org
The Global Fund for Women, San Francisco, CA
   *The Global Fund for Women raises money and gives it away to women's groups around
   the work working on female human rights issues.*
   http://www.globalfundforwomen.org
Global Network for Perinatal and Reproductive Health, Portland, OR
   *GNPRH brings together clinical researchers in the area of reproductive health to
   identify best practices, develop capacity building, and advance knowledge on diseases
   which affect reproductive health.*
   http://www.ohsu.edu/gnprh

Global Network for Women's and Children's Health Research, Research Triangle Park, North Carolina
The Global Network is a collaborative effort among teams of international investigators working to improve women's and children's health with a focus on pregnancy and birth outcomes.
http://gn.rti.org/index.cfm

Alan Guttmacher Institute (AGI), New York, NY
AGI conducts applied research on issues relating to family planning, and publishes International Family Planning Perspectives
http://www.guttmacher.org

Health & Development International (HDI), Svestadvn, Norway
HDI addresses eradicable debilitating diseases, such as guinea worm and fistula, through community-based approaches.
http://www.hdi.no

Hesperian Foundation, Berkeley, CA
Hesperian is a non-profit publisher of books and educational materials that help people take the lead in their own health care, and organize to improve health conditions in their communities.
http://www.hesperian.org

Human Rights Watch (HRW), New York, NY
HRW is a "watchdog" agency which produces reports on human rights abuses around the world.
http://www.hrw.org

Ibis Reproductive Health, Boston, MA
Ibis conducts clinical and social science research to promote policies and practices that support sexual and reproductive rights and health.
http://www.ibisreproductivehealth.org

International Center for Research on Women (ICRW), Washington, DC
ICRW conducts economic research on the situation of women and works to catalyze change in over 40 countries worldwide.
http://www.icrw.org

International HIV/AIDS Alliance, Brighton, UK
The Alliance is a global partnership of nationally-based organizations working to support community action on AIDS.
http://www.aidsalliance.org

International Planned Parenthood Federation, London, UK
IPPF is a worldwide network of family planning organizations
http://www.ippf.org/en

International Women's Health Coalition (IWHC), New York, NY
IWHC is a research and advocacy group focusing on reproductive health.
http://www.iwhc.org

Ipas, Chapel Hill, NC
Ipas works through training, research, advocacy, and direct aid to increase women's ability to exercise their sexual and reproductive rights and to reduce deaths and injuries from unsafe abortion.
http://www.ipas.org

Latin American and Caribbean Women's Health Network (LACWHN), Isis
  International, Santiago, Chile
  *LACWHN is a network of organizations and individuals in the women's health
  movement working to promote women's health and the full exercise of women's human
  rights and citizenship.*
  http://www.reddesalud.org/english/sitio/portada.htm
Marie Stopes International, London, UK
  *Marie Stopes International provides sexual and reproductive health information and
  services worldwide.*
  http://www.mariestopes.org.uk
National Committee on the United Nations Convention on the Elimination of
  Discrimination against Women (CEDAW), Beverly Hills, CA
  *For information, contact: Billie Heller, Chair, UN/CEDAW, 520 North Camden
  Drive, Beverly Hills, CA 90210; email: BilliCEDAW@aol.com.*
Pathfinder International, Watertown, MA
  *Pathfinder International offers women, men, and adolescents throughout the developing
  world access to family planning and reproductive health information and services.*
  http://www.pathfind.org
Population Action International (PAI), Washington, DC
  *PAI is an independent policy advocacy group working to strengthen political and
  financial support worldwide for population programs grounded in individual rights.*
  http://www.populationaction.org
Population Council, New York, NY
  The Population Council conducts research and advocacy on range of population issues.
  http://www.popcouncil.org
Population Reference Bureau (PRB), Washington, DC
  *PRB is one of the most credible sources for demographic and general information on
  international health topics.*
  http://www.prb.org
Population Services International (PSI), Washington, DC
  *PSI addresses malaria, reproductive health, child survival, and HIV through social
  marketing.*
  http://www.psi.org
Program for Appropriate Technology in Health (PATH), Washington, DC
  *PATH advances technologies for low resource settings, strengthens health systems, and
  encourages health behaviors, to enable communities to break the cycle of poor health.*
  http://www.path.org
Project Concern International, San Diego, CA
  *Project Concern improves child health around the world by preventing disease and
  providing access to clean water and nutritious food.*
  http://www.projectconcern.org
Project Hope International, Washington, DC
  *Project Hope International addresses human trafficking with a focus on Southeast
  Asia.*
  http://www.phi-ngo.org

Reproductive Health Matters, UK
Reproductive Health Matters is a women-centered journal on reproductive and human rights and ethics.
http://www.rhmjournal.org.uk

Society for Women Against AIDS in Africa (SWAA), Senegal
SWAA is a pan-African women's organization dedicated to women and their families in the fight against HIV/AIDS.
http://www.swaainternational.org

Swasthya Program, a Community Health Partnership, India
Swasthya utilizes a feminist approach to general dialogue on women's health at a community level and to support local action for health promotion.
http://www.geocities.com/swasthyaindia

White Ribbon Alliance for Safe Motherhood, Washington, DC
The Alliance is an international coalition of individuals and organizations formed to promote increased public awareness of the need to make pregnancy and childbirth safe for all women and newborns.
http://www.whiteribbonalliance.org

Women's Action & Resource Initiative (WARI), Bangkok, Thailand
WARI is a center for education, research, and training related to gender and human rights.
http://www.geocities.com/wari9

Women's Commission for Refugee Women & Children, New York, NY
The Women's Commission seeks to improve the lives of refugee women, youth, and children through monitoring and field visits, documentation of key issues, and development and promotion of policy and practice affecting these communities.
http://www.womenscommission.org

Women's Environment and Development Organization (WEDO), New York, NY
WEDO is an international organization that advocates for women's equality in global policy, seeking to achieve economic, social, and gender justice.
http://www.wedo.org

Women's Global Health Imperative (WGHI), San Francisco, CA
WGHI is a global research center devoted to improving the reproductive health of vulnerable women around the world.
http://www.wghi.org

Women's Global Network for Reproductive Rights, Amsterdam, the Netherlands
The Global Network is an autonomous network of groups and individuals around the world who aim to achieve and support reproductive rights for women.
http://www.wgnrr.org

Worldwide Fistula Fund, St. Louis, Missouri
The Fund supports the provision of high quality clinical care for women with obstetric fistulas, promotes training for fistula surgeons, and advocates for the unmet needs of women suffering from fistula.
http://worldwidefistulafund.org

Gratitudes

This book would not have been possible without the help of many people. It is truly the result of much collaboration.

I thank thousands of women around the world whose stories have both shocked and inspired me. I thank them for their courage and persistence and their faith in their own capacity to change the world in positive ways.

I thank my mother, Eleanor Mary Firth, above all, for exemplifying strength, resilience, and grace throughout her life.

I thank numerous students, whose thoughtful comments and questions helped shape many parts of this book. I offer special thanks to Hannah Leslie for her constant help with concepts and sources, Ariel Sklar for her essential and superb work on the chapter on aging and during the final review of the book, and Liz Vrolyk for her help with permissions and insights throughout the final review of the book, especially with the chapter on work and trafficking. When I think of Ariel, Hannah, and Liz, I smile with appreciation.

I thank these other students for particular help: Rebecca Allen, for insights about domestic violence; Heidi Boas, for her careful work as a teaching assistant and for thoughts on refugee women; Orion Courtin for his early reviews of a course reader; Charles Feng, for his personal stories, helpful conversations, and help with the chapter on work; Lauren Gong, for her general assistance; Irene Lu, for her help in drafting the chapter on conflict and refugee situations; and Ashni Mohnot, for her help on early drafts of the chapters on childhood and reproductive health.

I thank several people who were instrumental in my having the opportunity to go to Villa Serbelloni in Bellagio, Italy, to spend the month of October, 2004, thinking about the book and doing a first draft:

- Gianna Celli, who ensured that my time at Bellagio would be as useful as possible

- Paul Farmer, for his support in bringing me to Common Courage Press and ensuring the time at Bellagio

- Stina Katchadourian, for her enthusiasm and support for the book and the time at Bellagio

- Phil Lee, whose support over the years was once again demonstrated in his recommendation for Bellagio

- Vivien Tsu, who gave me the idea to apply to Bellagio

I also thank the Rockefeller Foundation itself for the very existence of Villa Serbelloni at Bellagio and the opportunities that beautiful place provides.

I thank the Global Fund for Women for financial and practical support in the course of putting together this book. Kavita Ramdas generously suggested that the Global Fund provide some financial support to make this book possible, and several staff members, most notably Ana Maria Enriques, Kellea Miller, and Randy Trigg helped me obtain information about individual women's groups. I thank Yvette Bozzini, Barbara Mnookin, and Anne Weinstone for their comments on various versions of the manuscript. I especially thank Lauren Rusk, without whose editorial help this book would not have happened. I thank Robyn Duby and Walter Reed for essential logistical support as the book finally took shape. I thank Chris Hall who stepped in to ensure that the design of the book would honor women's efforts. I thank Greg Bates of Common Courage Press, whose idea it was to write and produce this book, and whose constructive criticism and encouragement have been key to its completion.

Last but not least, I thank my partner, Barry Rose, without whose unwavering support this book (and its title) would not have been possible.

A Personal Note

This book grew out of courses I have been teaching since 2000 at Stanford University within the Human Biology Program on "critical issues in international women's health." Hundreds of students have taken the courses, which are taught in highly participatory classes of about thirty-six students. The goals of the courses, beyond the simple transmission of information, are to stimulate students' concern about the situation of women worldwide, and to communicate forcefully the reality of our interdependence and the possibility of change.

Much of my concern with women came through my experience as the Founding President of the Global Fund for Women, a global organization that raises money and gives it away to women's groups around the world. My vision for the Global Fund for Women at its creation in 1987 was that it would be a place where women could come to be helped to give reality to their hopes and dreams for positive change and empowerment. It continues with that mission and thrives. My definition of empowerment is this: Having a vision, having a plan to make that vision a reality, and having the capacity to take the steps toward implementing the plan. In the course of creating the Global Fund, I experienced such empowerment. I am one of the lucky people in this world—a person who had a vision and saw it become reality through the creation and development of the Global Fund for Women and through dynamic interaction with idealistic and committed students. I wish similar experiences for others.

Creating the Global Fund and working with other organizations brought me into the company of thousands of women who are changing the world. I heard testimonies and presentations about unspeakable human and women's rights abuses, and I met people who are doing something about them. I was shocked and inspired. These are the experiences and insights that I have tried to pass on to my students at Stanford and that I share in this book.

ANNE FIRTH MURRAY

Stanford University, California, July 2007

Permissions

Index

Rustavi, Georgia, 104
Rwanda
    children of rape, 140
    rape as weapon of war, 9
    refugees, 103
    Réseau des Femmes, 156
    survivors of rape, 156

Sakhi Kendra, Kanpur, India, 121
Salvation, Kathmandu, Bagmati, Nepal,
    181
Sama Resource Group for Women and
    Health, New Delhi, India, 26
Samoa, domestic violence in, 111
San Cristobal, Chiapas, Mexico, 88
San Cristobal Birth Center, San Cristobal,
    Chiapas, Mexico, 88
San Ramon, Alajuela, Costa Rica, 127
Santiago, Chile
    Fundacíon Margen, 186
    impact of conflict on women, 138–139
    Red Chilena Contra la Violencia
        Domestica y Sexual, 125
Santo Tomas, Mexico, 183
Saudi Arabia
    female genital mutilation in, 47
    inequality of women in, 9
Save the Children, 134
school enrollment
    barriers for girls, 45–46
    gender gaps, 46
    as measure of poverty, 4–5
    women's disadvantages, 3
school fees, 42, 46, 76–77
secondary schools
    female access to, 34
    prolongation of childhood and, 62–63
self-employment, 163
Sen, Amartya, 19, 23–24, 219
Sen, Gita, 160, 216, 217, 218, 219
Serbia and Montenegro
    domestic violence in, 111
    Women's Center in Uzice, 156
sex education, 77–79
sex selection, societal effects of, 26–27
sex-selective abortions, 24–26
sex work. see also prostitution; transactional
    sex

    agents of trafficking and, 182–191
    by choice, 187–189
    stigma of, 181
sexual abuse
    health problems and, 117
    by humanitarian workers, 147
statistics, 114
sexual exploitation of orphans, 44
sexual slavery
    across borders, 154
    poverty and, 56
    rape as weapon of war, 8
    trafficking in women and, 175–178
sexual violence
    during armed conflict, 139
    survivors of, 155
sexually-transmitted diseases
    burden of, 103–105
    maternal mortality and, 105
    prevention of, 69
    protection against, 96
    in the world's youth, 64
Sharma, Kumud, 115–116
Shuriye, Isnino, 54, 55
Sierra Leone
    exploitation in refugee camps, 151
    rape as weapon of war, 9
    sexual slavery in, 143
Simpson, Trudy, 93
Sinha, Indrani, 187
Sirleaf, Ellen, 138
Sleightholme, Carolyn, 187
social systems, subordination of women, 13
socioeconomic status. see also poverty
    health and, 6
    malnutrition and, 23
    sex-selective abortions and, 24
Solidarity for Social Equality, 18
Somalia
    female genital mutilation in, 49, 50,
        54
    prevalence of female genital
        mutilation, 47
    refugees, 103, 149
    rituals, 62
Sommers, Tish, 201
son preference, 18
    economic pressures and, 19–20
    infanticide and, 19–22

About the Author

 Anne Firth Murray, a New Zealander, attended the University of California, Berkeley, and New York University, where she studied economics, political science, and public administration, with a focus on international health policy and women's reproductive health. In the 1960s and 70s, she worked at the United Nations, taught in Hong Kong and Singapore, and spent several years with Oxford, Stanford, and Yale university presses.

For the past twenty-five years, she has worked in the field of philanthropy, serving as a consultant to many foundations. From 1978 to the end of 1987, she directed the environment and international population programs of the William and Flora Hewlett Foundation in California. She is the Founding President of the Global Fund for Women, established in 1987, which provides funds internationally to seed, strengthen, and link groups committed to women's well being. Her book *Paradigm Found: Leading and Managing for Positive Change* describes lessons learned from the early years of the Global Fund. Since 2000, she has been a consulting professor in human biology at Stanford University, where she teaches courses on international women's health and human rights.

Ms. Murray serves on several boards and councils of non-profit organizations, including the African Women's Development Fund, Commonweal, Doctors for Humanity, G.R.A.C.E. (a group working on HIV/AIDS in East Africa), the Hesperian Foundation, SPARK (a network dedicated to women's empowerment), and UNNITI (a women's foundation in India). She is the recipient of many awards and honors for her work on women's health and philanthropy, and in 2005 she was among one thousand women nominated for the Nobel Peace Prize. Ms. Murray has one daughter, who is an attorney in California, and two grandchildren. She lives in Menlo Park, California.

To learn more, please visit www.outragetocourage.org

Set by Ampersand Visual Communications
in Janson 10/14 and Myraid Pro 9/13